Antonia White and Manic-Depressive Illness

Antonia White and Manic-Depressive Illness

Patricia Moran

EDINBURGH
University Press

Edinburgh University Press is one of the leading university presses in the UK. We publish academic books and journals in our selected subject areas across the humanities and social sciences, combining cutting-edge scholarship with high editorial and production values to produce academic works of lasting importance. For more information visit our website: edinburghuniversitypress.com

Edinburgh University Press Ltd
The Tun – Holyrood Road,
12(2f) Jackson's Entry,
Edinburgh EH8 8PJ

Typeset in 11/14 Adobe Sabon by
IDSUK (DataConnection) Ltd, and
printed and bound in Great Britain.

A CIP record for this book is available from the British Library

ISBN 978 1 4744 1821 8 (hardback)
ISBN 978 1 4744 1822 5 (webready PDF)
ISBN 978 1 4744 1823 2 (epub)

Contents

In memory of David Van Leer
1949–2013

Acknowledgements

Many people helped make this book possible. James Acheson was the first to discern a possible book in a lengthy draft that articulated the key ideas I had about White and manic-depressive illness. His encouragement led me to approach Jackie Jones at Edinburgh University Press, whose enthusiasm convinced me that a book on this subject was indeed viable. Erica Johnson, collaborator and friend extraordinaire, has been there every step of the way. She read numerous drafts of each chapter and offered the kind of editorial advice and insight that has made my friendship with her one of the sustaining elements of my life. I couldn't be more grateful.

I owe a special debt to Lyndall Passerini Hopkinson, who generously offered to let me read her copies of her mother's diaries at her Palazzone in Cortona. Lyndall insisted on providing sumptuous meals in her lovely garden throughout my visit; getting to know her has been one of the most unexpected and welcome pleasures of undertaking this study. I am also grateful to Lady Susan Chitty, who kindly gave her permission for me to reference her mother's unpublished writing. I thank Carmen Callil and Jane Dunn for their timely and helpful advice. Louis Sass was never too busy to respond quickly to panicked questions about schizophrenia and psychiatry. Danai Dima helped me understand some of the genetic factors involved in bipolar disorder and kindly agreed to read through relevant sections of the manuscript. At Edinburgh University Press Adela Rauchova and Rebecca Mackenzie have overseen the production of this book with admirable efficiency.

I have been lucky to have the support and friendship of numerous colleagues. I thank my former colleagues in English at the University of Limerick, particularly David Coughlan and Sinéad McDermott, whose friendship made my years there some of the most enjoyable of my career. Rachel Hynes' enthusiasm for women writers and modernism makes working with her a pleasure. I also thank the members of my writing group, Tina Morin, Maggie O'Neill and Michaela Schrage-Frueh, for providing good company as well as good advice. I thank Head of the School of Culture and Communication, Tadhg Ó hlfearnáin for his wry but always sensible guidance on all topics academic, and for his support of a research grant that made it possible for me to travel to Italy in the summer of 2016. I benefitted from a book completion grant in the spring of 2016 that relieved me of some of my administrative duties: my thanks to Dean Tom Lodge of the Faculty of Arts, Humanities and Social Sciences for that support.

My colleagues in English at City, University of London have been a friendly and lively group as we worked together to turn our disparate strands of interest and practice into a department. I am particularly grateful to Mary Ann Kernan, who guided me with tact and good humour as I set out to master the labyrinthine mysteries of a new institution. Julie Wheelwright has been a mainstay from the beginning, and has generously shared her time and resources with me; her friendship has made my transition to London far easier and more enjoyable than it might have been. Clare Allan is a gem: not only do our intellectual interests coincide, but Clare's passion for dogs is matched only by my own, and her gift of 'dog-time' with Elsie and Meg is priceless. Minna Vuohelainen and David Ashford have helped immeasurably as we worked together to launch the BA English: Minna deserves special mention for her capable handling of numerous duties involved in setting up a new department and for helping me get the manuscript ready for submission. Dean Theo Farrell and Laurence Solkin believed in me more than I believed in myself: I thank them for their support.

My son Patrick Higgins has lived with Antonia White more than he would have liked: I appreciate his forbearance ('You're a nerd, Mom. But a nice nerd'). I also thank friends and colleagues from across the globe who have supported me in various ways. Joanne Feit Diehl, Kari Lokke and Ray Waddington, my former colleagues at the University of California, have continued to sustain me with their interest and affection. Shout-outs go to Claire Davison, Jane Garrity, Margaret Harper, Suzette Henke, Mark Hussey, Sydney

Janet Kaplan, Kathy Laing, Frann Michel and Julie Vandivere. Friends outside of academia provided much-needed perspective: I thank Jack LaPoint and Gayle Denealius, whose practical advice has been invaluable. I single out for special mention my oldest friend, Cindy Crampsey, who knows me better than anyone.

Finally, I must thank two people who did not live to see this book in print. My title pays tribute to the brilliant work of Thomas C. Caramagno, whose study of Virginia Woolf and mental illness was the starting point of this book. I did not know Caramagno personally, only professionally, but I returned to his study of Woolf again and again as I grappled with mastering the intricacies of manic-depressive illness. His demonstration of how humanities scholarship could build on the insights of other disciplines motivated me to tackle this topic. I think he would have been pleased to know that his work continues to inspire those who follow in his footsteps.

David Van Leer was my stalwart friend for more than twenty years. We weathered many storms together, both personal and professional, and his kindness and generosity of spirit kept me going during some very dark times. I wish he could have read this book. I miss him.

Introduction

Antonia White (1899–1980) is best known today for four novels that trace the fractured development of a would-be woman writer from childhood to early adulthood. Strongly autobiographical in content, the novels depict the protagonist's conversion as a child to Catholicism and her subsequent education in a convent school (*Frost in May*, 1933); her adolescent years in search of a vocation (*The Lost Traveller*, 1950); her disastrous and unconsummated marriage that ends in annulment (*The Sugar House*, 1952); and her three-week whirlwind romance that culminates in a psychotic breakdown and a nine-month incarceration in an asylum (*Beyond the Glass*, 1954). Undergirding all four novels are the protagonist's emotionally incestuous relationship with her authoritarian father and her fear of his disapproval, a disapproval made manifest when he denounces her as depraved after the nuns at the school discover a draft of an unfinished, sexually suggestive novel: '"I say that if a young girl's mind is such a sink of filth and impurity, I wish to God I had never had a daughter"' (*Frost in May*, p. 216). This denunciation crucially defines White's protagonist, as, indeed, it defined White herself:

> One sentence of her father's had torn right through every protective covering and shamed her to the very marrow. If he had stripped her naked and beaten her, she would not have been more utterly humiliated. Never, never could things be the same. (*Frost in May*, p. 217)

But it was White's inability to make sense of the years that followed her own incarceration for psychosis that brought her protagonist's story to a halt: she could not construct a coherent account of the life events that took place between 1920 and 1930, even though 'So much of my "life" was crammed into the years between 21 and 31 – madness, three marriages, both children born' (*Diary 2*, p. 39).

White believed that her inability to construct a coherent fictional account of these years reflected a fundamental incoherence in herself, for she used fiction as a therapeutic tool to work through her personal and emotional chaos.[1] She wrote in a letter:

> I can only deal with a difficult or painful situation in two ways – by facing or being made to face the full horror of it and then getting it into its right relation or by expressing it in what one loosely calls 'a work of art'. The second is really an extension of the first and one which I have not been able to use nearly enough, because I'm not yet able to write freely. (*The Hound and the Falcon*, p. 37)

Her writer's block only encompassed her projected *Künstlerroman* (a novel of artistic development), however, for, as she observed in the same letter:

> A great deal of the trouble crystallised round the actual act of writing [. . .] I can write what I really feel in notebooks and in letters [. . .] I can turn out any kind of journalism as a dressmaker makes dresses to any pattern, but of 'real' work I've done very little. (*The Hound and the Falcon*, p. 37)

Hence it is significant that White could not develop a plausible plot sequence for the fifth volume, despite twenty-six years of trying to do so (two abortive attempts appear in *As Once in May*). Given that the fourth volume ends with the protagonist Clara's recovery of her sanity and release from a mental hospital closely modelled on Bethlem, where White herself was incarcerated for ten months in 1922–3, White's inability to continue the narrative that would launch Clara as an artist and woman is sadly apt.

While stymied by her inability to come to grips with her chaotic twenties in her fiction, White obsessively revisited this period in her monumental diary and her extensive correspondence. Over time she came to believe that her writer's block, her psychotic breakdown, the misadventures that followed and her ongoing emotional problems were all rooted in her father's denunciation of her first manuscript:

> I could not say for myself where I first 'went wrong' and began that series of entanglements and sins and muddles and disasters which still affect my own and other people's lives. How appalled my father would be if he knew the results of that fifteenth birthday.

Yet I often feel as if I had never been a 'whole' person since that day. (*Diary* 1, p. 263)

But this explanation, plausible as it seems and widely adopted by scholars of White's work, has obscured the real nature of White's difficulties.[2] For the psychotic breakdown that landed White in the hospital at the age of twenty-three was only the most severe manifestation of the manic-depressive illness that recurred throughout her life, resulting in several further breakdowns and near breakdowns, an almost constant state of depression, compulsive behaviours that she could not understand or control (particularly in regard to sexuality and money) and troubled relationships with family members, including those with her two daughters, whose memoirs of their mother paint a painful picture of White's inadequacy as a parent. White's oeuvre thus constitutes an important and overlooked first-hand record of a woman writer's struggle to impose coherence on an identity fractured by the chaotic and kaleidoscopic ravages of manic-depressive illness. This study rereads White's writing within the context of manic-depressive illness to show how White's misinterpretations of her illness shaped her conceptualisations of herself and those of her fictional alter ego.

White's misinterpretations of her illness constitute an important historical record in other respects. The onset of her illness in 1921 coincided with the publication of the English translation of Emil Kraepelin's *Manic-depressive Insanity and Paranoia*, yet White herself never received a formal diagnosis of manic depression in her lifetime, although her daughter Susan did in 1978. (Oddly, White did not connect her daughter's diagnosis to her own illness, although she had noted clear parallels between their experiences during the emergence of Susan's illness in 1951: 'The swing from acute depression & total lack of confidence to wild optimism & extreme self-confidence seems suspicious. Her life in some ways is horribly like mine.')[3] Told she suffered from 'brain fever' following her recovery from her first episode, White did not receive a formal diagnosis until 1935, when she was misdiagnosed as schizophrenic by the analyst with whom she would subsequently undertake a four-year 'Freudian' analysis (in fact, it was far more shaped by the theories of Karl Abraham, as I show in Chapter 3). The psychoanalytic understanding of schizophrenia and the gendered assumptions that informed both her diagnosis and subsequent analysis played a key role in consolidating White's belief that her troubles had their source in her relationship with her father.

White would turn to analysis twice more, in the late 1940s with a Jungian-influenced follower of the Indian mystic Meher Baba, and in the mid-1960s with an analyst convinced that prenatal trauma underlay neurosis. These analyses expanded the scope of White's obsession with her father's influence on her – her second analysis in particular directed her to acknowledge her maternal inheritance and influences – but did not significantly alter her explanation of her illness. White's encounters with the newly emergent disciplines of psychiatry and psychoanalysis illuminate the limitations and biases of 'scientific' diagnoses and explanations of mental illness, and add rich nuance and detail to histories of these disciplines. White's four-year 'Freudian' analysis, which she documented in an 'analysis diary' that has never been published in its entirety, is itself a valuable archive for scholars of psychoanalysis, mental illness and women's modernism.

Psychoanalysis was not the only avenue White pursued in hopes of bringing her illness under control. When her first analysis ended and her symptoms returned, White reconverted to the Catholicism she had abandoned in her twenties. Thereafter White remained a Catholic – albeit one riven with doubts and anxieties about the validity of certain doctrines – even as she continued to struggle with recurrent episodes of depression and mania, and even as she turned twice more to analysis. As this study shows, her reconversion reinforced White's convictions about her father's central role in her illness, in part because it inevitably reminded White of her first conversion at the age of seven at her father's instigation and her subsequent traumatic expulsion from her convent school after the discovery of her 'fatal' first novel. One of White's motivations in returning to the Church was the hope that her problems had resulted from following her own will rather than that of God. But the Church that White returned to was itself in flux, culminating in the reforms of the Second Vatican Council of 1962 to 1965. White had grown up in a Church strictly adhering to the scholastic tradition of Thomas Aquinas, which promoted an 'orderly rationalism and a conceptual framework into which every discrete item of information can be fitted, showing its connection to the whole and to the divine will from which it springs'.[4] The process of modernisation, which sought to reconcile scientific advances with Church doctrine, undermined

White's quest for a system of coherence and stability as the Church began to modify its teachings about God's role in Creation.

This study focuses on White's repeated turns to psychoanalysis and Catholicism to resolve the emotional conflicts that she believed were the cause of her tumultuous moods, her inexplicable behaviour and her writer's block.[5] These discourses structure the way she conceptualises her moods: they provide patterns, motifs and plotlines for the stories that White tells about herself, her illness and her writing. Psychoanalysis and Catholicism thus function as master narratives that themselves embody and transmit dominant and often implicit cultural and social values and expectations. As Hilary Clark observes:

> The stories one tells [about oneself] are never one's own. The post-structuralist view that identity and knowledge are socially constructed by dominant narratives can lead to the more sceptical conclusion that [. . .] even the most heartfelt personal narratives [. . .] are always ideological, shaped by myths and metaphors that [. . .] have remarkable sticking power.[6]

In trying to order her life through the structures of psychoanalytic and Catholic paradigms, White's stories about herself, her illness and her writing bear striking resemblances to those of her fellow women writers Virginia Woolf (who similarly suffered from manic-depressive illness) and H.D. (who similarly sought to break the grip of a paralysing writer's block by entering analysis). But unlike Woolf and H.D., White did not come to terms with either her illness or her writer's block. Interpreting her affective disorder through the lenses of psychoanalysis and Catholicism, she came to believe that her chaotic moods and resulting actions attested to unconscious conflicts and/or moral failings: affective symptoms became psychological complexes; complexes in turn became sins. White's accession to psychoanalysis and Catholicism as self-defining templates thus enmeshed her even more powerfully in the patriarchal narratives from which she sought to disentangle herself, choking and finally silencing the story of the woman writer that White wanted to tell, the story that would authorise the writer White herself wanted to become.

White's interpretations of herself have skewed interpretations of her work. In particular, the failure to address the scope of manic depression in White's life and its impact on her work characterises almost all the scholarship on White since the mid-1980s, leading scholars to accept without question White's attribution of her writer's block to her father's repudiation of her first novel, an interpretation developed during her psychoanalytic treatment in the 1930s. This equation, and the erotic intensity between White and her father that she explored both in her diary and in her fictional treatments of the father–daughter relationship, have recently led some scholars to read White's writing as testimonials to a buried incestuous trauma in White's life.[7] Such readings sustain White's misreading of her illness – that it occurred solely as a result of her relationship with her father – and then reproduce her interpretation of her writer's block – that it developed out of her repression of unconscious conflicts generated by her father's repudiation of her writing. Scholars have thus virtually ignored how analysis shaped White's understanding of the father–daughter relationship and her subsequent formulations of it: vivid incestuous phantasies prompted and indeed produced by analysis have been taken at face value as evidence of actual incest. As this study shows, White's desperate search for a narrative framework to account for her psychic incoherence and inexplicable behaviour fuelled her accession to a psychoanalytic plot in which the female castration complex was then the dominant storyline; her subsequent return to Catholicism superimposes a startlingly similar storyline upon the psychoanalytic one. In focusing on the emotionally incestuous dimension of the father-daughter relationship, White exposes not only how that dimension damages the daughter's subjectivity but also how the master plots of psychoanalysis and Catholicism place the daughter's desire for the father and submission to his authority at the core of their narratives.

White's conviction that her illness had emotional roots is understandable, for, as Kay Redfield Jamison observes, manic depression is 'an illness that is biological in its origins, yet one that feels psychological in the experience of it'.[8] The biological and genetic basis of manic depression was not understood for most of White's lifetime; neither was there effective treatment for the illness. John Cade's inadvertent discovery in 1949 that lithium resulted in the significant remission of manic symptoms spurred widespread clinical trials, first in Denmark and then elsewhere, and by the late 1960s and 1970s lithium was widely accepted as a first-line treatment for the condition.[9] Research into other drug treatments generated neuroleptics, antipsychotics and antidepressants that could also help control the illness. The successful treatment of manic depression through drug therapies confirmed the biological basis of the illness. At the same time, studies centred on monozygotic (identical) and dizygotic (fraternal) twins and on adoptees and their families established that genetic transmission was involved in a host of psychiatric conditions, including schizophrenia and manic depression. Edward Shorter describes how such studies encroached on the classic terrain of psychogenesis:

> For a century, the doctrine had ruled that hysteria and the symptomatic psychoneuroses were the result of stress of dysfunctional family life. The genetic news implied that these illnesses must have a significant brain substrate, however much environmental circumstances might contribute to them.[10]

Neurobiological research has continued apace, and today a much greater understanding exists of the role of gene transmission and neurotransmitters in the illness, and the ways in which drug therapies produce the results they do.

But these breakthroughs in understanding manic depression were on the far horizon in 1921. Instead, White's history of illness coincides with what Shorter has called the 'psychoanalytic hiatus' in psychiatry.[11] He writes:

> For a brief period at mid-twentieth century, middle-class society became enraptured of the notion that psychological problems arose as a result of unconscious conflicts over long-past events, especially those of a sexual nature [. . .] Freud's psychoanalysis appears as a pause in the evolution of biological approaches to brain and mind.[12]

Psychoanalysis reinforced White's search for the emotional causes of her illness through its foundational stance that feelings, actions and speech symptomatically manifest unconscious motivations and desires which, when recognised in analysis, can be 'worked through'. Additionally, psychoanalysis directed White to believe that sexual desire for her father was crucial in the formation of her neurosis. Notably, all three of White's analyses focused on her childhood and her relationship to her parents. In this respect, the fact that she was misdiagnosed as schizophrenic instead of as manic-depressive by her first analyst made no difference, for the psychoanalytic understanding of these conditions at the time attributed both to regression and to conflicts with their roots in childhood. All three analyses, moreover, encouraged White to interpret her symptoms for herself, to read intent and meaning into them, to pursue 'the almost literary activity of viewing physical symptoms as metaphors for mental states'.[13] Susan Sontag's complaint about psychoanalytic interpretation seems germane here. Sontag writes:

> All observable phenomena are bracketed, in Freud's phrase, as *manifest content*. This manifest content must be probed and pushed aside to find the true meaning – the *latent content* – beneath [. . .] For Freud, the events of individual lives (like neurotic symptoms and slips of the tongue) as well as texts (like a dream or a work of art) – all are treated as occasions for interpretation [. . .] these events only *seem* to be intelligible. To understand is to interpret. And to interpret is to restate the phenomenon, in effect to find an equivalent for it.[14]

The ultimate aim of psychoanalytic interpretation is thus to find 'a subtext which is the true one'.[15] Analysis persuaded White that her symptoms were manifestations of a subtext in which her castration complex and relationship with her father constituted the plot.

The cause-and-effect linkage between meaning and symptom that White developed through analysis did not only affect her stories of self: the analytic stance towards symptoms as signs of repression convinced White that she was responsible for her own suffering. In other words, if she could come to grips with her unconscious conflicts and desires, she would not feel depressed or engage in compulsive behaviours or have trouble concentrating on her writing.

Psychoanalysts now acknowledge that traditional analytic approaches are inappropriate for those with mood disorders. As one explains:

> Most analytic treatment carries with it a strong implication that it is a major analytic task of the patient to accept responsibility for his actions. In the psychoanalytic view, this responsibility is nearly total. We are even responsible for incorrectly or exaggeratedly holding ourselves responsible. It is our job to change our harsh superegos, and it is our job to do battle with unacceptable impulses. However, it now seems likely that there are patients with depressive, anxious and dysphoric states for whom the usual psychodynamic view of responsibility seems inappropriate and who should not be held accountable [. . .] It may be that we have been co-conspirators with these patients in their need to construct a rational-seeming

world in which they hold themselves unconsciously responsible for events. Narcissistic needs may lead these patients to claim control over uncontrollable behaviours rather than to admit to the utter helplessness of being at the mercy of moods that sweep over them without apparent rhyme or reason. An attempt at dynamic understanding in these situations may not only not be genuinely explanatory; it may be a cruel misunderstanding of the patient's efforts to rationalise his life experience.[16]

White's analysis in the 1930s supports this view of the analyst as a 'co-conspirator' whose inadvertently 'cruel misunderstanding' of her condition meant that he encouraged her to construct a rational sequence of events for which she herself was responsible. Hence, whereas recent psychotherapies designed specifically for those with bipolar disorders emphasise patient education, recognition and management of relapse, and communication and coping skills, White's treatment only underscored her conviction that defects in herself precluded a return to health.[17] Indeed, contemporary psychotherapy for manic depression addresses this belief that the client is somehow responsible for having the illness: instead, it focuses on developing strategies for managing it. Thomas C. Caramagno writes:

> Most patients need short-term psychotherapy to help them examine how the disease has affected their judgements, emotions and memories and to encourage them to rebuild a coherent self-structure if it has been destroyed by the disease [. . .] an entrenched pattern of mood-induced misinterpretations will not be dissolved by drugs alone.[18]

Contemporary psychotherapies also pay close attention to the ways in which the illness affects interpersonal relationships and employment for, as one review of psychosocial interventions remarks, 'social, family, and occupational dysfunction are the rule rather than the exception in bipolar disorder'.[19] White's history of broken marriages, estrangement from her daughters and inability to hold on to jobs amply supports this conclusion. This history of dysfunction, moreover, added immeasurably to White's sense of personal failure and guilt.

The debilitation and devastation that untreated manic depression generates is not widely understood even today outside medical circles or those with personal experiences of the illness. An often-quoted statistic points to the fact that the person whose first episode occurs in their late teens or early twenties (as did White's) will lose fourteen years of productivity in adulthood (encompassing work and family roles) and nine years of life.[20] Suicide is a major risk: while most studies of completion determine a 15–19 per cent lifetime risk, other studies have found much higher completion rates, ranging from 30 to 50 per cent.[21] Even the lowest rate of 15 per cent completion is thirty times higher than that of the general population.[22] Because the term 'bipolar' highlights the division between the two extremes of mania and depression, moreover, it mutes the equally important factors of recurrence and chronicity. Yet, as a 2008 summary of recent research reports, 'More than 90 per cent of patients have recurrences of mania or depression over their lifetimes [. . .] Patients who have had one manic episode nearly always go on to have another, even if they are maintained on medications.'[23] The type of mood that initiates the illness – whether it begins with an episode of mania or an episode of depression – functions as a predictor of the illness pattern.[24] Manic episode onset has been associated with better outcomes than depressive episode onset, with the latter type more predictive of 'rapid cycling' (four or more episodes a year), resistance to treatment and suicidality.[25]

The role that life events play in the onset of illness and in subsequent episodes remains unclear. In general, life events and environmental conditions are thought to trigger or 'turn on' the biological predisposition for the illness at onset, but play a less important role thereafter.[26] Other studies, however, demonstrate a strong relationship between life events and relapse, although, admittedly, patterns of behaviour that develop from the illness may in turn contribute to creating stressful life events, in a vicious cycle that makes it difficult to determine causality.[27] One influential theory posits that, in a subset of illness cases, onset produces a 'kindling' effect: each recurrence increases the likelihood of further recurrences, and eventually stressors play a minimal role as the illness takes on a momentum of its own. In this subset, episodes increase in frequency and duration, while intervals between episodes decrease.[28] Even for those who do not fall into this subset, symptoms, particularly for depression, may characterise the intervals between major episodes: a 2002 study found that 'patients spent 47 per cent of their lives in symptomatic states, and depression accounted for three times as many weeks of illness as mania or hypomania'.[29]

White's illness seems to have been both chronic and predominantly depressive. Her diary indicates that it began with a severe bout of depression that preceded her marriage in 1921. As is still the case with depressive episode onset, she did not perceive herself as ill, nor did she ever connect this severe depression to the subsequent acute psychotic mania that led to her hospitalisation in Bethlem in 1922. White initially believed this manic episode was an isolated incident and unlikely to recur. Indeed, before her marriage to Tom Hopkinson in 1930, her future father-in-law raised objections to the marriage on the grounds of White's history of mental illness. Hopkinson located one of the doctors who had treated White in Bethlem, securing from him a letter 'declaring that her acute collapse in 1921–2 was due to prolonged mental stress, and was unlikely to be any kind of inherited disorder which could threaten any future children with mental disease'.[30] But the onset of a second serious breakdown in 1933 made it clear that her illness was recurrent, as White succumbed to suicide attempts, sleep disturbances and nightmares, violent outbursts and a general inability to function. And from this point on, White seems to have suffered almost constantly from 'mixed states', in which manic and depressive symptoms combine (although she evidences shifts between moods in which mania predominates with depressive symptoms – dysphoric mania – and depressions infused with manic symptoms – agitated depression). 'Bipolar', with its suggestion of a neat division between the two moods and the illness as one in which moods oscillate between the two extremes, is for White's condition a misnomer. She unmistakably endured both states together. The profound dysfunction and suffering this almost constant illness created is the subject of the next chapter.

Why did White's analyst, Dennis Carroll, diagnose her as schizophrenic in May 1935? There is no clear answer to this question. According to her daughter Lyndall Hopkinson, the notes for the case were destroyed after Carroll's death.[31] And Carroll did not convey this information to White: it came second-hand, conveyed to White by her second husband and lifelong mentor, who went to discuss the severity of her illness with Carroll on 27 May 1935 (*Diary* 1, p. 48). White's diary gives no indication that Carroll ever discussed this diagnosis with her directly. Several possibilities for Carroll's diagnosis exist. First, women were often misdiagnosed with schizophrenia in mid-century, so much so that Elaine Showalter has famously termed schizophrenia the 'female hysteria of the twentieth-century'.[32] The diagnosis, indeed, came loaded with cultural and gendered implications for White, which I consider in Chapter 2. But a second distinct possibility is that Carroll misdiagnosed White as schizophrenic based on her history of psychosis. White never became psychotic during her second breakdown. But her first and most severe manic episode meets the criteria for 'delirious mania', an acute state of insanity which Frederick K. Goodwin and Kay Redfield Jamison describe as underscoring 'the origins of the phrase "raving maniac"'.[33] This acute type of mania is characterised by 'sudden onset and symptoms of severe insomnia, loss of appetite, disorientation, paranoia, and extremely bizarre hallucinations and delusions'.[34] A recent (1999) description finds the following:

> Patients with delirious mania are excited, restless, fearful, paranoid and delusional. They sleep poorly, are often confused and disoriented, and they confabulate. The onset develops within a few hours or a few days. Fever, rapid heart rate, tachycardia, hypertension and rapid breathing are common [. . .] Garrulous, incoherent and rambling speech alternates with mutism. Negativism, stereotypy grimacing, posturing, echolalia and echopraxia occur. When examined, they are poorly oriented for place, date and time, are unable to recall their recent experiences or numbers given them.[35]

The medical records kept during White's hospitalisation and White's own descriptions of manic psychosis in *Beyond the Glass* conform to this description: White was so disoriented that she did not even remember her own name for many months.[36] She also suffered from fever, violent excitement – in *Beyond the Glass* Clara shreds a leather jacket with her bare hands, a detail probably based on White's own actions – and a loss of appetite so extreme that she would have starved to death if not force-fed. Incoherent rambling speech and incessant singing alternated with catatonic stupor. White also wrote in 'mirror writing' when on the verge of breakdown, an unusual and rare form of cognitive disorientation then linked to schizophrenia.[37] In White's time any symptoms of psychosis might be diagnosed as schizophrenia, and it is difficult to distinguish acute manic psychosis from schizophrenia even today. Stephen P. Hinshaw, whose bipolar father was misdiagnosed as schizophrenic as a result of manic psychosis in the 1930s, remarks that the misdiagnosis in any case was irrelevant, as there was no treatment for it.[38]

White's analyst may also have been misled by the common misperception of mania as a kind of pathological happiness. While euphoric mood indeed characterises some forms of mania, particularly the milder form known as 'hypomania', the dysphoric mania that seems to have characterised White's second breakdown was not widely understood or recognised. Karl Abraham, whose ideas about the 'female castration complex' were the basis of White's analysis in the 1930s, authored an influential essay on manic depression in 1911, subsequently collected in a 1927 edition of his writings published by the Hogarth Press. In that essay Abraham writes: 'The manic's frame of mind differs from both normal and from depressive states, partly in its carefree and unrestrained cheerfulness, partly in its increased irritability and feeling of self-importance.'[39] The manic mood is 'a kind of careless gaiety which bears an obviously childish character', he continues, in which the 'flight of ideas offers the patient considerable possibilities of obtaining pleasure' by making 'playful allusion to pleasurable things'.[40] This emphasis on pleasure, gaiety, cheerfulness and playfulness is a far cry from subjective reports of dysphoric mania, such as Jamison's description of her own experience of it:

> I felt infinitely worse, more dangerously depressed, during this first manic episode than when in the midst of my worst depressions. In fact, the most dreadful I had ever felt in my entire life – one characterised by chaotic ups and downs – was the first time I was psychotically manic. I had been mildly manic many times before, but these had never been frightening experiences – ecstatic at best, confusing at worst [. . .] Increasingly, all of my images were black and decaying.[41]

Indeed, Jamison points to mixed states – more often characteristic of women's manic-depressive illness – as part of her argument against the clinical term 'bipolar':

> 'bipolar' [. . .] perpetuates the notion that depression exists rather tidily segregated on its own pole, while mania clusters neatly and discreetly on another. This polarisation of two clinical states flies in the face of everything we know about the cauldronous, fluctuating nature of manic-depressive illness; it ignores the question of whether mania is, ultimately, simply an extreme form of depression; and it minimises the importance of mixed manic-and-depressive states, conditions that are extremely common, extremely important clinically, and lie at the heart of many of the critical theoretical issues underlying this particular disease.[42]

Why White's analyst misdiagnosed her as schizophrenic we will never know. What is clear, however, is that scholars have ignored the ways in which manic-depressive illness dominated White's life and shaped her thinking, even though Jane Dunn correctly identified White's illness in her meticulously researched 1998 biography. This critical oversight may reflect residual traces of the antipsychiatry movement of 1960s and 1970s. As scholars such as Michel Foucault and Roy Porter have shown, psychiatry has often functioned as a disciplinary practice that works to marginalise and punish those who deviate from social norms.[43] David A. Karp observes that the fact that mental illness has no 'demonstrable biological pathology' means that social judgements and evaluations play an enormous role in so-called 'scientific', 'medical' and 'psychological' conceptualisations of it. He writes:

> This is what makes the case of mental illness so especially fuzzy and warrants deep concern about the exclusive legitimacy of psychiatry to decide who should be labelled mentally ill and how they ought best to be treated. Such reservations seem well advised in light of what has been justified historically in the name of science and psychiatric medicine. Those deemed mentally ill have, at different moments in history, been subject to castration, involuntary incarceration, bloodletting, brutal 'electric shock' treatments, mind-numbing drugs inducing permanent neurological damage, and a variety of brain surgeries.[44]

Influential feminist critiques of psychiatry by Phyllis Chesler, Elaine Showalter, Jane Ussher and others have shown how femininity itself is often interwoven with and inextricable from definitions of insanity, mental instability and pathology.[45] (Indeed, Showalter uses White's case as an example of the abuses of psychiatric power.)[46] It is indisputable, moreover, that a psychiatric diagnosis can function as a debilitating 'label', isolating and marginalising an individual and resulting in profound material and social consequences.[47]

But it is also true that White was desperate to understand what was wrong with her, why she felt so badly, why she was unable to control her moods and actions. As I show in Chapter 2, diagnosis in the 1930s came as a great relief, confirming her sense that something was indeed amiss. Karp calls diagnosis 'a double-edged benchmark' in the acknowledgement of mental illness. On the one hand potentially stigmatising, diagnosis also

> imposes definitional boundaries onto an array of behaviours and feelings that previously had no name. Acquiring a clear conception of what one has and having a label to attach to confounding feelings and behaviours was especially significant to those who had gone for years without being able to name their situation.[48]

Over the years, moreover, White revised her conception of 'schizophrenia' to encompass her own actual lived and material realities of illness. An actual diagnosis, even though a misdiagnosis, authorised and legitimated her search for understanding her condition and taking it seriously.

Finally, I concur with Karp when he writes:

> Anti-psychiatry theorists undercut their credibility by taking their argument too far. To flatly claim that mental illness does not exist seems nonsensical when people are catatonic, visibly psychotic, or otherwise unable to understand or carry out even the most rudimentary behaviours necessary to function in a society.[49]

To discount the validity of mental illness adds immeasurably to the lived and tangible anguish of those who suffer, as White did, with an illness that was 'all in her head'. The contemporary critique of psychiatric practices notably differs from that of the 1960s and 1970s by not disputing the validity of mental illness but by instead disputing the ways in which those who avail themselves of mental health services are treated as objects without agency and insight and undeserving of respect.[50] In her study of psychiatric survivors' movements, Gail A. Hornstein champions in particular the value of first-person accounts of sufferers in understanding psychic distress. 'The more of these accounts I've read, and the more people I've met in the psychiatric survivor movement, the more convinced I've become that first-person experience is crucial to understanding madness and its treatment', she writes.[51] White's work constitutes an important and eloquent contribution to that understanding.

In the following chapters I trace the development of White's narratives of identity in tandem with her actual experiences of illness.

Because an understanding of manic depression is crucial to understanding the unfolding of White's stories of self, I begin with a chapter on the illness and the complex interplay of biological, psychological and environmental factors that constitute it. The three phases of the illness – mania, depression, and euthymia ('well' phases) – suggest a clear-cut demarcation that the illness itself confounds, for not only do the phases themselves overlap, but the disorder affects every aspect of being, including metabolism, speech, psychomotor activity, cognition, judgement and personality. I then compare White's experiences of illness to those of her better-known contemporary, Virginia Woolf. Such a comparison points up the different manifestations of manic-depressive illness, the approaches medical professionals and family members improvised to cope with the illness prior to the development of pharmacological interventions such as lithium and other mood stabilisers, and the aesthetic strategies each woman developed in response to the cognitive and emotional upheavals of the illness.

Chapter 2 contextualises White's stories of self within contemporary scholarship on narrative identity. White's search for an explanation of her illness that would account for her psychic turmoil and inexplicable behaviour is consistent with the emphasis in such scholarship that narrative is a central aspect of identity formation, that 'one can know oneself as a self only within the context of a (life) narrative'.[52] The possession of an identity narrative plays an integral role in both public and personal presentations of self. Yet the very principles an identity narrative embodies – principles of coherence, plausibility, causality, motivation and agency – conflict with the chaos and havoc created by severe manic depression. White's struggle to impose coherence on her stories of self thus sheds light on the construction of illness narratives in general and mental illness narratives in particular. Surprisingly little work has been done on how bipolarity impacts the formation of a sense of self. The typical onset of the illness (in the late teens or early twenties) ruptures the life narrative, opening up an unbridgeable gap between a lost 'healthy self' and a now-troubled one. White emblematises this rupture in her identification of her father's repudiation as the source of her illness. Her monumental diary bears eloquent witness to this process.

The following chapter explores the two main interpretative frameworks White adopted to conceptualise a sense of self in the face of her recurrent psychic distress and inexplicable behaviour. White's entrance into psychoanalytic treatment coincided with a moment in psychoanalytic history in which the thinking about female sexuality centred upon the 'female castration complex'. White's diary provides unmistakeable evidence that she developed an explanation for her illness that was heavily influenced by the ideas of Karl Abraham, whose 1920 'Manifestations of the Female Castration Complex' initiated this line of psychoanalytic theorising and who profoundly shaped British psychoanalysis.[53] The recurrence of manic-depressive symptoms following her supposed 'cure' by psychoanalysis impelled White to return to the Catholic Church at the end of 1940. Her account of her return to the Church in *The Hound and the Falcon* reveals White's ongoing preoccupation with developing a coherent self-narrative and shows how White superimposes Catholic doctrine on that of psychoanalysis. Together, these interpretative frameworks worked to affirm the centrality of father–daughter eroticism in White's identity narrative.

The final chapter examines how the consolidation of White's identity narrative influenced her later novels. Seventeen years separate the publication of *Frost in May* from the later trio, years in which White revised her imaginative reconstruction of the father–daughter relationship and the family constellation more generally to reflect her now unshakeable conviction that the daughter's illness emerged from her vexed relationship with her father. The later novels thus trace the emergence of 'schizophrenia' in White's protagonist. At the same time, however, White's fidelity to her own experiences of illness surfaces in the explorations of depression (in *The Sugar House*) and mania (in *Beyond the Glass*), providing a hitherto overlooked account of the onset of manic-depressive illness. The later novels also reflect the impact of White's second and informal analysis in the late 1940s with Dorothy Kingsmill, who drew White's attention to her neglect of her maternal heritage and who also encouraged White to free her imaginative faculties through dream analysis. White's more nuanced understanding of family dynamics is reflected in the later novels, which I read through Christine C. Kieffer's important work on the seductive father and the 'oedipal victor', the daughter who displaces the mother but who pays the price with her autonomy and her sense of herself as a woman.[54] In the novels, Clara's story ends with her emergence from the mental hospital, her restoration to her father and her loss of her fiancé, who, despairing of her recovery, has married someone else. It is a conclusion that poignantly captures White's assessment of her own life.

When asked in an interview whether her life had been happy, White hesitated a moment before responding that perhaps her life would be better characterised as interesting. White's was a troubled life, and her illness disrupted and in some cases irrevocably damaged her relationships with those closest to her. She did not have the kind of material and emotional support accorded Virginia Woolf, nor did she achieve the artistic reach and success of the latter. Yet it is impossible to read through White's diaries without an enormous sense of admiration and respect for this woman who courageously battled her inner demons, often alone, for decades. White's diaries have never been published in their entirety; the two published volumes represent, according to her daughter and editor Susan Chitty, only about a quarter of the manuscript material.[55] It is my hope that this study draws renewed interest to White's work and alerts scholars of life-writing, mental illness and histories of medicine and psychiatry to this rich and almost untapped archive. And by contextualising White's fiction within her struggles for self-understanding, I hope to call attention to the ways in which the novels offer competing explanations of psychic turmoil, thereby providing a new way of understanding and appreciating White's accomplishments.

White, literary scholarship and mental illness

Mental illness has received surprisingly little attention in White scholarship, despite the fact that much of her oeuvre focuses on it. In addition to the detailed accounts of depression and mania in *The Sugar House* and *Beyond the Glass*, three of White's eight published short stories – 'The House of Clouds' (1930), 'The Moment of Truth' (1941) and 'Surprise Visit' (1964) – depict the psychological disintegration of the main character. In *The Hound and the Falcon*, a collection of letters written in 1940–1 that documents White's reconversion to Catholicism, White discusses the history of her illness in depth. The two edited volumes of her diary provide ample evidence of her ongoing struggles with illness; her unpublished diaries provide even more. In addition to White's own writing, her daughters' memoirs make clear the devastating impact of their mother's illness on her life as well as theirs; Dunn's biography demonstrates the ongoing disruptions of White's illness throughout her lifetime.

In both her biographical and fictional writing, White represented her relationship to her father as the source of her illness and her writer's block. Since that account dominates not only her writing but critical assessments of it, it is worth examining here in some detail. White's relationship with her father was indeed fraught. An only child, White grew up idolising her father, a London classics master, and despising her mother, by her accounts a dreamy, frivolous and hyper-feminine woman. White knew her father wanted a son and in many ways she tried to be one, by sharing his intellectual passions and by engaging in 'boy's' games and interests. White developed an intense bond with her father, but at the same time she always felt that she never measured up to his ideals and she feared his disapproval. 'I always felt this impassable barrier between us, for he was a devout, but rigoristic man with no understanding of people unlike himself', White wrote. 'He centred everything on me, trying to force me into an exact replica of himself. I adored him, feared him and was never at ease with him' (*The Hound and the Falcon*, p. 82). When her father converted to Catholicism when she was seven, White followed suit: 'it would never have occurred to me to go against my father's wishes: I adored and revered him too much' (*The Hound and the Falcon*, p. 154). She attended the Convent of the Sacred Heart at his bidding, leaving at fifteen when she was expelled after the discovery of her adolescent manuscript. (In fact, she was not expelled: White would learn only many years later that her father used the discovery of her 'depraved' manuscript as a pretext: he withdrew her from the Convent so that she could attend a good secondary school and prepare for university examinations.) Although White tried to discuss her 'expulsion' from the Convent with her father before his death, he maintained a determined silence on the subject: 'To the end of his life he refused to discuss the matter or to let me state my side of the case. Thus for fifteen years there was a cloud between us which was never entirely dissolved' (*The Hound and the Falcon*, p. 155).

White attributes her enduring conflicts about femininity, sexuality and artistry to this event. Her father's authority, moreover, became entwined for her with the authority of the Catholic Church, and both fictional and biographical accounts stress the damaging impact of the Church's repressive attitude to sexuality on the female adolescent. White writes that the 'whole subject was so muffled and hedged round with horrors and pruriencies that one came to think "impurity" was in a class by itself' (*The Hound and the Falcon*, p. 55). Ignorant of the facts of life until the age of eighteen, White describes 'suffering ago-nies of shame and remorse and dreading going to Confession' after a boy kissed her when she was twelve; at fourteen the appearance of pubic hair caused 'shame and misery', for White thought she had 'committed some appalling crime and was being turned into an ani-mal for a punishment' (*Hound*, p. 65). Encounters with priests only made things worse. '[A]s a young girl it used to cost me tremendous efforts to confess any "sin against purity" because it was always the cue for the priest to begin what I can only call very prurient prob-ing and questioning. They never did that about any other sin', White recalled (*The Hound and the Falcon*, p. 68). White described the pro-cess by which the Church annulled her first marriage as an 'obscenity' that gave her her 'first real horror of it as an institution' (*The Hound and the Falcon*, p. 24). Not surprisingly, 'Actual sex became a kind of ordeal mixed up with all sorts of terrors and feelings of extreme guilt' (*The Hound and the Falcon*, p. 30).

This potent brew of feminine sexual desire and literary ambition mixed with patriarchal repression and served up as insanity and writer's block meant that White's work was tailor-made for revival as the women's movement gained momentum and created a demand for the lost work of women writers: Carmen Callil's newly founded Virago Press reissued *Frost in May* as its first Modern Classic in 1978, with *The Hound and the Falcon* and the three subsequent nov-els in the sequence following soon after; a collection of unpublished and unfinished pieces appeared in 1982. A four-part dramatisation of the novel sequence ran on the BBC in 1982. Early feminist stud-ies addressed the conflict between patriarchal authority and female literary ambition, discussing the relationship of White's work to the conventions of the *Künstlerroman* and the convent novel and evok-ing comparisons of *Frost in May* with James Joyce's *A Portrait of the Artist as a Young Man* (1916).[56] White's writing also attracted the attention of critics interested in her depictions of Catholicism.[57]

In the meantime, her daughters' memoirs appeared in 1985 and 1988, followed by the edited diaries in 1991 and 1992. Attention soon shifted to White herself. Mary Lynn Broe's influential 1989 study of Peggy Guggenheim's literary coterie at Hayford Hall, which included Djuna Barnes and Emily Holmes Coleman as well as White, sparked interest in this community as well as interest in the possibility that all three were incest survivors who described sexual trauma in their work.[58] Elizabeth Podnieks' groundbreaking analysis of White's diary appeared in 2000; Podnieks convincingly argues that White's diary should be read as a significant contribution to women's modernism, alongside the work of established diarists such as Virginia Woolf and Anaïs Nin.[59] Following Broe, Podnieks speculates about the role that incest may have played in White's difficulties. Podnieks also edited, with Sandra Chait, a collection on Hayford Hall (2005) that includes three chapters on White.[60] One examines the relationship between White's sexuality and spirituality (Sandra Chait) and another White's writer's block (Sandra Jeffery); both chapters support their analyses with White's account of her difficulties as originating in her relationship with her father.[61] The third chapter (Julie Vandivere) explores the formal differences between White's and Coleman's representations of psychosis in, respectively, *Beyond the Glass* and *The Shutter of Snow*.[62] The representation of psychosis in these two novels is also the subject of Kylie Valentine's 2003 article, included as a chapter in her monograph that appeared in the same year.[63] Valentine's monograph explores the ways in which psychoanalysis, psychiatry and modernism are implicated in one another but, somewhat surprisingly, Valentine does not address White's actual illness or her specific first-hand experiences of psychoanalytic treatment.

That literary scholars have by and large shied away from examining the role of illness in White's fictional and biographical narratives of self is understandable, given that our professional training leaves us ill equipped to evaluate the medical and scientific scholarship that would underpin that examination. In the single literary study that remarks the similarity of psychosis in *Beyond the Glass* to the manic pole of bipolar disorder, Philip F. O'Mara appends a disclaimer: 'A person with no clinical training must be cautious in any diagnostic claim about mental illness.'[64] Yet that caution has not extended to making diagnostic claims about psychosis based on the speculation that White was an incest victim. Podnieks, for example, writes that White's 'assertion that her "insanity" "had causes"' is 'clarified' by the fact that 'she was terrified of sex. It is arguable that the trauma caused by even the idea of intercourse was related to an earlier crisis brought on by her father's advances.'[65] Sandra Chait similarly attributes psychosis to White's conflicts about sexuality. White's sexuality offended her father, Chait writes:

> He attempted to control her every action, her every thought, even to
> the point of causing her mental breakdown under the stress of trying

to reconcile her supposedly divergent needs both to be loved and to express herself honestly, and therefore sexually too, in writing.[66]

Sandra Jeffery echoes this assessment. White's 'abnormal fear of sex' may have been 'sinister in origin': incest 'would provide an explanation for her irrational fear of a normal sexual relationship, as well as the cause behind her persistent inability to write fiction'.[67] Her retreat from sexuality into insanity 'was possibly exacerbated by the reawakening of the primal fear that had been repeatedly enforced by the negative attitude of her mother towards sexual matters'.[68] Such claims resonate throughout almost all recent scholarship on White.[69]

There are a number of problems with these claims. First, they overlook the chronology of White's discussions of the father–daughter relationship, which took on an explicitly sexualised character only after she entered the most orthodox of her analyses in the 1930s. Second, they blur not only chronology but also fictional and biographical depictions of the father–daughter relationship. Third, they uncritically adopt contemporary feminist models of traumatic and/or recovered memory that numerous scholars have challenged. Fourth, they make highly problematic assumptions about the relationship of psychosis to supposedly 'normal' or 'healthy' sexuality. And finally, they fail to address the evidence of serious illness and the role it may have played in White's representations of her illness and its relationship to her father.

I will bracket the last two problems for a moment and briefly review the foundations upon which readings of incest in White rest. When White entered analysis with Dennis Carroll in 1935, she experienced 'convulsive horror aroused by C[arroll]'s shaking his bunch of keys', which she linked to the sound of her father's latchkey and her fear of his disapproval (*Diary* 1, p. 51). Another early session established the layout of the family home, with White's nursery and her father's study separated only by a lavatory 'used almost exclusively' by them (*Diary* 1, p. 41). Podnieks writes that these early associations demonstrate how analysis 'triggered uncomfortable memories of her father',[70] but those memories need not be sexual: White always stressed her fear of her father's disapproval, and the proximity of her nursery to his study meant that if she made noise her father would storm into the room and demand silence. Mary Therese Strauss-Noll suggests that her analyst may have even been eliciting memories of her father, thereby resembling 'the current practice today of some counsellors convincing their patients that they were victims of childhood sexual abuse'.[71] As the analysis drew to a close in 1938, White recorded two startlingly lurid entries in her diary in which she ponders the implications of the female castration complex, whereby the daughter desires the father's penis or a child by him (*Diary* 1, p. 140). In the second entry, she launches into an angry tirade about her father; an asterisk in the edited edition notes that this entry 'is in a handwriting quite alien to Antonia's usual small neat style' and in her introduction to the volume Chitty observes that White's feelings about her father were so strong 'that in the one passage of the diaries where she obscenely abuses him her handwriting deteriorates into a childish scrawl' (*Diary* 1, pp. 141, 8). Lyndall Hopkinson also takes note of this unusual handwriting.[72] In addition to these entries, White recorded a number of sexually explicit dreams about her father, one of which she called the 'Ritual Rape Dream' in which she dreamt that her father penetrated her.[73] Hopkinson additionally recounts waking her mother from a nightmare that her mother then refused to describe to her because the content about her father was too obscene to share.[74]

White's fiction records no explicit sexual scenes between father and daughter, although the father–daughter relationship in the novel sequence does conform in some aspects to what Judith Lewis Herman has called 'covert' or emotional incest, which 'does not involve physical contact or a requirement for secrecy' but, rather, a pattern of eroticised behaviours that betray the fathers' 'intrusive sexual interest'.[75] Indeed, one of White's achievements in the sequence is to convey what her protagonist terms the 'disquieting' feelings such behaviours induce as well as the long-term repercussions they have on the daughter's sense of self and her relationship to her sexuality (*The Lost Traveller*, p. 126). One scene in *The Lost Traveller*, the second novel in the series, has been cited by several scholars and by Chitty herself as possible evidence of buried incest in White's own life: the father, angry with the daughter and consumed by jealous fantasies, makes overtly sexual and aggressive overtures to one of her schoolfriends, falling on his knees before her, pulling her coat open and kissing her neck, 'almost groaning: "So white, so soft"' (*The Lost Traveller*, p. 278). Chitty comments, 'But Antonia's neck was the one that was white and soft. She later admitted that the passage was pure invention, "to explain things in Daddy"'.[76] Chitty implies that those 'things' are incestuous in nature; Podnieks argues that this 'incident crystallises [White's] interpretation of her father'.[77] In a long passage in the unpublished diaries, however, White writes that this scene is a 'clue' to show that the father is a passionate man, which the daughter has never realised;[78] another unpublished diary entry records that she wants to make it clear that, while her father had a sensual and passionate nature, he never gave in to it.[79] In the context of the novel as a whole, the passage conforms to a pattern whereby the father projects his lustful urges on to women who remind him of family members. Structurally and thematically, it forms part of a deliberate attempt to represent the dynamics of unconscious incestuous fantasies underpinning family relationships. To pluck it out of context as biographical evidence of buried and repressed incest trauma gives White very little credit for the ambitious plan she developed in the novel.

White's interest in the incestuous dynamics of family life bears the indelible imprint of her lengthy analysis in the 1930s. I explore the trajectory of this analysis in detail in Chapter 3. Here I want to draw attention to psychoanalytic orthodoxy in this period, for Freud's contention that incest fantasies structure children's development and are at the root of adult neurosis was both controversial and well known: Freud himself relates an anecdote in which an hysterical girl, asked why she did not consult 'Dr F.', responded, 'What good would that be? I know he'd say to me: "Have you ever had the idea of having sexual intercourse with your father?"'[80] White's discussions of her analysis in the 1930s clearly reveal that her analyst saw the source of her problems as White's repressed rage about not receiving her father's 'gift' of a penis. He may have been particularly adamant that she accept this assessment, since he was not yet fully qualified and was still seeking full membership in the British Psychoanalytical Society.[81] White certainly perceived Carroll as aggressively insisting on the 'love transference' whereby he would replace the father in her unconscious conflicts; she likened analysis to 'being under torture . . . one will confess anything for relief. I'm perfectly willing to say I'm raging with lust for you if that will satisfy you & you'll leave me in peace.'[82] As analysis continued, White did develop a positive transference to her analyst and did perceive him as both father and lover.[83] The lurid passages in her diary – recorded in June 1938, prior to completing analysis in September that same year – hence document the 'successful' resolution of her castration complex: White acknowledges her rage at her father for his 'castration' of her, his withholding of the 'gift' of the penis. Notably, these entries also record White's sense that her father certainly did not want to have sex with her; the passage in the second entry where her handwriting deteriorates records her rage at his withholding approval and love for her unless she conformed to his standards, including his standards for her handwriting.

This 'successful' resolution of White's 'neurosis' suggests iatrogenesis, the process by which doctors or therapists inadvertently induce the conditions they purportedly treat: White, like the girl in Freud's anecdote, has come to believe she wanted to sleep with her father. In the first entry, moreover, she refers to an illegal abortion she underwent with the help of her father; the reference to this abortion and the strange circumstances surrounding it underscore the way in which analysis may have impelled White to concretise and literalise the female castration complex. This pregnancy resulted when a man she had been seeing was invited by her father to spend the night at the family home; he crept into her bedroom that evening when she was asleep, wearing her father's dressing gown. White never could explain her acquiescence to this unsettling encounter, for she was still a virgin and in the process of annulling her first marriage on the grounds that it had not been consummated; her inability to account for her behaviour would eventually thwart her continuation of the novel sequence (see Chapter 2). White related this story to her daughters, both of whom refer to it in their memoirs: Chitty calls it 'very strange, something so outlandish that my mother never spoke of it to anyone except my sister and myself, and then only once or twice'.[84] To Chitty, White 'confessed that she put up little resistance – on the contrary, she was rather encouraging'.[85] In the diary entries that announce her acceptance of her 'castration' and her desire for her father's 'gift' – a 'gift' she equates with both her adolescent novel and aborted baby boy – White observes that her father could not have been kinder had he been her husband in his care for her after the abortion.[86] In making notes for the novel she could not finally write about the episode, White describes the father's trip to Paris with the daughter afterwards as 'definitely a sort of honeymoon' (*Diary* 1, p. 293). White and her daughters always stressed the father's dressing gown as a key detail in recounting this story. 'Because of those references to the familiar dressing gown, it is very tempting to think she believed she was having sex with her father', Strauss-Noll writes, in one of the only critical accounts that examines this incident.[87] Analysis may have encouraged White to focus on (or perhaps even add) this detail.

The sexually explicit references and dreams about her father in the 1940s, following the 'resolution' of her 'female castration complex', thus record White's incest fantasies, fantasies encouraged and elicited by analysis as part of her supposed 'cure'. A number of White's entries suggest that her analyst employed aggressive methods in convincing her to accept this interpretation. One entry, for example, records White's fear of 'still more humiliation and suffering than I have yet undergone' in analysis (*Diary* 1, p. 109), another her sense that her analyst used 'sneering and jeering' to convince her of her 'castration'.[88] (In that entry, she defensively continues that just because she doesn't have a penis doesn't mean she has nothing.)[89] A dream White records features a 'brisk-looking Jewish doctor' who addresses her in a 'sneering, patronising voice', leaving her 'tongue-tied' and feeling as if 'something unspeakably humiliating and agonisingly painful was going to happen' (*Diary* 1, p. 111); it is hard not to see this figure as a representation of Freud himself. By the end of analysis, however, White records her strong attraction to her analyst, even imagining him as a potential husband, while she simultaneously wonders why the Judeo-Christian tradition punishes disobedient daughters for their forbidden desires, whereas the Greeks created a god who could have 'incestuous relations' with his daughters without any apparent sexual guilt.[90]

Researchers in the fields of cognitive psychology have studied the ways in which memory is a form of interpretation and reconstruction rather than an accurate transcription of 'what really happened'.[91] Martin A. Conway writes:

> A vast body of research from the psychological laboratory and, increasingly, from more real-world studies demonstrates that human memories are inaccurate, incomplete, open to distortion, and wholesale fabrication. Indeed, experimentally inducing false memories in healthy young adults appears almost trivially easy [. . .] the implication being that in the context of therapy, with a patient who is psychologically dysfunctional and actively seeking help, the probability of memory distortion and fabrication is multiplied many times over.[92]

I am not suggesting that White's memories are false: rather, I am suggesting that her analytic 'treatment' during the 1930s played a key role in shaping her interpretation and representation of father–daughter relationships, whereby incestuous desire is seen as normal and the problem lies in the repression of those desires. White was seriously ill and on the verge of complete breakdown when she entered analysis; her terror of the asylum, reflected in persistent nightmares about her incarceration, was a strong motivator in her submission to Carroll's therapy and guidance:

> Carroll says that, without treatment, I should certainly become insane again. It is by no means certain that, even with treatment . . . I can avoid insanity . . . I think I must accept analysis meekly since it is difficult for me to accept, to blot myself out, become featureless, a 'case'. (*Diary* 1, p. 58)

In the years following analysis, White interpreted some of her most sexually explicit dreams about her father as evidence of her reconciliation with him.[93] In one, White discovers that her father is not dead after all: they embraced with 'love and relief' and White comments that in her dream she 'was so happy, so relieved. I would not be lonely any more'; she awoke 'aware of a very faint sexual tremor' (*Diary* 1, pp. 251–2). She interpreted this dream as evidence that she had forgiven her father, although several days later she wonders about the '"suspect" elements' in it: 'Fear . . . about my novels. Slightly wrong love . . . the sexual element. A touch obviously of wanting the father as a *husband*' (*Diary* 1, pp. 252–3). 'Fear' results not from the dream but from her fiction – and public exposure of the daughter's incestuous desires. The Ritual Rape dream is even more evocative. The entire dream occupies pages in White's unpublished dream diaries, and formed part of White's Jungian analysis with Dorothy Kingsmill in 1947. It is an extraordinary piece of writing, in which White evokes the medieval pageantry attendant to a great cathedral ritual that concludes with a holy virgin deflowered on an altar: no child will be born from this 'sacred incest' carried out by a white-bearded knight who is and is not her father, 'an august and sacred personage, almost like a druid priest'. White describes wanting the 'full act' despite being a virgin; she includes a graphic account of penetration and the terror and desire it inspired: 'there was no lust in this rape. It was a real act, but a sacred one, an initiation, not the fulfilment of a passion'. She woke with 'cold rhythmic shudders' passing through her body, 'in a kind of awe and thankfulness'.[94]

Critical readings of White's dreams, particularly this one, reductively understand them as evidence of actual incest rather than as inscriptions of forbidden, transgressive desire.[95] Podnieks, for example, interprets the Ritual Rape Dream as possibly evidence of

'Freudian desire' – presumably female oedipal desire – or an 'alternative, earlier discourse of hysteria':

> White's sexual preoccupation with her father could stem from early sexual abuse. The description of the 'ritual rape dream' fits well with Broe's argument of how the daughter-incest-survivor is exiled 'from the realm of childhood, where, as the child bride of the father, the mother's husband, she must now act as an adult woman'.[96]

This interpretation ignores the lush sensuousness of the dream and the power and intensity of the writing – the literary qualities of this extraordinary text – despite the fact that it draws upon and revises a tradition of graphic descriptions of black masses in writers ranging from the Marquis de Sade to Sacher-Masoch and Huysmans.[97] In limiting interpretation to the inscription of literal incest, White's complex collapsing of the sacred with the profane, the spirit with the flesh, and God/Mary with father/daughter disappears. The context of White's production of the dream, moreover, is important, for Jungian dream analysis encourages the identification of the personal unconscious with the archetypes of the collective unconscious (see Chapter 3). Finally, White's own interpretation of these dreams – as evidence of acceptance and forgiveness by her long-dead father – points back to the paralysing shock of White's adolescence, when her father repudiated her as a daughter because she had produced an erotic text. At a symbolic level, the dreams celebrate the father's full acceptance of the daughter and her sexuality, resulting in the scenario of the second dream, in which the emphasis is not on the Incarnation of the Holy Child – the Word made flesh – but rather the opposite, the flesh made Word.[98]

It is easy to see why White has been seen as an incest victim. White's daughter Susan Chitty initiated this interpretation, writing in her introduction to the edited diaries that 'It is hard not to suspect that Cecil may have, even if only to a small degree, sexually abused Antonia as a child'[99] and citing the usual reasons: the proximity of the nursery to the study; the passages in the diary in which the handwriting deteriorates; the explicitly sexual dreams and so on. Chitty's 1985 memoir implicitly invites such a reading, for, without access to biographical information about White's early life, Chitty creates a highly suggestive collage of erotically tinged incidents drawn from the novels.[100] Chitty's memoir and edited volumes of the diaries appeared in the charged atmosphere of the 1980s and 1990s, as controversies over 'recovered memories' of sexual abuse became ubiquitous in the United States. 'The women's movement of the 1960s and 1970s gave political momentum to the cultural "recovery" of memory around family violence, with sexual abuse at the forefront of challenges to the private control of men over women and children', writes the American psychologist Janice Haaken.[101] But by the late 1980s discussions of sexual abuse had changed. 'Whereas earlier accounts of childhood sexual abuse were based on continuous memories of abuse, by the late 1980s women with no prior known history of abuse began to "recover" such memories in the course of psychotherapy.'[102] Popular self-help books and memoirs of recovery, as well as more scholarly studies, many of which included 'lists of signs and symptoms indicating a possible history of abuse', created a new conviction among therapists and clients 'that the source of female disturbances was in a forgotten childhood trauma'.[103] As Haaken's study demonstrates, the 'recovered memory' controversy reignited long-standing debates over the credibility of women's stories. Hence the tendency for feminists was 'to close ranks around women's allegations, whatever they may be' and 'to insist that women's remembrances be taken literally as imprints of past events'.[104]

But this closing of ranks also serves a defensive purpose, Haaken argues. Haaken does not question either the pervasiveness or the traumatic impact of childhood sexual abuse. She does ask us to consider what cultural and social purposes the emergence of the 'recovered memory' narrative serves. An assumption that underlies both sides of the recovered memory controversy is that 'women are incapable of generating disturbing sexual imagery on their own' and thus the existence of such imagery must indicate an intrusion from an external source.[105] To be sure, the trauma model offers 'a corrective to the cultural tendency to view females as more prone to mental disorders' by 'locating the source of female disturbances within an external set of events imposed on the psyche through a discrete sexual assault that exerts a powerful pathogenic effect through the deferred action of the trauma memory'.[106] But this insistence on literal memory also forecloses the role of fantasy, desire and imagination in women's subjective lives. Haaken notes that sexual-abuse narratives allow women 'to speak about the forbidden: sexuality, aggression, rivalry, and fantasies of submission and domination', but then require the recovery of a traumatic memory to validate and normalise those responses.[107] Continuous memories become less revelatory than shadowy, fragmentary and inconclusive or ambiguous ones, as the trauma narrative fills in the gaps and locates the source in the abusive events of the past.[108] Indeed, the terminology that developed out of the recovered memory movement – 'trauma', 'survivor', 'witnessing' and 'testimonial' – makes memory a 'sacral function'.[109] The process of remembering and resurrecting the buried events of the past takes on 'the power of a conversion experience', while the recipient of the narrative 'bears witness' to its truth: 'once a person introduces her or his position as being that of a witness, invoking the moral and sacral discourse of the testimonial, questions about both the veracity of the testimony and the motivations of the witness are silenced'.[110]

Feminist readings of White as an incest victim developed out of this framework. In 1989 Mary Lynn Broe opened her interpretation of White by remarking that 'According to Antonia White, the only "unsafe subject" was her relationship with her father.'[111] Broe references a letter of 1941, in which White described her work on the novel that would eventually become *The Lost Traveller* (1950): 'The book I have in mind (I've made several false starts on it in the last six years) *will* be "unsafe". It is an "unsafe" subject the relation of a father and a daughter' (*The Hound and the Falcon*, p. 71). White does not state that her relationship with her father is the 'only' unsafe subject; rather, she states that it is her book that will be 'unsafe'. Given White's conviction, developed during analysis and in tandem with her composition of the early chapters of the novel, that incestuous fantasies are normal but also repressed and the source of guilt about sexuality, her remarks suggest that she plans to explore the incestuous dynamics between father and daughter, a subject she well knew to be 'unsafe' in terms of conventional social and cultural norms (she also explores other transgressive sexualities in the novel; see Chapter 4). Broe follows her opening remark by reproducing Chitty's highly suggestive collage of erotically tinged moments – two drawn from *The Lost Traveller* – which Broe claims 'suggest an unfinished text' for White's writer's block.[112] Following Chitty's lead, Broe implies that the fictional scene in which the father makes aggressive sexual overtures to the daughter's schoolfriend is a coded biographical event: 'The friend, Antonia White later admitted, was pure invention "*to explain things in Daddy*"' (Broe's emphasis).[113] Broe's dramatic conclusion follows:

Explaining Daddy. By 1937, although Antonia White had begun six novels (including two written at school), the only one she had actually

completed was *Frost in May* (1933). A series of breakdowns, marriage annulments, divorces, conversions, reconversions, bouts with
psychoanalysis, and severe writer's blocks punctuated her life.[114]

Implying that these experiences can all be explained by something
revealed by White's silence, and noting that White could produce
copious amounts of writing in diaries and letters ('a "safe" form of
intimacy') but could not produce finished fiction after 1954, Broe
attributes White's writer's block to the silence imposed on the incest
survivor.[115] White's *Frost in May* then becomes 'the daughter's struggle
to reveal the father's secret' and the fictional daughter's repudiated
novel 'the incest survivor's embattled discourse in and on textuality'.[116]

Podnieks builds on Broe's reading of White. In this pioneering
analysis of White's diaries, Podnieks demonstrates White's relevance to
numerous strands of women's modernism, including her engagement
with psychoanalysis; her efforts to combine work, artistry and mother-
hood; her relationship to sexuality; and her attempts to work through
her conflicted feelings about her father and Catholicism.[117] Throughout
her analysis, Podnieks stresses the possibility that White was an incest
victim; these reiterated suggestions acquire weight simply by virtue of
repetition. Psychoanalysis, instead of promoting the fantasy that White
wanted to sleep with her father, 'allowed White to confront the domi-
nating personality of her father and to identify the traumatic psychological and possible sexual abuse she had endured from this man as a
child'.[118] The diary functions as a safe space, in which White 'inscribes
the discourse of hysteria as she contemplates the likelihood that she
was a victim of incest'; in fact, her 'analysis diary' of the 1930s 'may
have been one of her best hopes for dealing with childhood abuses'.[119]
Thus, while White herself dates her keeping of diaries to an episode
of depression in 1921, Podnieks finds it 'likely that it was the convent
novel coming up against the male authorities of father and God that
motivated White to begin her diary', a finding Podnieks confirms by
referencing the connection between the convent novel and the diary
that White develops in her 1952 novel *The Sugar House*.[120] Podnieks
is definite about the source of White's inability to continue the novel
sequence: 'It is precisely because White failed to win her father's love
through writing that she suffered from writer's block.'[121]

Attributions of White's problems to incest proliferate in the section
focused on White's sexuality, many anchored in Judith Lewis Herman's
work. White's 'persistent' fear of sex 'reinforces the likelihood that

Herman's research applies to White as a subject'.[122] The suicide attempt that preceded the onset of psychosis in 1922 is a 'common practice among incest survivors', while psychosis itself, evidencing White's 'terror of sex', may have been caused by 'an early crisis brought on by her father's advances – hence, for instance, her "terror" at the sound of his latchkey in the door announcing his arrival home' and the fictional episode that 'explains Daddy': 'Once again this interpretation is corroborated by Herman.'[123] White's second breakdown in the 1930s, following the publication of *Frost in May*, developed from 'her guilt or distress at publicly treating the subject of her painful relationship with her father'.[124] White's choice of sexual partners and practices is also evidence of incest. Her oscillation between frigidity and promiscuity 'reads to a large extent like Herman's case studies of incest survivors'.[125] Her marriage to an older gay man may be understood 'in terms of Herman's research that shows that many incest survivors "had affairs with much older or married men," hoping to "fulfil their unsatisfied childhood longings for protection and care"'.[126] A masochistic relationship enabled White 'to fulfil her longing for what Herman describes as masochistic punishment', while the masochistic fantasies recorded in White's diaries are also explained by Herman,

> who states in *Father-Daughter Incest* that the incest survivor often carries 'a deviant and debased self-image' and demonstrates 'a masochistic search for punishment'. If White was indeed such a survivor, then her diary can again be read as an hysterical text.[127]

Although Podnieks briefly considers the repressive effect that Catholicism may have had on White's sexuality, that consideration is drowned out by the drumbeat of reiterated suggestions of incest. Her mother's stories about the brutality of sex and the misery of pregnancy and childbirth and White's own revulsion towards her mother's body do not even merit mention.

This thematic section ends with a dramatic revelation. Podnieks is one of only a very few people who have had access to the manuscript diaries (at the time of the publication of Podnieks' study, the only person who had seen them aside from White's daughters and Virago publisher Carmen Callil was White's biographer Jane Dunn). The deterioration of White's handwriting in the June 1938 entry that marks White's accession to the female castration complex – her admission that she wants 'my father's penis or a child by him e.g.

a work engendered with his loving approval' (*Diary* 1, p. 140) – becomes the site for Podnieks of the emergence of 'sacral memory'. In this entry White 'unconsciously revealed the truth' that her father had destroyed her ability to write:

> I use the word 'unconsciously' because in the entry in question, her small, always controlled handwriting breaks into what her daughter so aptly describes as 'a childish scrawl'. For me as a reader of this manuscript, coming upon this dramatic and horrific passage was almost chilling, for I realised that I was witnessing what Broe has described as the incest survivor's writing 'out of that paradoxical link between survival and exile, between bodily memory and repression of that memory'. White literally reverted to being a child as she uncharacteristically lashed out at her father in large block letters.[128]

Podnieks' conclusion that White's handwriting reveals incest and the subsequent destruction of her ability to write is perplexing. White states in this entry that 'I couldn't have had intercourse with him anyway because presumably apart from morals *he didn't want it*' (*Diary* 1, p. 140, my emphasis). Her handwriting deteriorates as she rages – at both parents – about their withholding of love and approval, and it marks her defiance of her father's standards: 'I will write backhand in spite of my father' (*Diary* 1, p. 140). Although White may seem childish, she does not 'literally revert to being a child' – except in the incest survivor narrative, which requires the recovery of a buried and literal memory of childhood sexual abuse. Podnieks' 'witnessing' locates the 'truth' of incest trauma in her own reaction to the literal manuscript page. Given that this passage is marked in the published *Diary* with an asterisk and discussed by Chitty in her introduction to the volume, Podnieks' reaction of chill and horror seems somewhat disingenuous.[129] But this 'witnessing' of incest in White's handwriting reinforces the conclusion of this section that White's writer's block 'was likely related to early sexual abuse by him'.[130]

These interpretations of incest trauma in White's life and writing have been extremely influential, but they do White a disservice: ironically, what White does write becomes less important than what she doesn't. The subtlety of White's fictional analysis of father–daughter desire disappears as critics substitute what White 'really' wanted to say but couldn't. In *Frost in May*, for example, White indicates the father's sexual arousal with almost-but-not-quite-innocuous gestures:

shaking hands that reveal his excitement even as he tries to conceal it by lighting his pipe (!); holding his daughter 'longer than usual as she kissed him good night, smoothing her hair from her forehead and looking into her eyes' (*Frost in May*, pp. 177, 179). Broe identifies these passages as a 'courtship ritual', which is fair enough, if a bit overstated.[131] But as Broe continues, these passages alone merit her conclusion that the daughter is an 'incest survivor' and that White's novel unequivocally enacts the battle of the 'incest survivor's paradoxical stories': 'The violation of the daughter, the incest survivor, and her compromised family situation, but most important, her battle for a textuality not yet infiltrated, is re-enacted in *Frost in May* as the absolute sovereign silencing by the father.'[132] But surely the terror and fear the daughter experiences when the father repudiates her 'depraved' novel develops out of her confusion about what that novel supposedly reveals about her: she cannot 'name' sexuality because she does not know what it is. She only knows that he perceives her as 'a sink of filth and impurity', but she does not know why (*Frost in May*, p. 216). The father's insistence that she fulfil his narcissistic ideals of purity and perfection – that she sacrifice her sexuality in the interests of his own redemption – sets up an intense psychic conflict: vaguely sensing something 'not quite right' about her father's behaviour but without the language to name it, she internalises his conviction that sexuality is shameful and corrupt – that she herself is shameful and corrupt – even as she also senses, at a deep and wordless and hardly graspable level, his erotic preoccupation with her.

The translation of ambiguity into certainty and the foreclosure of other possible meanings characterise these interpretations. More egregious is the rewriting of White's texts to support the meanings that are not actually there but which 'should' be there. Her 'convulsive horror' about hearing her father's key in the door can only mean her terror about forthcoming sexual abuse, although White herself attributes her terror to her intense fear of his disapproval. Her childish handwriting can only mean sexual abuse, although White herself attributes her outburst to 'repressed rage' in an entry that explicitly states that her father didn't want to have sex with her. As Strauss-Noll points out, 'Nowhere in her Diaries, Autobiography, or fiction does Antonia White (or her fictional counterparts, Nanda and Clara) record her conviction that her father sexually abused her as a child.'[133] Given that White wrote freely in her diaries about a range of taboo subjects – including defecation, masturbation, masochism and a range of non-normative sexual fantasies – it seems unlikely that she would censor herself about this topic. Yet White's explicit writings about sexuality are also suspect. Incestuous dreams and masochistic fantasies are signs of sexual abuse. Her sexual behaviour is also suspect. Her marriage to a gay man is a sign of sexual abuse. Her enjoyment of a masochistic relationship is a sign of sexual abuse. Whether she refrains from sex or indulges in it, the conclusion is the same: virtually everything is a sign of sexual abuse.

As Haaken points out, the opposing forces of the recovered memory controversy converged in their conviction that women's disturbing memories and fantasies could never be internally generated but had to be 'imported into the psyche from an external source'.[134] This conviction speaks to the narrow range of permissible behaviours accorded women, she argues, but 'to view sexual fantasies that deviate from domesticated versions of femininity as merely derivatives of sexual abuse is to strip the female subject of her complexity'.[135] The recovered memory paradigm permits women 'to express a broad array of sexual, aggressive and rebellious imagery, but it requires the production of a trauma memory to redeem and make sense of this therapeutic process'.[136] If disturbing material is literal, 'women are permitted to experience it as a normal upsurge of traumatic material and as part of the healing process', but if that 'same imagery is identified as fantasy – that is, as internally generated material – its fate is less certain'.[137] White's incest fantasies are acceptable as long as they are perceived as signs of her victimisation. But if they are perceived as positive – that is, if they are perceived the way White herself perceived them – something is amiss. In fact, White's second analyst, Dorothy Kingsmill, for whom White produced the Ritual Rape Dream, crushed White when their work together ended unhappily: 'she has cast me out very crudely and definitely. Something all wrong with me. .I am "depraved", and she must "withdraw from me and my situation"' (*Diary* 1, p. 217). This 'mention of "depravity" obviously touched a very raw place' in White, making her feel 'a kind of leper' whose irredeemable corruption made her unlovable, since once people discovered it they would turn away from her in horror (*Diary* 1, p. 215).[138] Indeed, at least one element at play in White's inability to publish fiction after 1954 was her ongoing worry that her material was offensive and corrupt.

But what about White's psychosis and the 'terror of sex' that supposedly drove her out of her mind? Doesn't this 'abnormal' and 'irrational' reaction to sex indicate the likelihood of sexual abuse? White's own writing suggests a less clear-cut conclusion. Writing in 1937 that she had never learned 'the language of the body' and that this ignorance made her feel 'false and shallow and incomplete', White connects her current sexual desire for a lover to the passion she felt before her breakdown: 'I felt the same thing without quite understanding it with Robert [. . .] but I was not ready for it and the shock drove me out of my mind' (*Diary* 1, p. 94). White does not say that she was 'terrified of sex', but rather that the unfamiliar 'language of the body' overwhelmed her. (She will fictionalise this interpretation in *Beyond the Glass*, where the too-rapid release of sexual inhibitions triggers the protagonist's mania.) It is true that childhood sexual abuse can predispose a person to psychosis, but so can a range of other psychosocial factors, including poor parenting (encompassing verbal and other forms of emotional abuse), cognitive styles and temperamental characteristics.[139] Significantly, however, abuse and maltreatment can trigger psychosis only in those who already have the genetic predisposition to develop such disorders. Hence, while not everyone who suffers from some form of childhood abuse will develop bipolar disorder or schizophrenia, childhood abuse may increase the likelihood or even function as a causative factor in 'turning on' such illnesses in those with the neurobiological vulnerability for developing them. (At the same time, neurobiological vulnerability alone can 'turn on' these illnesses as well.)

Does this link support a reading of White's psychosis as a response developing from childhood sexual abuse? Not really. Since, as Strauss-Noll points out, White never recorded anywhere in her writing that her father sexually abused her, and since such illnesses can switch on for a range of other reasons, it is impossible to state with any certainty why she developed psychotic mania in 1922–3 or what might have played a role in triggering the depressive episode that preceded it. White herself has provided some possible explanations. Her father's repudiation of the convent novel plays an enormous and even defining role in her construction of biographical and fictional identity narratives. Some research suggests that individuals with one particular genetic expression of susceptibility for developing bipolar disorder – those who carry the Val66 allele on the BDNF (brain-derived neurotrophic factor) gene – are at increased risk for developing the illness if they experience abusive childhoods.[140] BDNF plays a role in the main biological stress-response systems, and stress has been linked with irregularities in its expression and functioning. This increased sensitivity can also mean that stressful experiences that would not seem overwhelming or deeply traumatic to unaffected people may have significant impact upon children or adolescents with the Val66 allele. The trauma caused by her father's reaction to her adolescent novel – which White always identified as the origin of her illness – may, in fact, have contributed to its onset.

That is, of course, only one possibility among many. Another intriguing possibility arises from White's characterisation of her father as stern, punitive and autocratic, centring everything on her and trying to force her into becoming an exact replica of himself (*The Hound and the Falcon*, p. 82). White developed an intense fear of his disapproval, and as an adult had an 'aversion to people appearing to make too many claims on me or in any way to force me, even when it is done out of affection' (*The Hound and the Falcon*, p. 77). 'Too much stress was laid on fear in my childhood and my own nature was too responsive to fear, anyway', she comments (*The Hound and the Falcon*, p. 35). It is possible that White's numerous depictions of her sense of fundamental inner corruption reflect emotional damage generated by insensitive parenting more attuned to the parent's need for narcissistic affirmation than to the child's need for love and acceptance. Studies of adults with bipolar disorder and a history of emotional neglect or emotional or physical abuse in childhood found that they experienced high levels of internalised shame. 'The experience of CEA [childhood emotional abuse] directly attacks the individual's self-worth by continued and repeated criticism, humiliation, invalidation and belittlement', writes one group of researchers.[141] The bipolar adults they studied had developed 'a fundamental sense of incompetence and inferiority, which results from enduring and intense levels of shame during childhood'.[142]

In the end we simply do not know why White's illness switched on, and we will never know. But it is clear that she suffered from a debilitating mental illness throughout her life, and that she repeatedly searched for 'clues' that would explain it. This study focuses on her quest for those clues and the manner in which she wove them into biographical and fictional narratives. It is, of course, risky for a humanities scholar with limited knowledge of the medical and scientific fields to undertake this work. In her study of long-dead writers that she believed suffered from manic-depressive illness, one of the leading experts on the illness, Kay Redfield Jamison, maps out the parameters that must frame such study:

Despite the difficulties in doing diagnostic studies based on biographical material, valid and highly useful research can be done by using in a systematic way what is known about manic-depressive illness: its symptomatic presentation (for example, pronounced changes in mood, energy, sleep, thinking and behaviour), associated behaviour patterns (such as alcohol and drug abuse, pathological gambling, pronounced and repeated financial reversals, and chaotic interpersonal relationships), suicide (70 to 90 per cent of all suicides are associated with manic-depressive or depressive illness; therefore, if an individual has committed suicide, it is almost always the case that a mood disorder was at least contributory), its natural course (an episodic, cyclic course of symptoms, with normal functioning in between; usual onset of symptoms in the late teens or early twenties, with temperamental signs often exhibited much earlier; seasonal aspects to the mood and energy changes; and, if untreated, a worsening of the illness over time), and very important, a family history, especially in first-degree relatives (parents, siblings or children), of depression, mania, psychosis or suicide.[143]

It is my contention that the study of White's writing fulfils Jamison's criteria of symptomatic presentation, associated behaviour patterns, suicide attempts, natural course, age of onset, seasonal changes and family history. In developing this analysis I draw on her diaries, including those still unpublished, that record her life from 1926 to 1980; Jane Dunn's excellent biography as well as the memoirs published by her daughters and her third husband Tom Hopkinson; discussions with several family members and friends, including her daughter Lyndall Hopkinson, Tom Hopkinson's daughter Amanda by his second wife, and Virago publisher Carmen Callil; and all of White's fiction. White's monumental diary is an important resource in this respect, for although White does not always know what is wrong or why she feels the way she does, she usually records her symptoms, thus making it possible to chart the course of her illness over the years. (It is true, however, that White's diary in the 1930s often has long gaps, when she was too ill to record anything.) I have also benefited from colleagues whose expertise in the biological determinants of bipolar disorder supplements my own deficiencies. 'Making a retrospective diagnosis is, in many ways, like putting together the pieces of an elaborate psychological puzzle or solving a mystery by a complicated but careful marshalling of elements of evidence', Jamison comments.[144] It is to that task I turn in the next chapter.

Chapter 1

The Beast in White's Jungle: Manic-Depressive Illness

The illness White termed 'the Beast' forms the nucleus around which the tangled threads of her chaotic emotions and actions cluster. Despite repeated attempts to come to terms with her illness, through psychoanalysis as well as through religious practice and writing, the Beast hounded White from her early twenties until her death.[1] Her breakdown in her early twenties was the most severe, when she lapsed into a violent and suicidal psychotic mania and was committed to Bethlem by her father: her doctors believed that she might never recover or that, if she did, she would do so only in her late forties or fifties (perhaps reflecting their belief that her insanity was linked to hormones that would subside at menopause).[2] A severe depression accompanied by delusions and 'violent suicidal impulses' took hold after the publication of *Frost in May* in 1933 (*The Hound and the Falcon*, p. 37), lasting through 1938 with brief periods of remission, and again White and those around her feared that she would lapse into complete insanity; a final and less severe breakdown occurred in the 1960s. Between these debilitating episodes, White grappled with frequent bouts of depression, often linked to seasonal changes and preceded by flu, severe headaches and a feeling of pressure behind her eyes. She suffered from disrupted sleep, frequently awaking screaming and distraught from powerful nightmares (several times she tried to throw herself from the window after waking from one).[3] Her weight fluctuated as well: during her first severe manic episode, she lost weight rapidly over a period of three weeks, and while hospitalised in Bethlem she had to be force-fed to be kept alive.[4] During phases of depression, on the other hand, she rapidly put on weight, and her diary records her shame over bouts of compulsive binge eating. The connection between her moods and her body was so marked, in fact, that White and her family and friends commented on the extraordinary way her very appearance reflected her emotional state.[5]

This chapter discusses White's illness within the context of medical and subjective accounts of bipolar disorder. The chapter thus develops three strands of analysis. It opens with a selective overview of White's life that highlights key sites of disruption and signs of illness. My goal is not to provide a comprehensive account of White's life – that can be found in Jane Dunn's excellent biography – but rather to discern the pattern of her illness. I then turn to an overview of manic-depressive illness, followed by a more detailed discussion of the characteristics of manic, depressive and mixed episodes. The chapter ends with a brief comparison of White's experiences of illness to those of Virginia Woolf. This comparison demonstrates not only the diverse expressions of manic-depressive illness but also the different approaches that the writers themselves as well as family members adopted to cope with it. A brief discussion of White's response to Woolf's writing concludes the chapter.

A selective overview: the illness pattern

White's twenties were a record of chaos. White herself described the 'muddled' events of her life between the ages of twenty-one and thirty-one as a 'very queer sexual record' (*Diary* 1, p. 274) in which she contracted three marriages – two annulled for non-consummation – had three unplanned pregnancies, embarked on a number of unsatisfactory transient affairs, and underwent a traumatic incarceration for total insanity in Bethlem. Her first marriage to an impotent alcoholic in 1921 ended in an annulment sanctioned by the Catholic Church, an ordeal she described as 'obscene' (*The Hound and the Falcon*, p. 24), in which White underwent examination by two doctors in order to be certified *virgo intacta*. Within weeks she met a man with whom she shared telepathic communications, but after a hectic three-week courtship she became psychotic and was incarcerated for nine months. After her release she lived again with her parents. At this time she lost her virginity in an unsettling way: a friend of her father's entered her bedroom when she was asleep, wearing her father's dressing gown; in an incident that remains obscure they had sex. White subsequently became pregnant and with her father's help obtained an illegal abortion, only bothered by the fact that the baby had been a boy. She married her second husband a year later; although she knew he was gay, she considered her bond with him a 'mental blood tie' (*Diary* 2, p. 245), and he became an important father figure to her and an ongoing source of emotional and financial support until his own remarriage in the late 1940s. White lapsed from Catholicism at this time and had several brief affairs. Eventually, White writes, 'the inevitable happened. I fell in love in the ordinary way and very soon found I was going to have a child' (*The Hound and the Falcon*, p. 26). Her second marriage also ended in annulment when White decided she wanted to marry this man, Silas Glossop, in hopes of building a 'natural' life (*The Hound and the Falcon*, p. 26); Glossop went to America to work while she waited for the birth of their child and the decree of dissolution. White's daughter Susan was born in August 1929 and she left the baby with her parents, returning to London in November to work. Her father died suddenly and unexpectedly several weeks later (he was only fifty-nine). The next month White fell 'violently' in love with a co-worker, Tom Hopkinson. When Glossop returned to marry her in September 1930, she wavered between the two men for several months before finally deciding to marry Hopkinson after discovering she was pregnant again. (This second daughter, Lyndall, born in July 1931, may have been Glossop's child also.) White never fully understood her motivations for her affair and subsequent marriage to Hopkinson, writing as late as 1954, 'I shall never understand the Tom thing [. . .] Tom, whom I had always rather disliked . . . suddenly assumed this violent, almost compulsive importance soon after my father's death. Why?' (*Diary* 1, p. 274).[6]

Because she later destroyed the two 'enormous old journals' of the years 1921 to 1933, it is difficult to trace her moods in this period. An important entry recorded in 1934 suggests that low moods were recurrent throughout this time. In that entry White remarks that she is in bed with tonsillitis and the 'profound depression that accompanies even a day of illness with me' (*Diary* 1, 27). She goes on to observe:

> [I don't] seem to learn anything from the fact that these moods recur – & I have noticed their recurrence on & off for thirteen years. Each time they attack me I begin all over again with the awful feeling that never, never can I get out of this blackness.[7]

White's description makes clear the intense physical sensations that accompany this profound sense of a suffocating blackness from which she feels she will never escape: her head feels as if it will burst; her bowels seem tied in an iron knot.[8] She also notes that sometimes these moods make it impossible to write. At other times, however, they give her 'a kind of acuteness of perception and feeling' and that to get rid of them through analysis might deprive her of something she values and that is valuable for her writing.[9] This important entry suggests that White has already begun to notice a pattern in her symptoms: they accompany illness; they possess chronicity; they oscillate between crippling black depression and a hyper-acuity characteristic of the manic pole of the illness.

White's impulsive sexual liaisons are also commonly recognised symptoms of manic behaviour. Both Glossop and Hopkinson have left accounts in which they describe their frustration with White's habits of overspending, another behaviour typical of mania.[10] Both also describe 'rage storms' in 1929–30 that are strikingly similar. Glossop writes that White had a 'vicious temper':

> When she was upset or angry, and for her to be upset was always to be angry, her whole appearance changed and she seemed another person. Her expression became sullen, her complexion sallow, her hair lustreless, she looked ten years older, and she gave the illusion of having put on weight. One look at her and I saw that trouble was coming.[11]

Hopkinson's description is almost identical: 'With anger her whole appearance was transformed. Her body seemed to thicken and her features set into a stony mask like that of an outraged Roman emperor.'[12] Such dramatic physical changes, and the anger and irritability that give rise to them, again are symptomatic of mania. Symptoms of mania hence stretch back to 1929 or earlier, but went unrecognised.

The onset of a second serious breakdown in 1933 was, by contrast, unmistakable, as White succumbed to suicide attempts, sleep disturbances and nightmares, violent outbursts and a general inability to function. In the summer of 1934 White experienced 'a complete disintegration, physical, mental, nervous & emotional' that 'had something of the same quality as the asylum' but was 'worse because it all went on in actual life & ordinary surroundings'.[13] In 1935 she records 'bad' days of headaches, languor, tears and depression followed by days of feeling 'so restless as if something in me would burst if it weren't expressed'.[14] Sleeping became difficult: White records trying to 'lie quiet' but her thoughts 'raced too fast & I was afraid if I did not do something they would rise to a hysterical climax'; in that same entry she comments on the 'fearful strength' of her 'fears and anxieties' and remarks that 'the symptoms of this illness [. . .] poison my life'.[15] Both White and Hopkinson date the onset of this second breakdown to the publication of *Frost in May*, and both connect its recurrence to White's father, albeit with different emphases. Chitty writes that Hopkinson believed White's breakdown 'was caused by Mother's guilt at betraying her father in *Frost in May*. She had exposed his cruelty to the world because she thought him dead, but he had risen again.'[16] White connects her breakdown to her father via Hopkinson's infidelity. Hopkinson, also a writer, had begun an affair with another woman at a party where he had been introduced as the 'husband of Tony White who's just written that marvellous book';[17] White had been able to finish the novel after fifteen years only with his encouragement, and his infidelity seemed to her a repetition of her father's denunciation of her first novel.[18]

These retrospective accounts of the onset of White's second breakdown seek to establish causality for it. Determining causality is particularly tricky in manic depression because environmental stressors – any change that disrupts daily routines and/or that affects mood – can exacerbate or 'turn on' the biological predisposition for it. Certainly the upheavals of the years between 1928 and 1933 – the ending of her second marriage; emotional and sexual entanglements with two prospective third husbands; the birth of two children, both unplanned and one illegitimate; her third husband's infidelity; the death of her father – constitute an extraordinary range and number of potential stressors. Nor were these events the only source of stress. These were also years of financial strain, as White left yet another job and decided to try to support herself doing freelance work, a risky move that caused her a great deal of anxiety, particularly given her inability to control her spending.[19] White's home life underwent an enormous shift, as the newly married Hopkinson and White set up a household for the first time with two children under the age of two. White's social life expanded considerably, and she sometimes kept very late hours. Circadian rhythms, the twenty-four hour 'clock' that regulates the body's sleep–wake cycle, have been found to play a crucial role in affective disorders, with disruptions to sleep potentially triggering episodes or causing existing episodes to worsen.[20] To imagine that White's relationship to her father was the sole and determining factor in precipitating her second breakdown is ludicrous.

When White's second breakdown was at its worst, she decided to seek help in analysis, a step that was central in establishing her conviction that her relationship to her father was the key source of her difficulties and that I explore in detail in Chapter 3. In the meantime White's third marriage was disintegrating – she had moved into a separate flat in 1935 – and in 1936 she moved back into the family flat, Hopkinson moved out and White was left in charge of her two daughters. This move, which her analyst may or may not have suggested but which he certainly read as a normalising sign of White's improvement, seems at best 'rash', as Dunn observes.[21] White had begun the year 'with a calm intention of suicide', deterred only by her second husband's suggestion that she wait six months and then carry out her plan if she still felt her pain was unbearable.[22] Furthermore, the consequences of having a severely depressed and unstable mother replace a competent father were devastating for both daughters, who both recall this period in their memoirs: Lyndall Hopkinson describes it as the sisters' '"Babes in the Wood" phase of our childhood [. . .] our only remaining security was each other'.[23] Chitty recalls her mother as 'strangely promiscuous' after her return to the family flat, when White's affairs became 'virtually continuous': Chitty calculates that White engaged in a dozen love affairs in a two-year period, all ending 'painfully and prematurely'.[24] White's diary also records other compulsive behaviours, including binge eating and overspending. She took a highly paid job in advertising at the beginning of 1937 – her first full-time job in four years, since the onset of her second breakdown – only to find that 'My debts are as bad as they were before I started.'[25] She was sacked before the end of the year.

White was more stable in the closing years of the 1930s than she had been for a very long time. In 1938 she landed a job she enjoyed as fashion editor for the *Sunday Pictorial*. She began work on 'The Moment of Truth', her first work of fiction since *Frost in May*, and published several poems as well as a reprint of 'The

House of Clouds' in *Delta*, one of the experimental little magazines of the period.[26] In that year she also initiated divorce proceedings from Hopkinson and ended analysis, although she recorded worries about losing the stabilising influence of her analyst and being left alone with the need to support herself and her daughters. A relationship with a much younger man, the son of a friend, became her first fulfilling sexual relationship, one that came to an end only when White returned to the Church in 1940.[27] Her relationship with her daughters also improved. In 1939 the three moved into a new flat, and Chitty writes that 'In that all-female household we came nearer to being a family than we ever had.'[28] That year was also the most prosperous year of White's life: in addition to steady work for the *Sunday Pictorial*, she contributed to *Picture Post*, whose editor was Tom Hopkinson, as well as other periodicals; and Penguin reissued an edition of *Frost in May*.[29]

But this increased stability did not fully alleviate White's sense that something was still deeply amiss. Her diary records her continuing sense that she had not been cured by psychoanalysis and finds her wondering whether returning to the Church would accord her a more peaceful mind. More ominously, White's diary records compulsive eating and spending in response to '*emptiness* . . . like annihilation [. . .] complete numbness of mind and extreme depression' (*Diary* 1, p. 169). And, characteristically, White connects these symptoms to her father and her writing. To Emily Holmes Coleman she wrote that writing about her father 'has the most awful effects. All my demons wake up, determined to shake me off it [. . .] and they do. Sometimes it is awful recurring dreams about my father & fearful depressions.'[30] Still, she determined that 'If some of the trouble comes from having my father inside me, I should get him out' (*Diary* 1, p. 168).

England's entry into war with Germany, not surprisingly, changed everything. In Chitty's words, 'When war was declared on 3 September [1939] Antonia's life fell apart. All her jobs went, and with them her money.'[31] White's household broke up: she put her furniture into storage, sent her daughters off to live with Hopkinson's parents, and became a paying guest of friends. By 1940 she had re-established herself in London, sharing a flat with another friend and working for the BBC. In December of that year she reconverted to Catholicism, a step detailed in *The Hound and the Falcon*, an extensive correspondence with a former seminarian. Ironically, life in London, and particularly during the Blitz, initially proved salutary for White; she appreciated that 'the excitement of being in a job again and the slight danger which certainly whets one's appetite for life made me begin to feel alive again' (*Hound*, p. 12). Later, she would write that she preferred the Blitz to accidia (her term for depression) and that the Blitz 'wasn't nearly so upsetting as the inner assaults in the bad days of mental breakdown' (*The Hound and the Falcon*, p. 121; *Diary* 2, p. 185). But by 1942 White records reading through her analysis diary 'in the hopes of finding some clues' to familiar signs of trouble (*Diary* 1, p. 178). In 1943 she lost her job at the BBC, and in a long entry in June White recognises her plight as 'one of those old familiar situations in which everything has boiled up together – losing job, physical illness, religious uncertainty, angst, apathy and depression' (*Diary* 1, p. 180). White enumerates the 'outward signs':

> maniacal reading [. . .] complete jam in writing . . . desire to eat, drink, smoke . . . Careless & unorganised spending. Inability to feel. Irresponsibility, touchiness [. . .] reading mania but do not read slowly and intelligently. Try and swallow books whole . . . No one to whom I can go for advice, who knows *all* the circumstances [. . .] Everywhere conflicting creeds, opinions. Church offers security, but do I really believe in the Church? (*Diary* 1, pp. 180–81)

A new job, translating English into French for propaganda pamphlets air-dropped into occupied France, provided welcome relief and distraction, but by August 1944 she had to take sick leave:

> Once again have had a prolonged bout of the usual state. The same symptoms (except there were many fits of weeping and in the end I broke down in the office). Inertia, paralysis, depression, extreme sleepiness, maniacal reading, the eternal book trouble. (*Diary* 1, p. 181)

Searching for causality, White wonders 'But why, just now, should I have "panicked" again?' (*Diary* 1, p. 181).

White's working life stabilised to a large degree when she began to translate French novels into English for her publishers in 1947. Her first effort, Guy de Maupassant's *Une Vie* (*A Woman's Life*) won the Clairoun prize for translation in 1949, and thereafter she supported herself mainly through translations, completing 34 titles in total by the end of her life, many of them works by Colette.[32] In the late 1940s she also entered analysis for the second time, a step she considered responsible for finally freeing her to write three novels of the quartet in quick succession (in 1950, 1952 and 1954).

Her personal life remained tumultuous, however. In these years White channelled much of her energy into what Chitty describes as 'religious mania' (*Diary* 1, p. 184), inspired in part by her erotic entanglement with another woman. Her relationship with her daughters also deteriorated. Her daughters had mostly lived apart from White since 1939–40, attending boarding school and visiting White for vacations. Even these limited interactions proved difficult. Susan, whose own illness was beginning to emerge, was drawn into her mother's 'religious mania'; her subsequent breakdown frightened White, who recognised in Susan her own extreme moods: White ordered her out of the house in 1951, creating a rift between them that never fully healed.[33] Both daughters were also subjected to White's rages, particularly if the rigid routine she had established for herself was in any way disrupted. Lyndall Hopkinson, who developed habits of subterfuge and stealth to stave off her mother's temper and who lived with White for several years while attending drama school, described her mother as 'a complicator of life who could not improvise. Her attempts to keep on an even keel meant she had to plan everything ahead and make lists'.[34] The evening meal in particular became a time of tension. If Hopkinson's plans unexpectedly changed and she telephoned that she would not be home for dinner, she reports that she 'received such a blast of indignant rage about my inconsiderateness that I would continue to shake long after I had put down the receiver'.[35] Similarly, showing up when not expected

> created such a drama about there not being anything cooked for me to eat that I learned the easiest way for a quiet life was not to make an early appearance on those occasions. Rather than roam the streets or linger in some sordid café, I came home and sat on the stairs outside [. . .] until I heard no more bustling around and knew it was safe to creep up to my room.[36]

White often stated that the last twenty-five years of her life were her happiest.[37] With her daughters grown, White lived alone, sharing her flat with a succession of boarders. She had by now established herself as a distinguished translator, a mode of work she could accomplish at home and one that freed her from the mind-numbing routine and stresses of office work. She brought out a number of publications, including a collection of short stories (*Strangers*), the correspondence detailing the process of her reconversion (*The Hound and the Falcon*), and two children's books about her cats. But the projected sequel to *Beyond the Glass* never materialised. To characterise White's inability to complete a fifth instalment as writer's block gives a misleading impression of what actually transpired: White wrote and wrote and wrote but, always dissatisfied with what she had written, destroyed almost all of it. Her 'block' in part grew out of her difficulty in establishing coherence for the chaotic events of her twenties. But it also grew out of what Chitty terms 'pathological indecision. She teased a sentence like a cat with a mouse, until the page was black with crossings out and rewritings [. . .] Often one barely legible page was all she had to show for a morning's work.'[38] Chitty describes editing her mother's autobiography and finding that her mother 'would sometimes revise a paragraph she had written ten years earlier'.[39] White herself wonders why it is that she is incapable of control or selection as she writes draft after draft of the unfinished 'Clara IV' in 1957 (*Diary* 1, p. 318); in 1962 she observes while rereading *Frost in May* that what depresses her now is 'that I *then* seemed to "select" automatically and *right*' (*Diary* 2, p. 72).

White's struggles to impose coherence on her life story through writing fiction constitute one source of ongoing distress in these later years. Struggles with her faith constitute another. These came to focus on what White came to call her 'Adam and Eve troubles', the question of whether the Biblical account of creation was fact or myth: if the latter, White felt that the whole secure structure of her faith was in doubt. She repeatedly questioned several priests about this issue, all of whom told her that her worries seemed more emotional than doctrinal (*Diary* 2, p. 201). In addition to these continual sources of mental turmoil, White continued to experience financial difficulties as a result of overspending. Numerous diary entries record calculations as White worries about how she will meet her obligations. Nor did her other symptoms recede: in fact, in her annual summation for December 1954, White records the miracle of not having experienced one of her 'black depressions' that year (*Diary* 1, p. 283), a notation that suggests how pervasive that state had become.

In the mid-1960s a visit to a doctor following months of ill health revealed that another breakdown was imminent. Treated for the first time in her life with antidepressants, White felt her debilitating depression lift: '"Fresh air?" *That* is how all this feels' (*Diary* 2, p. 137). Her doctor seems to have thought that White was suffering from manic depression, as a number of diary entries record his concern that she is becoming elated or euphoric. These queries suggest that he was aware that antidepressants could provoke mania in bipolar disorders if not taken in tandem with mood stabilisers, which then didn't exist or, in the case of lithium, had not been approved. Although the antidepressants initially worked and White was able to work productively for several months, her depression returned and she was referred to another analyst, who again interpreted her symptoms as psychological conflicts. After three years he had to end her analysis in order to concentrate on his in-patients. Finally giving up her attempts to write her autobiography in 1968, White noticed with relief that the physical pressure behind her eyes had gone.[40] Her health declined in the 1970s, even as her work was brought back into the public eye by Virago publisher Carmen Callil: *Frost in May* was the inaugural Modern Classic of the newly founded press. White died in 1980 in the midst of this revival.

White's diary demonstrates that by the 1930s she had begun to recognise a pattern to her illness; as time went on she also noted symptoms as well as the duration and intensity of her low moods and the time of day and year when they occurred. Hence an entry for 2 January 1953 records that she had had two 'bad spells' in the previous year, one in the spring and a very bad one that began in October and lasted until the end of the year (*Diary* 1, p. 259), including a crisis in December 1952, when she felt her depression rising to 'a paroxysm of nightmare blankness and terror when I feel I simply CANNOT go on. Only being a Catholic stops me from taking an overdose' (*Diary* 1, p. 256). The restless moods frequently became more intense in early spring and mid-autumn. In February and March White found herself full of energy and prone to bursts of extravagance; March in particular, as the restless energy subsided, was 'Always a trying time of year for me [. . .] always a chilled sense physically and mentally, reinforced by weeks of cold weather' (*Diary* 1, p. 1956). Holy Week and Easter are typically low times, which White connects to the repudiated convent novel. Low moods also intensified in September or October, usually reaching a nadir of a trance-like depression in November, always a 'peculiar' month for her.[41] Another entry records how 'The autumn, especially Oct–Nov is always a significant time for me. The most important changes in my life happen at this time' (*Diary* 1, p. 79): she recalls here her escalation into psychosis among other events. White also notices a daily rhythm to her depression. In 1953 she counsels herself to take a walk after lunch and rest before tea 'since that is the most "depressive" part of my day' (*Diary* 1, p. 261). A similar entry almost thirteen years later records her awareness that her 'worst melancholy is in the afternoon: about 6 my spirits begin to revive' (*Diary* 2, p. 151).

White also identifies patterns in her symptoms. She frequently refers to familiar 'spells' or 'states of mind' and calls her nature 'episodic'.[42] She grew sensitive to the early signs of onset, recording how '[r]estless nights and bad dreams' herald something 'going on inside' (*Diary* 1, p. 252). Particularly vivid dreams usually signal something 'boiling up' and function as a warning that all is not well (*Diary* 1, p. 278).[43] Physical illness, which seems to strike during the periods in which her moods intensify, generates feelings of profound depression, something White had recognised as early as 1934 (*Diary* 1, p. 27). More than thirty years later an entry sounds an almost identical note: 'These states of mind are of course familiar. Any physical illness demoralizes me terribly. I feel stale, listless, poisoned all through. In these states I really feel as if I could go mad' (*Diary* 1, p. 120). Headaches, feeling as if her head will burst and pressure behind her eyes ('lead spectacles') are all 'warning symptoms' that must be heeded.[44] Office jobs intensified these mood states, for White loathed monotony and boredom: their routines left her 'checked and at a standstill though longing for action' (*Diary* 1, p. 88). She attributes the profound discomfort she experienced in the late 1930s and early 1940s to the dullness of office work, which she thought prevented her violent nature from expressing itself.[45] 'I suppose, if one *can't* bring oneself to accept boredom, the price is losing all capacity for enjoyment & then one needs some kind of drug, to stimulate in the grey state or muffle in the acute depression acute excitement', she writes.[46] But even in later years, when she worked from home, White would often identify moods in which she felt herself suffocating in a 'blank meaningless automatic state' and consumed by feeling that '*something* must happen – some kind of change, explosion, even illness' (*Diary* 2, p. 113).

White connects certain kinds of behaviours to different moods. By 1940 she connected her 'wild spending and wild lovemaking' to a particular nervous 'strain': 'I know that sudden irrational attachments and a disposition to spend money I haven't got are warnings to me to be careful!' (*The Hound and the Falcon*, p. 40). In the 1930s she had learned 'to be suspicious of myself when anyone suddenly assumes a violent importance to me' and she found it 'disconcerting how frequently and irrationally I change my love object. I fall in love with a schoolgirl rapidity and grown-up intensity' (*Diary* 1, pp. 69, 87). She realised that her impulsive love affairs had had disastrous consequences, and thus grew wary of 'the sort of situation in which I've always taken the wildest risks – and most of my hardest knocks' (*The Hound and the Falcon*, p. 52). The events of 1929 to 1930, which she pondered for years as part of her effort to compose a fifth novel based on her life, frequently surface in her entries, as she tries to account for the compulsive feelings that she suddenly developed for Tom Hopkinson following her father's death, thereby setting in motion the chain of events that shaped the following decades.

Overspending remained a problem throughout her life. She often embarked on redecorating her flat in February and March: despite cautioning herself not to overspend, she often did, and spent the rest of the year worrying about meeting her expenses. In February 1962 she wonders whether her 'neurotic fidgeting' about the flat and her similar neurotic fidgeting about her writing have a common cause (*Diary* 2, p. 65); the next month she notes that she is 'unable to get over this crazy restlessness about the flat' (*Diary* 2, p. 67). In February 1965 she reprimands herself for the same reason:

> I should have tried to get on with the book instead of having this orgy – an expensive one too – of getting the flat redecorated. I deserve to be punished! It's the old thing – this compulsive spending that I seem unable to control. (*Diary* 2, p. 120)

In the same entry she notices that, although she now feels 'paralysed', 'exhausted' and 'apathetic', two weeks earlier she had been tired but 'full of energy – though not mental energy. All my energy seems to go into the wrong things – painting the flat, not writing'.[47] White did recognise that 'the pleasure of spending money freely [. . .] can appear to one as creative activity. Or consolation, as a woman buys a new hat when she is depressed' (*Diary* 1, pp. 267–8). But despite her insight into 'the misery extravagance brings on' and her realisation that the 'delicious pleasure of "blueing" – and no one enjoys it more than I do simply isn't worth all the misery of months of worrying how to make ends meet', she was never able to control her finances (*Diary* 1, p. 307).

This admittedly selective review of White's life reveals the pattern of her illness, the response of both professionals and non-professionals to it, and its devastating consequences on White's life. White seems to have experienced very few periods in which she was completely symptom-free: possibly her twenties (about which information is scanty), the early years of the Second World War and some intermittent years during the 1950s. Aside from these brief periods, White suffered from debilitating moods almost without respite. Illness interfered with her life at virtually every level: employment, personal relationships, writing, financial stability and even daily life. White herself acknowledged that both sexuality and spending functioned as sites of trouble. But as is so often the case with manic depression, the behaviours driven by her symptoms generated further stress, which in turn exacerbated the existing symptoms or engendered new ones. White's compulsive spending, for example, was a constant source of worry and anxiety, contributing to the ruminative patterns of thought typical of depression, in which shame and self-loathing predominated. Similarly, while White abstained from sexual relationships after her return to the Church in 1940, prior to her reconversion her impulsive liaisons created havoc in the lives of those around her, not least the two daughters whom her impulsive sexual behaviour generated. And finally, her ruminative patterns of thought – which obsessively centred on her father, her illness and her writing – resulted in her so-called 'writer's block', whereby she compulsively wrote, revised and destroyed 'Clara IV' for twenty-six years.

Manic depression: an overview

Today the 'Bible' of psychiatry, *The Diagnostic and Statistical Manual of Mental Disorders* 5th edition (*DSM-5*), would probably classify White's illness as bipolar 1 disorder, the 'classic' form of manic depression that afflicts approximately 1 per cent of the world's population. This diagnosis requires a single lifetime episode of mania, which *DSM-5* defines as:

> a distinct period of abnormally and persistently elevated, expansive, or irritable mood and abnormally and persistently increased goal-directed

activity or energy, lasting at least 1 week and present most of the day, nearly every day (or any duration if hospitalisation is necessary).[48]

In addition, *DSM-5* requires three or more of the following symptoms, or four if the mood is irritable: grandiosity; a decreased need for sleep; an urgent and excited need to speak as well as rapid speech ('pressured speech'); racing thoughts ('flight of ideas'); distractibility; 'increase in goal-directed activity or psychomotor agitation'; and 'excessive involvement in activities that have a high potential for painful consequences', such as impulsive sexual liaisons or spending sprees.[49] Mania may be mild ('hypomania'), moderate or severe, depending on the level of impairment. Acute or severe mania, such as White suffered in 1922–3, may include 'hallucinations and delusions, marked formal thought disorder, and/or grossly disorganised behaviour'.[50]

Although a diagnosis of bipolar 1 disorder requires only a single episode of mania, the illness typically encompasses a range of other factors, such as depressive episodes, recurrence and an astonishingly wide array of physiological and emotional expressions. Recent research has confirmed the strongly genetic component of the illness, with genetic factors accounting for up to 80 per cent of the liability for its emergence.[51] The average age of onset, in the late teens or early twenties, accompanies the maturation of the frontal lobe of the brain, but identifying the precise genetic factors involved is difficult, since the disorder is polygenic, consisting of 'thousands of variants of very small effect that together act to increase or reduce risk'.[52] As the standard medical textbook observes, 'a true understanding of the pathophysiology of manic-depressive illness [. . .] must address its neurobiology at different physiological levels – molecular, cellular, systems, and behavioural'.[53] The authors explain that the illness results from 'a complex interaction between the dysregulated signalling systems and activation of existing physiological feedback mechanisms designed to compensate for extreme changes'.[54] Thus 'the constellation of symptoms – including not only mood but also autonomic, endocrine, sleep/wake, and circadian activity determinants – reflects both the stage and progression of the illness and unique individual characteristics conferring heterogeneity'.[55]

Bipolar disorder is recurrent, with an almost 'near-total likelihood' of further episodes following onset.[56] Cycles, 'defined as the time from the onset of one episode to the onset of the next', become more frequent as the illness pattern establishes itself, typically slowing down after three to five episodes and approaching 'a levelling off, or maximum frequency of episodes' within a given time period.[57] White's diary suggests that her illness eventually established a predictable pattern of two lengthy episodes annually, one beginning in early spring and another beginning in mid-autumn (although her diary also suggests that she was rarely symptom-free). This pattern is consistent with studies that have shown that hospital admission rates for depression generally peak during the spring and the autumn, although hospitalisations more accurately reflect the severity of the depression rather than its onset.[58] Rates of suicide broadly correlate with this seasonal pattern, with a rise that begins in March and peaks in May and, for women, a second, smaller rise in September with a peak in October.[59] Manic episodes, on the other hand, tend to occur in late spring or early summer.[60] Mixed episodes have a 'significant autumn peak' of depressive episodes with manic characteristics.[61]

The striking seasonality of mood disorders is linked to changes in light: the spring and the autumn are 'times of the year when the ratio of sunlight to darkness is changing most rapidly.'[62] Those with mood disorders seem to suffer from 'fragile' biological clocks that do not 'reset' easily in response to environmental changes, particularly those environmental changes that disturb sleep.[63] As the psychiatrist Peter C. Whybrow explains:

> Any environmental signal capable of resetting the clock is called a *zeitgeber*, from the German meaning 'time giver'.'[64] While sunlight is the most powerful such zeitgeber, interpersonal relationships and daily routines – meal times, work habits, exercise – can similarly function as factors that either synchronise or disrupt circadian rhythms.[65] [. . . M]any of the social zeitgebers emerge as of great practical importance when one is working to re-establish a daily rhythm in manic-depressive illness. Individuals with bipolar disorder frequently are driven by an internal cycle that disregards external cues, and they find organizing themselves in synchrony with the day very difficult.[66]

White's establishment of an extremely rigid routine for herself – one that could not be disturbed without provoking intense irritation and rage – suggests a self-fashioned response to this internal chaos. Hence, while she records as one sign of her 'cure' in 1937 the ability to sit up all night, by the 1950s she often mentions how even one late night has repercussions on her mood the following day or for even longer.[67]

White's first manic episode was the most clear-cut in terms of adhering to clinical descriptions of 'classic' mania; thereafter she seems to have had mixed episodes of either dysphoric mania ('characterised by anger and irritability') or agitated depression ('characterised by depressed symptoms'), with the latter particularly characteristic of her moods in later decades.[68] White's irritability, often escalating into rage, is the characteristic that those who knew her well often single out as the most destructive element in their relationships with her. Goodwin and Jamison note that irritability 'constitutes the most common feature of mania':[69] 'Manic mood, frequently characterised as elated and grandiose, as often as not is riddled with depression, panic, and extreme irritability'.[70] This irritability easily gives rise to rage, especially if the patient '"comes up against opposition to his wishes and inclinations; trifling external occasions may bring about extremely violent outbursts of rage"'.[71] Recent studies have further refined the equation of mania with euphoria and grandiosity by identifying significant factors that in turn encompass clusters of symptoms:

> The first and strongest factor was described as 'dysphoria'. It involved depressed mood, mood lability, guilt, anxiety, and suicidal thoughts and behaviours. It had a strong negative relationship with euphoric mood. The second factor was 'psychomotor acceleration', involving key diagnostic features such as racing thoughts, pressured speech and increased motor activity. The third factor was labelled 'psychosis' and involved grandiosity, psychotic symptoms and paranoia. 'Increased hedonic tone' constituted the fourth factor and involved the diagnostic features such as euphoric mood and increased sexuality. The fifth and final factor loaded on dimensions of irritability and aggression.[72]

From this division, the authors of the study proposed four subgroups of mania – depressed, irritable, euphoric and psychotic – with psychomotor agitation common to all of them.[73]

The manic pole

Researchers have distinguished three stages of manic escalation: a first prodromal stage characterised by mild euphoria and elevated mood (hypomania); a second active stage characterised by elation, grandiosity, impulsivity, hyperactivity and decreased sleep; and a third acute stage characterised by delusions and hallucinations, rapid and/or incoherent speech, dysphoria or panic, and loss of insight.[74] Goodwin and Jamison note that, while the onset of manic episodes is 'abrupt, developing over a few days', the first stage or 'hypomanic alert' may extend over 'a period of days or even weeks [. . .] before the switch into mania'.[75] The most common prodromal syndrome is the decreased need for sleep, although family members and others close to the individual are likely to discern other signs of incipient mania.[76] The acute manic phase, on the other hand, may last anywhere between two weeks and four to five months.[77] The delirious mania White experienced in 1922–3 was extremely debilitating and potentially lethal: the combination of violent excitement and agitation, weight loss, rapid pulse, fever and refusal of food could lead to dehydration, heart failure and death from 'manic exhaustion'.[78] Virginia Woolf's cousin James Stephen died from a similar combination of symptoms at St Andrew's Hospital in Northampton in 1892;[79] and a 1933 report attributed 44 per cent of in-hospital deaths of manic patients to exhaustion of this type.[80] Death from manic exhaustion is by no means entirely a thing of the past. A 1986 study of 'lethal catatonia' explores the progression of coma, cardiovascular collapse and death in mania.[81] In a 1997 study of the link between acute excited states and sudden death, the authors attribute death to 'high circulating adrenaline concentrations, lactic acidosis, dehydration [and] heart arrhythmia': they observe that 'agitation is centrally driven regardless of context, leading to physiological exhaustion without subjective fatigue'.[82] Their recommendations for intervention to stave off death recapitulate the treatment imposed on White in Bethlem: 'restraint, seclusion, and medication'.[83]

The manic episode White fictionalised in *Beyond the Glass* closely follows the trajectory of escalation through mild and moderate stages to psychosis. Mild mania or hypomania can be both pleasurable and creative, expressed in 'profusion of ideas', 'associational fluency' and 'quickened senses'.[84] This heightened sense of reality may include states of ecstasy, in which the manic person experiences 'a sense of benevolence and communion with nature [. . .] analogous to the beatific and mystical experiences of saints and other religious leaders'.[85] Perceptual acuity increases: colours seem vivid and intense; surfaces and textures are invitingly tactile and finely detailed; sounds are amplified beyond their actual level and pitch.[86] This mild stage of mania is often highly valued as a source of creative vision and fluency by writers and other artists;[87] even for those who do not express themselves artistically, the pleasure of the manic 'high' can serve as a powerful inducement to forego lithium and other drug treatments that dampen and dull hypomanic intensity.[88]

Gradually the level of impairment increases. One of the most common symptoms of manic onset is a decreased need for sleep in conjunction with an increase in energy and activity levels. *DSM-5* reports that the manic person 'may sleep little, if at all, or may awaken several hours earlier than usual, feeling rested and full of energy. When the sleep disturbance is severe, the individual may go for days without sleep, yet not feel tired.'[89] Boundlessly energetic and uncritically self-confident, the manic person may embark on a multiplicity of new endeavours, for nothing seems unachievable.[90] This inflated sense of self easily shades into grandiosity, a belief that one has been singled out for special and exalted missions on behalf of humankind and the world. This same inflated self-confidence and grandiosity fuels the impulsive, reckless and often disastrous behaviours – promiscuity; risky financial ventures; extravagant spending sprees – particularly associated with manic episodes.[91] Because those in the throes of mania do not perceive themselves as being ill, moreover, they may 'vehemently resist efforts to be treated'.[92]

Eventually, the rush of thought and sensory impressions can become unbearable: thinking becomes 'fragmented and often psychotic', 'incoherent', and 'racing and disjointed'.[93] In her memoir about living with manic depression, Jamison describes her distress at feeling her mind go into overdrive and her sense of helpless inability to stop it:

> The fast ideas are far too fast, and there are far too many; overwhelming confusion replaces clarity. Memory goes. Humour and absorption on friends' faces are replaced by fear and concern. Everything previously moving with the grain is now against – you are irritable, angry, frightened, uncontrollable, and enmeshed totally in the blackest caves of the mind. You never knew those caves were there. It will never end, for madness carves its own reality.[94]

Mania may induce paranoia and a conviction of threat and persecution. As the *International Statistical Classification of Diseases* 10th revision (*ICD*-10) observes:

> Inflated self-esteem and grandiose ideas may develop into delusions, and irritability and suspiciousness into delusions of persecution. In severe cases, grandiose or religious delusions of identity or role may be prominent, and flight of ideas and pressure of speech may result in the individual becoming incomprehensible.[95]

The flight of ideas may be 'evidenced by a nearly continuous flow of accelerated speech, with abrupt shifts from one topic to another [. . .] speech may become disorganised, incoherent, and particularly distressful to the individual'.[96] In the most extreme cases of manic psychosis, the individual may experience a 'total chaotic disarray of the senses', in which mania results in 'visual, auditory, and olfactory experiences unrelated to existing physical phenomena'.[97] At the same time, '[s]evere and sustained physical activity and excitement may result in aggression or violence, and neglect of eating, drinking and personal hygiene may result in dangerous states of dehydration and self-neglect'.[98]

As mania subsides, the individual may experience the sequence of escalation in reverse – proceeding from acute mania to active mania to hypomania – or s/he may cycle into a depressive episode.[99] In the trajectory of de-escalation, 'hallucinations – the least common of symptoms – [are] also the first symptoms to disappear [. . .] followed in turn by delusions, flight of ideas, push of speech, and distractability'.[100] Shame and humiliation often follow in the wake of mania (and may contribute to the cycling into depression) as the individual confronts the consequences of the episode. Jamison eloquently summarises the overwhelming embarrassment and very real and material reminders of post-episode turmoil, an embarrassment intensified by the realisation that she does not fully know exactly what she did or why she did it:

> finally there are only others' recollections of your behaviour [. . .] your bizarre, frantic, aimless behaviours – for mania has at least some grace in partially obliterating memories. What then [. . .] All those incredible feelings to sort through. Who is being too polite to say what? Who knows what? What did I do? Why? And most hauntingly, when will

it happen again? Then, too, are the bitter reminders [. . .] Credit cards revoked, bounced checks to cover, explanations due at work, apologies to make, intermittent memories of vague men (what *did* I do?), friendships gone or drained, a ruined marriage. And always, when will it happen again?[101]

Others' reactions may intensify such feelings. Some families and friends may respond with an embarrassed and polite silence about what has transpired, a response that, albeit well intentioned, may intensify feelings of isolation, stigma and shame. Other families may respond with anger, criticism and hostility, termed 'expressed emotion' by family-focused therapists.[102] This kind of response has been associated with higher rates of relapse.[103]

The depressive pole

Although mania is the essential and defining feature of a diagnosis of bipolar 1 disorder, most of those who experience a manic episode also experience depressive episodes as well,[104] and in fact the depressive pole of the illness is often more debilitating, more chronic and more difficult to treat than the manic pole.[105] In general, depressive episodes develop more gradually than manic episodes – over weeks rather than days – and the stages are less clear-cut.[106] Depression can range in severity from 'mild sadness, [to] deep sadness with sleep disturbance and suicidal preoccupations, to emotionally deadened states with psychomotor immobility and lethargy'.[107] 'Sadness' encompasses a range of feelings – emptiness, hopelessness, ennui, despair – that may not even be recognised as depression. Typically depressive states must persist and deepen before people admit that their 'inchoate feelings' are not just 'blues' but represent something more sinister.[108]

As White wrote of her second breakdown, 'for a long time, I did not think it was any more than tiredness, nerves and general strain. But when it came to delusions, a depression so deep that even now I don't like to think about it and violent suicidal impulses (one very nearly successful), something had to be done' (*The Hound and the Falcon*, p. 37). Even now, when depression is widely recognised, the majority of depressed patients initially seek medical help for a range of somatic symptoms – bodily aches and pains, headaches, digestive problems, shortness of breath – without realising that they are depressed.[109] Similarly, irritability, tearfulness, withdrawal from activities and other people, sleep disturbances and weight changes can all signal depression, even though the individual may not make that connection for him- or herself.[110]

Like mania, depression alters metabolism, and changes in sleep and appetite are common. Sleep disturbances include difficulty in falling asleep or staying asleep as well as sleeping too much.[111] White's history of sleep disturbances is unusual: mood episodes in her case induced terrifying nightmares and during her second breakdown these in turn provoked suicide attempts. White's weight also fluctuated depending on her mood. She gained weight quickly when depressed, which in turn intensified the self-loathing typical of depression, for she then disliked her body: 'I know I'm too fat. I don't like being too fat. I know ways of making myself thinner. Yet as soon as I see a nice piece of food I eat it, even if I'm not hungry. Then I get morbid about it and I think that because I'm too fat I must be physically repulsive in every way' (*Diary* 1, p. 100). Weight gain may occur in part because depression leads to less physical activity, but atypical features of bipolar disorder – 'hyperphagia [excessive hunger], hypersomnia, "leaden paralysis," and carbohydrate craving' – may also contribute.[112] White's binge eating, recorded in a number of diary entries, may thus have been a sign of a mixed state, since binge eating has a specific association with hypomania.[113] White notes that 'When I am writing, I must always be smoking or nibbling. I *feel* that it helps me to concentrate. Actually I am pretty sure that it *prevents* me from concentrating' (*Diary* 1, p. 168). Later in the same entry she returns to the subject:

> Is the craving for a cigarette expression of horror of the void? Daren't experience *emptiness*..like annihilation. Starvation diet produced complete numbness of mind and extreme depression. I am always so busy stuffing something into my mind or my mouth that I very seldom experience real hunger. (*Diary* 1, p. 169).

White's inability to concentrate and binge eating suggest the restless energy associated with hypomania, while the 'emptiness like annihilation' and 'numbness of mind' speak to depressed mood.

Depression often induces guilt, self-loathing and self-condemnation. For White, raised in a harsh and authoritarian religious climate, dysphoric moods frequently provoked feelings of inner corruption and putrefaction, 'bad spells when one feels corrupt and poisoned right through' (*The Hound and the Falcon*, p. 112). She vividly portrays this state of internal putrefaction in her short story 'The Moment of Truth', when the protagonist comments on her fear of thinking: 'Her very thoughts were tarnished. They split and unravelled into meaningless ends. Often she believed she was going insane. Something inside her seemed to have died and to be filling her mind, even her body, with corruption' (*Strangers*, p. 29). 'I am poisoned, poisoned right through', she tells her husband, while he for his part listens to her raving self-accusation: 'the terrible words multiplied and multiplied, till he seemed to be watching the multiplication, cell by cell, of a cancer' (*Strangers*, p. 41). For White, as for many who are depressed, the body itself seems to rot in tandem with the mind: as Andrew Solomon observes, 'If your hair has always been thin, it seems thinner; if you have always had bad skin, it gets worse. You smell sour even to yourself'.[114] In an image later made famous by Sylvia Plath, White describes depression as a slow suffocation brought on by breathing the noxious fumes of one's own stinking, stale decay: her fictional alter ego likens herself to 'sour soil where nothing will grow' and feels overwhelmed by the sense 'of being utterly cut off from life, gasping for air inside a bell jar' (*The Sugar House*, pp. 210, 212). White also images depression as engulfment: of a 'wonderful and terrible passage' in St John of the Cross's *The Dark Night of the Soul* White remarks how 'the soul seems to disintegrate and to be swallowed up by a great beast. I know the psychological equivalent' (*The Hound and the Falcon*, p. 92). Over time, she believed it was necessary to

> stand still and let the sea close over you [. . .] chances are you'll come to the surface and float [. . .] But when you're in it it is impossible to believe that you were ever in any state but this stagnation or will ever emerge from it. The only thing is to go on mechanically with one's daily routine – if one can. (*The Hound and the Falcon*, p. 138)

White's depression made her feel cut off not only from life but from other people, whose responses often amplified feelings of isolation and exile. The very intangibility of depression makes it harder for others to comprehend, a fact of which the depressed themselves are often aware. Solomon finds himself incredulous that he is 'split and racked by this thing no one else seemed able to see'.[115] Other reactions range from well-intentioned but obtuse exhortations to 'cheer up' or 'snap out of it' to more debilitating insinuations that the sufferer can simply decide – indeed, has a moral duty to decide – to stop being depressed. This kind of response exacerbates the feelings of guilt, worthlessness and self-blame that depression itself already generates.[116] Even those who are more supportive of the sufferer may eventually be worn down as the episode persists. Goodwin and Jamison note that 'depressive symptoms such as irritability, loss of energy and enjoyment, heightened sensitivity to criticism, and defeatist and pessimistic attitudes' can 'erode the initial concern and patience' of a spouse;[117] furthermore, 'individuals may correctly perceive that they are a burden to others, a reality that may serve to heighten their depression [. . .] others tend to reject depressed persons and express preferences for avoiding them'.[118]

Suicide is the most tragic and pernicious endpoint of depression and, even if there is no attempt, suicidal ideation is common.[119] 'I asked for deliverance,' Andrew Solomon writes. 'I would have been happy to die the most painful death, though I was too dumbly lethargic even to conceptualise suicide. Every second of being alive hurt me.'[120] The American writer William Styron excoriates those who cannot fathom how severe depression can lead to suicide. Family members and close friends often deflect or disclaim suicidal intent, Styron observes, a response that is understandable but finally misguided: 'The sufferer [. . .] is often, through denial on the part of others, unjustly made to appear a wrongdoer.'[121] Indeed, it was the reaction to Holocaust survivor Primo Levi's suicide that inspired Styron to write the essay that would eventually become *Darkness Visible*. 'It was as if this man whom they had all so greatly admired, and who had endured so much at the hands of the Nazis – a man of exemplary resilience and courage – had by his suicide demonstrated a frailty, a crumbling of character they were loath to accept', Styron writes. Their reaction 'was helplessness and [. . .] a touch of shame'.[122] Styron's 'straightforward' conclusion is that 'the pain of severe depression is quite unimaginable to those who have not suffered it, and it kills in many instances because its anguish can no longer be borne'.[123] White echoes this conclusion in a letter describing how her second husband helped her during a suicidal crisis in 1936:

> Some years ago when the beast was at its worst and from violent suicidal impulses I'd subsided into a state of hopeless, blank despair, I thought seriously the most reasonable thing to do was to kill myself

deliberately because there seemed no hope of getting better. Instead of arguing against that he said: 'Hang on for six more months. Then if it hasn't got any better, I think you would be perfectly justified in committing suicide.' And I did hang on. (*The Hound and the Falcon*, p. 114)

If, as seems likely, White's episodes took the form of mixed states, it is hard to overestimate the turbulence and anguish she endured over almost sixty years of illness. Jamison reports that the 'most virulent' predictor of suicide in manic depression is

the mix of depressed mood, morbid thinking, and a 'wired', agitated level of energy [. . .] It is singularly and dangerously uncomfortable. Excess energy produces a kind of unhinging agitation, an 'almost terrible energy' [. . .] Mixed states, whether they occur as depressive manias or agitated depressions, make people who experience them more likely to kill themselves.[124]

White's breakdown in the 1930s, in which she not only contemplated suicide but attempted it on multiple occasions, bears out Jamison's observation. The irritability and angry outbursts that disrupted White's personal relationships and that in some cases permanently alienated family members are some of the clearest markers of these dangerous states. It is also likely, moreover, that White's episodes of illness lasted for longer periods as she aged. Records of untreated manic-depressive illness kept prior to 1950 indicate that the illness becomes progressively worse.[125] Emil Kraepelin, for example, observed that attacks that initially lasted from six to eight months lasted longer and longer as time went by; the 'disease showed a tendency to evolve more quickly, with shorter intervals between the attacks, and a gradual increase of their duration'.[126] He also noted that manic episodes tended to decrease between the ages of fifty and sixty, whereas depressive episodes increased.[127] Kraepelin further observed that these mixed states tended to become more common as the disease progressed, and to be more common in women.[128]

Woolf and White: a brief comparison

Individual patterns of manic depression vary widely; Kraepelin notably remarked that the variations are 'absolutely inexhaustible'.[129] The variations involved in individual manifestations of manic depression are amply illustrated by comparing White's experiences of illness to those of her contemporary Virginia Woolf. Both women suffered from debilitating and chronic episodes, and they even shared similar symptom patterns. Both, for example, suffered from headaches, which they describe as a feeling of the head encircled by a tight band; for both women these headaches were early signs of illness. Both also suffered from frequent bouts of flu, which seemed to cause or exacerbate episodes; as Goodwin and Jamison note, physical illnesses 'are sometimes not recognised as significant precipitating factors for manic or depressive episodes, but they should be'.[130] White always connected flu with a peculiarly unpleasant mood, writing in a letter that 'I'm still in a black, sour and rebellious mood – partly physical, for I always get this accidious melancholy with even a whiff of flu' (*The Hound and the Falcon*, p. 111). Woolf similarly struggled with the connection between her moods and flu:

> But – oh damn these medical details! – this influenza has a special poison for what is called the nervous system; and mine being a second-hand one, used by my father and his father [. . .] I have to treat it like a pampered pug dog, and lie still directly my head aches.'[131]

Both found physical sexuality difficult. The illness may have complicated the two writers' relationship to their physicality more generally, for they both describe themselves as cut off from spontaneous physical expression and, by extension, trapped within the limiting parameters of the mind. In a well-known passage in 'A Sketch of the Past', Woolf describes her 'looking-glass shame' and observes that she could feel 'ecstasies and raptures spontaneously and intensely and without any shame or the least sense of guilt so long as they were disconnected from my body'.[132] White similarly writes that she has never learnt 'the language of the body' (*Diary* 1, p. 94) and she often mentions her sense of being 'rigid, unable to let myself go or live by my instincts, unaware of other's people's feelings and frequently bludgeoning and indelicate' (*Diary* 1, p. 163). Finally, however, their experiences of illness were more divergent than similar.

In his brilliant study of Woolf's illness, Thomas Caramagno charts Woolf's moods from the onset of her illness after her mother's death in 1895 to her suicide in 1941, basing his calculations on Quentin Bell's biography of his aunt, Leonard Woolf's records of his wife's moods and Woolf's own diary and letters. His chart demonstrates that Woolf suffered severe or psychotic episodes of mania and depression in 1895, 1896, 1904, 1910, 1912–15, 1936 and 1941.[133] These severe or psychotic episodes gradually increased in length between 1895 and 1915, beginning with single months of illness in 1895 and 1896 and increasing to three or four months in length by 1915.[134] Thereafter, although very few years were altogether symptom-free, episodes were brief and for the most part remained at mild and only occasional moderate levels. The severe depression of 1936 persisted for two months; the psychotic depression that resulted in Woolf's suicide came in March 1941.[135]

Several aspects of Woolf's pattern of illness stand out. First, her illness, triggered by the sudden death of her mother in 1895 when Woolf was thirteen years old, falls into the category of early-onset bipolar disorder, typically a predictor of a debilitating pattern of illness in which episodes increase in frequency, severity and duration.[136] And, in fact, Woolf's episodes did worsen between 1895 and 1915. But the fact that she suffered from a recurrent illness was established early on in her life and meant that she entered adulthood with that knowledge. Second, Woolf seems to have experienced relatively clear-cut swings between mania and depression. When her manic symptoms did not escalate into severe or psychotic states, she benefited from the creative intensity of hypomania, states that have been associated with greater combinatory thought processes and greater associational fluency.[137] Finally, and in some ways most importantly, Woolf benefited from significant levels of support and understanding for her illness from adolescence on. Her family was extremely familiar with a variety of mental illnesses, and Woolf herself understood her illness to have its origins in her genetic inheritance. Her mother's devotion to nursing, moreover, meant that the family was situated within a network of doctors and medical practices long before Woolf herself fell ill. Even before Leonard Woolf began to monitor her moods, her family was able to arrange competent care for her and to afford extended stays in private nursing homes, where she was often cared for by friends of the family and others known to her. While Woolf certainly resented her doctors' obtuseness and the sexism that informed their attitudes to women, she benefited from coming from a privileged background that protected her from incarceration in the public asylums or from certification under the Lunacy Act of 1890.

Above all, Woolf benefited from Leonard Woolf's devotion to maintaining her health. It is no accident that from 1915 on Woolf's episodes remained at mild and only occasional moderate levels. When Woolf's most prolonged episodes of illness began soon after their marriage in 1912, Leonard 'cross-examined' (his term) Woolf's doctors and embarked on a study of what was then known of mental disturbances, correctly identifying her illness as manic depression.[138] In addition, he began to keep a daily diary of her symptoms, what would now be called a 'mood chart', a widely recommended practice for those diagnosed with mood disorders. From 1913 to 1919, Caramagno explains,

> Leonard kept an almost daily journal of Virginia's moods (time of onset, duration and intensity), her sleeping and eating patterns, temperature, weight, dose of drug taken, and date of onset of menstruation. Correlations between bodily rhythms and mental states helped him anticipate what level of care she would need. In later years, whenever Virginia felt ill, Leonard returned to his monitoring, using his measurements as a predictor of impending breakdown.[139]

Leonard himself provided an overview of the Woolfs' approach to managing the illness:

> If Virginia lived a quiet, vegetative life, eating well, going to bed early, and not tiring herself mentally or physically, she remained perfectly well. But if she tired herself in any way, if she was subjected to any severe physical, mental or emotional strain, symptoms at once appeared which in the ordinary person are negligible and transient, but with her were serious danger signals. The first symptoms were a peculiar 'headache' low down at the back of the head, insomnia, and a tendency for the thoughts to race. If she went to bed and lay doing nothing in a darkened room, drinking large quantities of milk and eating well, the symptoms would slowly disappear and in a week or ten days she would be well again.[140]

In his attention to patterns of sleeping, eating and daily routines, Leonard anticipated research that stresses the role that the body's daily biological rhythms, or circadian rhythms, play in affective disorders. Leonard clearly grasped these connections, commenting that:

> It was a perpetual struggle to find the precarious balance of health for her among the strains and stresses of writing and society. The routine of everyday life had to be regular and rather rigid. Everything had to be rationed, from work and walking to people and parties.[141]

To a contemporary reader familiar with research on managing manic-depressive illness, Leonard Woolf's grasp of the connection between psychosocial stressors and biological rhythms seems extraordinarily prescient in the light of recent clinical findings. Leonard's conviction that pregnancy might compromise Woolf's health, for example – a conviction that some critics have condemned – is in fact borne out by contemporary statistics: the postpartum period 'is clearly a time of greatly increased risk for relapse, especially into mania and psychosis, rates of which are estimated at 50 to 75 per cent'.[142] Still other bipolar women develop severe postnatal depression. In an era without psychotropic drug therapies, pregnancy and, particularly, childbirth did represent a significant risk of illness of indeterminate character, length and treatment for women with a history of mental disturbance. Indeed, Woolf's family history included such a case: Isabella Makepeace Thackeray, the mother of Leslie Stephen's first wife and the maternal grandmother of Woolf's half-sister Laura Stephen, lapsed into a severe postpartum depression resulting in permanent insanity.[143] Even today, clinicians recommend that women with bipolar disorder consider the risk of illness with care and caution before embarking on pregnancy.

Leonard's regime of managing Woolf's sleep also deserves mention. Sleep disruption is one of the earliest and most common symptoms of episode onset, and clinical studies have shown that any kind of sleep disruption may trigger mania.[144] Leonard monitored Woolf's sleeping carefully, and resorted to sedatives such as chloral and veronal when she suffered from insomnia.[145] More intriguingly, his insistence on her resting in a darkened room – a vestigial remedy derived from the Victorian 'rest cure' – has recently been confirmed as an antidote to rapid cycling in bipolar disorder.[146] In a pioneering experiment, researchers hypothesised that the suprachiasmatic nucleus of the hypothalamus, an area of the brain situated above the optic nerve which receives input from special photosensitive cells in the retina, could become desensitised by too much light and activity in the evening in those with the rapid cycling form of bipolar disorder. Rapid cyclers, in other words, 'have lost their ability to respond to the timing of natural day and light'.[147] When a man with a history of severe rapid cycling rested in darkness for fourteen hours, from 6 p.m. to 8 a.m., over a period of weeks, his mood stabilised without any drug therapies at all. The researchers concluded that 'fostering sleep and stabilising its timing by scheduling periods of enforced bed rest in the dark may help to prevent mania and rapid cycling in bipo-lar patients'.[148] Leonard reached the same conclusion. In a letter to Vita Sackville-West, he notes that Woolf is 'still not right & is more or less in bed. The slightest thing is apt to bring symptoms back.'[149] Her symptoms, he continues, derive not from physical illness

> but simply to her overdoing it & particularly not going to bed at 11 for all those nights running. It has been proved over & over again in the last 10 years that even 2 late nights running are definitely danger-ous for her & this time it was 7 or 8.[150]

Throughout Woolf's life, Leonard would similarly insist on rest in a darkened room when he perceived signs of episode onset.

Records for White are far less reliable and complete, but overall the history of her symptoms and treatment reads quite differently from that of Woolf. In contrast to Woolf, whose illness began in early adolescence, White's conformed to a more typical trajectory, begin-ning in her early twenties, the average age of onset. White's illness began with a protracted episode of severe depression, followed by a psychotic and protracted manic episode. Available records suggest that White did not suffer such clear-cut distinctions between moods again. In contrast to Woolf, who seems to have had frequent hypo-manic moods that enhanced her writing and productivity, White suffered primarily from mixed episodes of a depressive cast that drained her physically and mentally and made it difficult for her to concentrate or work. Not only did manic energy infuse her depres-sive moods – leading to 'maniacal' reading, eating, shopping and the like – but depression itself has been shown to interfere with cog-nition, memory and decision-making. Cognitive psychologists have long known that 'memory and mood fluctuate together; the sadder the mood, the more morbid are the memories the depressed person recalls'.[151] Recent studies suggest that depression may cause changes in the brain that result in 'internal rumination over morbid past experiences'.[152] White's crippling inability to process her relationship with her father and the chaotic events of her twenties may have been in part a consequence of such depressive rumination.

The treatment White received for her illness also differed mark-edly from that of Woolf. White's incarceration in Bethlem is a case in point. White's family, unlike Woolf's, did not have much experience with psychiatric illness, and the sudden onset of her manic episode in November 1922 apparently took her parents completely by surprise.[153] The decision to commit her in Bethlem developed from a number of factors. Although White's mother wanted to try and nurse her at home, White's father and the family doctor believed that the violence and severity of her psychotic state made professional care imperative. The choice of a public hospital rather than a private nursing home was in part medical, in part financial. Dunn reports that the family doctor 'argued for Bethlem [. . .] because it had a reputation for employing experienced psychiatric doctors. It had no commercial interest in its patients, and its waiting list meant that the administrators would not be tempted to hold a patient incarcerated for any longer than was medically necessary.'[154] The actual medical treatment of White's mania seems to have been quite competent. Like Woolf, White was sedated with chloral and veronal, then-standard treatments for mania, and dosages were reduced as it subsided.

Other aspects of her hospitalisation, however, would haunt her for life, chief among them that she had been treated like an animal. White's fictional treatments of Bethlem adhere so closely to the medical records that it seems as if, even in her psychotic state, some part of her mind retained awareness of what was happening to her.[155] This phenomenon of being an observer of one's own activity from another point in the mind has been noted by others suffering mania, and apparently involves stimulation of the limbic or temporal lobe.[156] White's memories of restraints, water treatments and padded cells vividly capture not only the dehumanising character of such 'treatments' but also the way psychiatric institutions often intensify the fear and terror that already infuse psychotic conditions. White's memories of contemptuous and dismissive medical staff and the depersonalisation and dehumanisation of patients similarly underscore the ways in which institutional psychiatric care often disempowers those who are already suffering. This kind of treatment is the focus of multiple critiques of psychiatry today.[157] In fact, contemporary research shows that psychiatric patients often leave hospitals with an additional diagnosis of post-traumatic stress disorder as a result of the terrifying and dehumanising experience of 'treatment'.[158] Hence, while Woolf certainly took issue with the sexism and limited insight into psychiatric suffering she experienced from doctors, she was spared the kind of institutional horrors to which White was exposed. White's nightmarish memories of Bethlem led her to a profound fear of relapse, memorialised in the 1964 story

'Surprise Visit', in which the protagonist lapses into a state of insanity simply by revisiting the scene of her prior incarceration.

The long hiatus between White's first serious episode of illness in 1922–3 and the second in 1933–8 is another factor that distinguishes White's experiences from those of Woolf. White left Bethlem with the assurance that her illness was an aberration, not a chronic condition. Her breakdown in 1933 therefore came as a surprise, both to her and to Tom Hopkinson, her third husband. As I note in the opening to this chapter, the events of 1929–30 suggest that White may have been at least mildly manic at this time, but no one, not even White herself, recognised the signs. Thus, like the majority of those suffering with bipolar disorder today, White's illness went unrecognised for ten years.[159] A lag between the onset of bipolar disorder in one's early twenties and its recognition as a chronic illness means that this crucial decade of early adulthood – in which many people make significant choices about partners, families, employment and education – can generate a lifetime of harsh consequences for actions impelled by manic energy and poor judgement. White's broken marriages, unplanned pregnancies and job losses attest to the havoc the illness can generate. And while both Tom Hopkinson and White's second husband Eric Earnshaw Smith did their best to locate treatment for White, neither had Leonard Woolf's dispassionate, objective and methodical approach to charting symptoms and devising strategies for coping with them. Here, too, White's illness conforms to the more typical trajectory. For while the support and care of partners and family members can help prevent relapse, all too often the illness interferes with and even destroys interpersonal relationships.[160] Goodwin and Jamison observe that women's depressive moods frequently lead to marital conflict and are 'fraught with friction, inadequate communication, dependency, overt hostility, resentment and guilt, poor sexual relationships, and a lack of affection'.[161] Such was indeed the case for White and Tom Hopkinson, and the breakdown of their marriage left White a single unemployed mother who had to cope with her two young daughters in addition to coping with her illness.

Finally, White developed a very different attitude to her illness than did Woolf. Woolf seems to have accepted her illness as an inevitable component of her life, and her diary and letters attest to the way she taught herself to detach her moods from events and circumstances, to see them as phenomena possessing an internal rhythm and logic of their own. 'I must note the symptoms of the disease, so as to know it next time,' she writes in a diary entry. 'The first day one's miserable: the second happy.'[162] Another entry records how her own psychology interests her: 'I intend to keep full notes of my ups & downs, for my private information. And thus objectified, the pain & shame become at once much less.'[163] The early onset and frequency of episodes, her family history of affective disorders and the support of others, particularly her sister Vanessa Bell and Leonard, aided her in this approach.

White, however, repeatedly sought a permanent cure for her illness. She thought herself cured following the end of analysis in 1938 and believed herself cured by Catholicism in the late 1940s; her near-breakdown in the 1960s – following months of feeling paralysed in a 'blank automatic state' – came at a point when she 'prided myself on being – sane' (*Diary* 2, p. 130). Although, over the years, White recognised patterns in her illness, she sought explanations, asking herself where she had gone wrong, as if the answer lay in some flaw in her character. Both psychoanalysis and Catholicism buttressed this conviction that she was in some way responsible for her symptoms and could eradicate them with due diligence. Hence, as her analysis with Carroll drew to an end, White celebrates having the 'last clue, the one it seemed almost impossible to find' and observes that 'Whatever happens, the missing piece is found, and if things go wrong after this, it will be my own fault'.[164] Indeed, at times White demonstrates compelling insight into her symptoms, only to 'correct' herself by substituting explanations drawn from her analyst or priest. Thus, for example, she notes that 'Extravagance is I am sure a symptom of anxiety with me' (*Diary* 1, p. 169), whereas her analyst connects her overspending to her angry, cruel impulses (*Diary* 1, p. 152). Similarly, in another entry White observes that 'I am getting very fat very fast again but believe it is psychological and that physical measures, even if I could stick to them, won't be much good'; the next sentence in the entry records her analyst's interpretation that White feels 'it safer to have things *inside*' (*Diary* 1, p. 145).

White's fear of her illness and her belief that she could cure it permanently by identifying its causes may have contributed to her writer's block. White's name for her illness, 'the Beast', was a term she took from Henry James's story 'The Beast in the Jungle', whose protagonist fears the inevitable spring of a terrible crouching Beast that could overwhelm or perhaps even kill him. White remarked during the Blitz that she was 'much more afraid of the beast than of death'

(*The Hound and the Falcon*, p. 16). White's fear of 'letting go' and her terror of 'getting carried away' may have developed out of her fear of losing control of her mind (*Diary* 2, p. 59). In 1937, for example, as she began to emerge from her second crippling breakdown, White describes her efforts to 'track something down which keeps eluding me . . . Now the odd thing is that in a sense I *know* the beast in my jungle and have even stated the thing in speech and on paper and *yet*, try as I will, cannot feel it fully and so escape from it. Obviously I am terrified . . . but of what?' (*Diary* 1, p. 109). The rest of the entry describes her fear of exposing herself to the risk of failure, but ends on a revealing note: 'I am a very serious failure . . . because I have no control over my emotions or actions' (*Diary* 1, p. 109). Other entries at this time record White's sense that 'It is a great art to let oneself go in the right place; does not mean disintegration as I always feel. And part of me just pants to let go. *What* am I frightened of?' She answers this question for herself: 'as soon as I let go, or want to let go, I feel a menace of annihilation'.[165]

This fear of 'letting go' emerges in her changing attitude to Woolf's writing. Throughout White's life Woolf served as a crucial touchstone for White. As early as 1925, while working in an advertising firm, White cut Woolf's picture out of *Vogue* and kept it over her desk. 'It used to comfort me while I wrote advertisements for corsets and disinfectants and baking powder', she would later write to Woolf in a letter of appreciation in 1931.[166] In that letter White identified *Mrs Dalloway* as a source of inspiration. Dunn explains that White felt 'excitement, recognition, acceptance; "This is it [. . .] the real, right thing." She wrote to tell Virginia Woolf that in this book she had shown her there was a reason and pattern in madness. Antonia passionately identified with Virginia Woolf as a survivor.'[167] White had herself just completed 'The House of Clouds', a short story that depicts the experience of psychosis and that White would later revise as the psychosis section of *Beyond the Glass*. Although it remains unclear when White actually read Woolf's novel, whether before, during or after writing 'The House of Clouds', White's excitement about Woolf's portrayal of madness suggests a commonality in perception – a commonality rooted in their shared affective disorder.

But a diary entry recorded in 1970 evidences misgivings. Calling Woolf 'the great heroine-writer of my youth', White reflects:

She will always interest me extremely. I still feel *To the Lighthouse* is her one real masterpiece. And of course she was mad too – more officially mad, in a way, than I am. I understand very well her intense sense of the thousand things pressing on one's mind simultaneously which one can never capture when one writes. She is very much an 'impressionist' as a writer. Yet this enormous accumulation of detail and speculation – marvellously observed – can be fatiguing: everything dissolves and becomes, as it were, brilliantly nebulous and one is left stimulated yet unsatisfied. Only in the *Lighthouse* do I feel she reached a point of stability and that there are bones beneath the flesh. (*Diary* 2, p. 216)

Still appreciative of the power and intensity of Woolf's writing, White finds reading Woolf disturbing. The accumulation of sensory detail overwhelms but then dissolves, leaving White with the sense that there is nothing behind it, no point of stability, no structure. This generalisation echoes White's reactions to *Jacob's Room* in 1939 and to *The Years* in 1968. The former 'exasperated yet charmed' White: 'She lays her little strands side by side instead of working them into a pattern. But perhaps it is because there is no solid structure underneath that it leaves me with this curious and dissatisfied feeling' (*Diary* 1, p. 164). Similarly, although White records that she is 'fascinated' by *The Years* – '*How* marvellously she writes – or rather *paints*' – she also calls it 'a beautiful, but utterly frustrating book. But she creates something out of that very frustration. We don't know ourselves, we don't know others' (*Diary* 2, p. 197). By 1978 *A Writer's Diary* produces 'extreme depression [. . .] I can't follow her mind at all' (*Diary* 2, pp. 294–5).

Why did White's reaction to Woolf's writing change? The answer may lie in White's experiences of affective illness. When she pinned Woolf's picture above her desk, read *Mrs Dalloway* and wrote Woolf an enthusiastic fan letter, White did not realise that her illness was chronic and recurrent. But by the time she recorded her reactions to *Jacob's Room* and *The Years*, White had struggled through years of chaos and upheaval and almost constant illness. It seems significant, moreover, that White never wrote anything like 'The House of Clouds' again, since the psychosis section in *Beyond the Glass* is a revision of the earlier piece. If in 1931 White found in *Mrs Dalloway* a way to locate reason and pattern in madness, by 1939 and thereafter Woolf's writing seems to elicit in White deep discomfort, uneasiness, even fear.

White's objections to Woolf's writing turn on qualities highly relevant to a discussion of manic depression. The fluency and flood that White finds disturbing are qualities characteristic of divergent thinking, which Jamison also finds characteristic of manic thinking.[168] Such thinking is rapid, seemingly random flights of ideas that are only loosely tied together. White's desire for stability, structure and 'bones beneath the flesh' suggests a more constrained form of thought, convergent thinking. John Guilford, a psychologist whose research on creativity underpins Jamison's argument, defines convergent thinking as a process in which 'almost always one conclusion or answer [. . .] is regarded as unique, and thinking is to be channeled or controlled in the direction of that answer', whereas divergent thinking is 'less goal-bound. There is freedom to go off in different directions'.[169] Significantly, 'The House of Clouds' and the psychotic sections based on it in *Beyond the Glass* – two of the most powerful pieces of writing White ever produced – are examples of highly divergent thinking. These pieces evidence the fluency, rapidity and intensity of divergent thinking. They also evidence 'combinatory thinking', the 'merging of "precepts, ideas, or images in an incongruous fashion [. . .] loosely strung together and extravagantly combined and elaborated"'.[170]

White's response to Woolf's writing thus suggests that she was disturbed by writing that evoked manic thinking after the ordeals she underwent in the 1930s. Notably, she finds herself both 'stimulated' and 'fatigued' by reading Woolf, much as those in the grip of mania cannot turn off minds that are running in overdrive, no matter how exhausted they are. Although it is impossible to know why White found herself so blocked in writing fiction when she could write so easily in other forms, at least one possible explanation may lie in White's distrust of the very divergent thinking that makes 'The House of Clouds' and the psychosis sections of *Beyond the Glass* such powerful pieces of fiction. And the desire for coherence, stability and pattern – the desire for the more constrained kind of thinking that Guilford calls 'convergent' – similarly suggests the desire for control and coherence that White would search for in psychoanalysis and Catholicism, and that she would attempt to incorporate as structures of coherence for her troubling incoherence of self. That search for coherence forms the subject of the next chapter.

'I am a schizophrene': Narrative Identity, Affective Disorder and White's Stories of Self

White's desire to construct a coherent narrative of self, one that would serve as a 'kind of testimony', resonates with contemporary scholarship on life-writing in general and on illness narratives or 'pathographies' in particular. For several decades, scholars across a number of fields have explored the idea that identity itself is a narrative construction. In a much-quoted formulation, Oliver Sacks observes that 'It might be said that each of us constructs and lives a "narrative," and this narrative *is* us, our identities'.[1] Jerome Bruner writes that 'self is a perpetually rewritten story';[2] a sense of self, he argues, develops out of stories that 'impose a structure, a compelling reality in what we experience':[3] self *is* story, 'a product of our telling and not some essence'.[4] Yet identity narratives do not develop in a vacuum: the structures we impose reflect dominant cultural and social norms that function as regulatory and disciplinary mechanisms. Psychoanalysis and Catholicism function as such structures in White's life-writing, for these discourses provide narrative models that organise White's feelings (moods) along a striking number of parallels. Both models privilege male authority (Freud/analyst and God/priest); both foreground family structure (the Oedipal complex; the Holy Family); and both emphasise female inferiority (the castration complex; fallen Eve). The Catholic sequence of sin, repentance and redemption, carried out under the auspices of God's representative, the priest, finds its correlative in the psychoanalytic sequence of transference (repetition, recognition and working through), carried out under the auspices of Freud's representative, the analyst. Interpreting her affective disorder through the frames of these narrative models, White came to believe that her chaotic moods and resulting inexplicable actions attested to unconscious conflicts and/or moral failings: affective symptoms became psychological complexes; complexes in turn became sins.

White's desperate search for cure/grace, documented in her diary and other writing, constitutes a significant contribution to the field of identity narratives that focus on mental illness. Illness narratives, as well as those that treat the related categories of trauma and disability, receive heightened attention in the scholarship on narrative identity precisely because such afflictions disrupt the dominant and normative models of development and health that serve as a kind of unacknowledged meta-narrative of human life. 'Disease, disability, and trauma disrupt the body, the self, and the life-as-story', write the editors of *Unfitting Stories: Narrative Approaches to Disease, Disability, and Trauma*.[5] Anne Hunsaker Hawkins and Arthur W. Frank have shown how stories enable sufferers to find meaning in what has happened to them, thereby restoring coherence to broken narratives of self.[6] As in other identity narratives, master narratives and pervasive myths and metaphors play a key role in how the afflicted interpret their afflictions and how they represent them. Motifs of battle and the journey or quest, for example, are common.[7]

Yet recurrent illnesses, and particularly recurrent mental illnesses, may not lend themselves readily to conventional narrative patterns.[8] Mental illness is more nebulous in character than physical illness, and may not assume an identifiable pattern initially, or indeed ever. 'Chronic emotional illness poses especially difficult problems of sense-making because the source of the problem is unclear and its course uncertain', Karp writes in his study of depression. It is 'an exercise in negotiating ambiguity and involves the evolution of an illness consciousness extending over many years'.[9] The editors of *Unfitting Stories* note that 'the imposition of artistic form may provide coherence, re-establishing a wholeness or healing lacking in life', yet that is not always the case: 'An existence interrupted or disrupted by disease, disability, or trauma may be conveyed narratively by an aesthetic structure that reflects the fragmentation and patching together of a broken life, or through a story which presents an enigma rather than a "remedy" or solution'.[10] But such a fragmented or enigmatic narrative may rebound upon the teller and increase the isolation and stigma associated with mental illness, for one of the biggest challenges facing those who construct narratives of mental illness is that mental health is to some extent linked to the ability to tell a coherent story of self, a story that makes sense: it is this very coherence and sense that mental illness undercuts.[11] In this respect, narratives of mental illness may resemble what Frank typifies as 'chaos stories', in which 'Events are told as the storyteller experiences life: without sequence and without causality'.[12] Such stories provoke anxiety in the listener, he observes, for not only is the sufferer not telling a 'proper' story, but 'the teller of the chaos story is not heard to be living a "proper" life, since in life as in story, one event is expected to lead to another'.[13] Such a story is a 'non-self-story [. . .] In stories told out of the deepest chaos, no sense of sequence redeems suffering as orderly, and no self finds purpose in suffering.'[14]

Frank underscores the necessity of honouring the chaos story, observing that our discomfort with such stories lies in the way that they 'reveal the hubris of other stories. Chaos stories show how quickly the props that other stories depend on can be kicked away.'[15] His stance echoes that of the editors of *Beyond Narrative Coherence*, who similarly urge the honouring of stories told by the disabled, brain-damaged or traumatised that do not conform to narrative norms; 'the imperative of coherence', they charge, 'works to legitimate certain narratives while excluding or marginalising others'.[16] Yet incoherent stories of self may actually endanger those who tell them. The ability to tell a coherent life story plays a key role in social interactions: Charlotte Linde notes that it is a 'social obligation that must be fulfilled in order for the participants to appear as competent members of their culture'.[17] Paul John Eakin similarly points out that

> we inhabit systems of social intercourse in which the ability to articulate an identity narrative – whether written, related orally, or simply dropped piece by piece into the social discourse of daily life – confirms the possibility of a working identity. Accordingly, when brain disorders of various kinds impair or prevent our saying to others who we are, our claims to recognition as persons may suffer irreparable harm.[18]

In short, 'no satisfactory narrative, no self'.[19] The absence of a coherent identity narrative, moreover, can carry harsh consequences, such as a diagnosis of insanity and involuntary incarceration in a mental hospital.[20] The inability to tell a life story may mean not only being labelled abnormal but also being perceived as 'without personhood' altogether.[21]

White's own quest for a coherent narrative identity developed out of the chaos of her illness: fundamentally, she felt she had no identity. A diary entry in 1937, almost three years into her first analysis, captures what was to remain an enduring lament: 'I wish to heaven I knew who I was – my eternal cry. And no one can tell me.'[22] Such laments thread the diary throughout White's life: in 1953, she writes 'I don't understand my self. I don't understand my life'; in 1970 she complains that she has 'NO character'.[23] Even her multiple names come to signify the absence of an identity.[24] Observing that she has had five Christian names and four surnames, that she doesn't write under any of them, and that her nom de plume derives from her mother's nickname and her mother's own surname, White notes 'No wonder I feel I have no identity: am confused at introductions: cannot bear to be asked my name'.[25] White frequently refers to her fiction writing as representing therapy and cure, whereby she could explain herself not only to other people but to herself as well.[26] As her writer's block took hold after the publication of *Beyond the Glass* in 1954, however, her inability to construct a coherent fictional form for her life came to underscore her conviction that she lacked an identity, and White frequently characterises herself as a ghost. And underlying and intensifying her sense of uncertain and shadowy existence lurked the mood swings that constantly destabilised her: depression, which left her feeling inert, paralysed and impotent; and mania, which left her feeling restless and unsettled and which triggered compulsive and destructive behaviours. Her need to formulate stories of self, and her use of psychoanalysis and Catholicism to structure those stories of self, developed out of this constellation of factors.

White's framing of herself through master narratives worked not only to identify her father as the powerful patriarch who warped her sexuality, blocked her writing and motivated her illness; it also maintained him in that position and became the dominant theme of both her life-writing and her fiction. But the desperation that fuelled her accession to these narratives began with the onset of manic depression in White's early twenties. This chapter explores how illness in general and manic depression in particular destroyed White's sense of a coherent self and motivated her to construct identity narratives through the master narratives of psychoanalysis and Catholicism.

Manic depression and identity: the incoherence of 'self'

The fractures of psychosis, mania, depression and mood swings pose challenges to creating a coherent narrative of self for obvious reasons. Jamison has spoken eloquently to the incoherence of identity that manic depression creates. 'Which of my feelings are real?' she asks. 'Which of the me's is me? The wild, impulsive, chaotic, energetic, and crazy one? Or the shy, withdrawn, desperate, suicidal, doomed, and tired one?'[27] Jamison identifies here a fundamental problem the manic depressive encounters: the challenge of separating mood and emotion from self. Whybrow describes emotion as 'memory and feeling intertwined', and he goes on to distinguish emotion from mood: whereas emotion is 'usually transient and responsive to the thoughts, activities, and social situations of the day', mood is 'the consistent extension of emotion in time' and 'may last for hours, days, or even months'.[28] Hence, as Jamison suggests, the manic depressive is never sure of what is 'valid' or 'sane' or 'normal' and what is symptomatic, an uncertainty that deepens because a 'valid', 'sane' or 'normal' feeling can easily intensify into a disturbed one. This uncertainty undercuts an ability to trust or believe in 'the authenticity of identity and the reality of emotion', since 'a seemingly normal depressive reaction (to bad news, the loss of a loved one, a marital squabble) can sometimes deepen into a major episode of psychotic proportions', while 'a feeling of well-being, or happiness and creativity, can sometimes escalate into hypomania or mania'.[29] As Goodwin and Jamison note:

> Many common emotions range across several mood states [. . .] irritability and anger can be part of normal human existence or alternatively can be symptoms of both depression and hypomania. Tiredness, sadness, and lethargy can be due to normal circumstances, medical causes, or clinical depression. Feeling good [. . .] can be either normal or pathognomic of hypomania.[30]

To separate mood and emotion from self is extremely difficult, because they seem to be one and the same. Whybrow writes:

> Moods develop from our emotions, and because emotional life lies at the very core of being a person, to accept that mood and emotion can be 'dis-ordered' calls into question the very experience that most of us take for granted – the presence of a defined, predictable, and unique subjective entity that we fondly refer to as the intuitive 'self'.[31]

Beyond the challenge of finding a way to identify a sense of a coherent self through such contradictory changes, the interface between biology and psychology impacts the kind of narratives that the manic-depressive constructs. Explanatory strategies develop out of the need to make sense of moods, but 'a mood disorder fulfils its own prophecies by affecting what evidence the subject attends to and how he interprets it'.[32] Whybrow describes moods as having a 'halo effect', whereby they 'recruit memory and any ongoing experience and color these with the prevailing mood state'.[33] Depression, for example, can induce a false sense of guilt that thereby serves to explain feelings of worthlessness and self-loathing. Similarly, the manic impulsivity that fuels spending sprees, sexual indiscretions or violent outbursts can provide a logical focus for feelings of depression and guilt. While some manic-depressives, like Woolf, learn to detach moods from events and circumstances, White looked for causality: the guilt she experienced in depression was linked to the castration complex in analysis, to original sin in Catholicism. In a letter in which she observes that a nervous breakdown often results from 'choosing the wrong kind of life', she continues, '"Madness", apart from the manias concomitant with disease and injuries to the brain, is nearly always connected to the emotions' (*The Hound and the Falcon*, p. 39). White's lifelong efforts to discover the source of her conflicted and contradictory feelings thus tragically reversed cause and effect: manic-depressive illness motivated her behaviour and coloured her responses, not the other way around.

Sheri L. Johnson and Randy Fingerhut explain how White's efforts to discover originary sources for her illness in life events are a common response:

> People want to believe that their episodes were triggered, explainable, and that they will be predictable in the future. Life events are a particularly reassuring explanation. This creates the potential for systematic error as people may want to believe and present certain scenarios. Over time, memories of life events become more biased to support the idea that life events triggered episodes.[34]

White's conviction that her father's repudiation of her first novel was responsible for her psychic torment bears out this finding: as the years passed and her illness persisted, her memory of this event became ever more deeply woven into her stories of self. Here, too, the linkage between feeling and memory that Whybrow describes as the basis for mood plays a key role. 'Memories of past experiences and feeling are so intimately woven that each can access the other', he writes. 'A mood of sadness, as it occurs in depression, thus selectively recruits memories of other sad events.'[35] Depressed and unable to write, White would obsessively dwell on her father's role in her life, increasingly convinced that his repudiation of her and her writing was the precipitating event of her ongoing misery.

Mood disorders wreak havoc on the life story not only because emotion and mood are untrustworthy but because they disrupt the coherence that is the basis for autobiographical reasoning, the 'process of self-reflective thinking about the personal past that involves forming links between elements of one's life and the self in an attempt to relate one's personal past and present'.[36] More than just autobiographical remembering, autobiographical reasoning is a deliberate process of 'enhancing understanding through actively creating coherence between events and the self'.[37] The process of developing a life story is a gradual one, beginning in early childhood when children first begin to grasp the concept of 'temporal coherence', the ability 'to put the happenings of a single event into a sensible order'.[38] By adolescence, children have grasped the other key elements conducive to a plausible life story, including the concepts of causal and thematic coherence and what researchers variously term 'the cultural concept of biography' or 'content expectations'.[39] The latter refers to 'the narrative cultural notion of the facts and events that should be included in life narratives', which varies among cultures, 'both in terms of typical or normative life sequences and in what is considered to be a significant life event';[40] the term references the master narratives of a culture that establish the norms for plots and characters.[41] Temporal coherence and content expectations combine 'to form a basic, skeletal life narrative consisting of an ordered sequence of culturally defined, major life events'.[42]

These elements are then joined by causal and thematic coherence, which express 'the unique interpretive stance of the individual'.[43] Through thematic coherence, the narrator 'tries to explain a general self-attribution in terms of a recurrent theme that can be traced through different elements in the life story'.[44] Strategies may include developing a central metaphor for the self; statements that foreground thematic coherence, including introductions, conclusions and turning points; episodic memories, 'childhood events that substantiate family myths, reveal the narrator's present character, or are assumed to have determined the narrator's later life course'; comparisons of key events or the selection of one key event that typifies others; and evaluative trajectories or templates of stability, progression or regression.[45] Thematic coherence intertwines with causal coherence, the ability 'to link separate events into causal chains. The events themselves become the key episodes to explain a current aspect of self or a future goal.'[46] As with thematic coherence, causal coherence takes a variety of forms: it may link events and episodes; relate life phases to one another; account for changes in value or personality over time; and draw on either external events or internal causes to account for the individual in the present moment.[47] Causal coherence endows the life story with plausibility, and hence the narrator must account for any seeming discontinuity or contradiction.[48] For this reason, challenges to identity, such as role transitions, traumatic experiences or major life events may necessitate the reconstruction of the life story.[49]

These four elements – temporal, thematic and causal coherence and content expectations – combine to create the 'global coherence' of the life story:

> A coherent life narrative must account for change and development over time. Thus, it is essential to interrelate past and present selves by establishing causal links between life circumstances or events and one's personal development. Global causal coherence provides a diachronic understanding of how individuals remain themselves in spite of change (i.e., maintain self-continuity) and a biographical understanding of how previous experiences have shaped oneself.[50]

The narrator of the life story must simultaneously address 'the problem of being understood in a social context': 'stories that depict characters whose actions seem to have no motive or goal, or lay out plotlines that go nowhere, or fail to provide a causal account for a sequence of events, or never reach a culmination, resolution, or satisfying sense of an ending' will strike audiences 'as incoherent, or at least incomplete'.[51] White's inability to continue her serial fictions developed out of her inability to account for her motivations at two key points in her twenties: the loss of her virginity to the man in her father's dressing gown (the 'Dougal episode') and the affair with Tom

Hopkinson following her father's death. In both cases, White could identify temporal order and thematic coherence, but she could not formulate causal chains that would provide plausible motivations for her behaviour. She could not, for example, account for her acquiescence in the 'Dougal episode': 'The impossible thing to explain to myself is the Dougal thing' (*Diary* 1, p. 293). Similarly, while she clearly identified the main plotline of the second topic – her oldest daughter's birth, her father's death and her subsequent affair with Tom Hopkinson – she could not understand her motivations. In one diary entry she wonders '*was* there some connection between [my father's] death and my sudden falling in love with Tom? There is something there I don't understand.'[52] Three years and many, many drafts later she reiterates her confusion – 'Those 2 things – my father's death & Tom were most certainly connected. I hadn't even *liked* Tom before' – before breaking off in frustration: 'It's all so complex. How can I write about what I don't understand myself?'[53]

The controversial nature of her material also presented difficulties. The Dougal story, for example – which White termed the 'subject the most unpleasant I've tackled yet'[54] – was to fictionalise her father, a devout Catholic who nonetheless provided the money for his daughter to obtain an illegal abortion and afterwards took her to Paris for what was 'definitely a sort of honeymoon' (*Diary* 1, p. 293). White worried that her material was 'squalid' and 'shaming' and that she might be 'exposing' herself and her father to public censure.[55] Further, she felt that it would 'destroy any sympathy the reader may feel for Clara'.[56] Yet, despite her efforts to eliminate this episode, the abortion became a 'King Charles' head' which seemed to materialise upon the page despite White's efforts to keep it out.[57] White's terminology is telling, for the phrase 'King Charles' head' alludes to Dickens' *David Copperfield* and to the hapless Mr Dick, who cannot keep references to the beheading of King Charles out of his own biographical manuscript. David's Aunt Betsey describes this persistent and irrelevant intrusion as allegorical, explaining that Mr Dick 'connects his illness with great disturbance and agitation, naturally, and that's the figure, or simile, or whatever it's called, which he chooses to use'.[58] White's compulsive return to this episode and her inability to account for it amply justifies her usage.[59]

White's second plotline presented similar difficulties. Here, White wanted to fictionalise the conception and birth of her oldest daughter, her father's death and her subsequent affair with Hopkinson.

Yet despite the fact that she considered her daughter's conception 'the point where my life took its sensational "wrong turning"' and the sequence of events 'the crucial turning point of my life' she could not work out plausible motivations for her protagonist.[60] Although she hoped to 'understand much through this book. Certainly things I couldn't have understood then', White found it impossible to account for the seeming compulsion which drove her into the affair and she worried that she would alienate the real-life models of her characters, particularly her oldest daughter.[61] Hence White's fictional stories of self foundered on the combination of narrative incoherence and public norms of acceptable behaviour. Dan P. McAdams emphasises the prescriptive nature of coherence and plausibility in the construction of life stories. '[A]ny consideration of narrative coherence must eventually come to terms with the characteristic assumptions regarding what kinds of stories can and should be told in a given culture, what stories are understandable and valued among people who live in and through a given culture', he writes. 'And the same consideration cannot be divorced from cultural expectations regarding what kinds of lives people should live'.[62] White's chaotic twenties certainly did not conform to the 'cultural expectations regarding what kinds of lives people should live', as she very well knew, and her inability to create causality in her life story made it impossible to explain her behaviour to anyone, including herself.

Inevitably, White would trace her sense of incoherence back to her father and her repudiated novel:

> I could not say for myself where I first 'went wrong' and began that series of entanglements and sins and muddles and disasters which still affect my own and other people's lives. How appalled my father would be if he knew the results of that fifteenth birthday. Yet I often feel as if I had never been a 'whole' person since that day. (*Diary* 1, p. 263)

White's identification of her incoherence as having its source in adolescence is deeply telling, for the ability to construct a life story emerges in adolescence and has profound implications for the manic-depressive, whose illness also typically emerges in late adolescence or early adulthood. Adolescence is a time of upheaval in terms of both psychosocial identity and biological development; it is also the time 'when the life story is first constructed and most intensively rehearsed'.[63] Hence the onset of the illness, particularly if it is severe, as in White's case, inevitably disrupts the manic-depressive's life story just as that life story has taken shape: the illness may shatter the life story irrevocably even as ongoing mood episodes make (re)construction difficult or impossible, particularly if the illness goes unrecognised and untreated, as in White's case. Contemporary therapies designed for bipolar disorder in fact single out deficits in self-construction as a focus for therapeutic intervention. Cognitive-behavioural therapy designed for bipolar disorder, for example, focuses on how its onset in late adolescence or early adulthood compromises the development of a sense of self. 'One of the goals is to help the ill person to rebuild a more solid sense of "self"', writes Irene Patelis-Siotis:

> Individuals with BD [bipolar disorder] frequently report being lost or not knowing who they are [. . .] early onset of the illness impacts on critical phases of development resulting in marked deficits in self-esteem or identity . . . it appears that the impact of hypomania and depression at an early age are significant precisely because they dramatically affect sense of self and postpone important developmental milestones, such as educational achievements, early work experience and important interpersonal relationships.[64]

Even more crucially, the illness can create dysfunctional core beliefs, including 'a disturbed sense of autonomy or personal capability, vulnerability to harm or illness and a sense of defectiveness and unlovability'.[65] Another recent therapy has incorporated 'grief for the lost healthy self' as an integral element of treatment, after the researchers discovered that bipolar patients tended to divide their lives into two parts, before and after diagnosis. Patients perceived themselves as two different people, and the sense of loss of who they had been before the bifurcation of illness exceeded that of other role transitions, 'because "becoming bipolar" has a kind of unalterability that is more like a death than the loss of a job or even a divorce'.[66] White's identification of the 'fatal' first novel and her father's condemnation of it as the origins of her psychic torment memorialises the death of the girl who had been able to write freely: she felt she had been healthy until her fifteenth birthday, when his repudiation of her and her writing set her illness in motion.

Even if recognised and treated, the kaleidoscopic nature of severe manic depression may render any conventional notion of self-coherence null. At least one contemporary psychiatrist questions whether a coherent sense of self is even possible for the manic-depressive:

> I contend that because of the nature of this illness affective patients emerge with particular problems in organizing a sense of self that is specific to this illness. . . .
>
> When a patient has a major affective episode, his or her normal self disappears. The patient becomes someone foreign, another self. By definition, this self has a different affective organization from the normal self. There are different thoughts, behaviors, and personality traits. Physiological rhythms and drives are dramatically altered [. . .]
>
> [. . .] The spectre of a recurrence can become a vivid phantom self, something or someone who might again take them over. Who, then, is the real self for someone who has been up and down and in between? Is the real self who one is when one is euthymic [well]? Is it possible or even necessary to construct a whole self out of an amalgam of the 'self-in-episode' and 'self-out-of-episode'? Can this integration ever achieve the same coherence of self-structure that the patient previously took for granted?
>
> [. . .] To switch unpredictably into highs and lows that are not in your control, when you have no clear sense of stable, differentiated identity to start with, leaves you without a critical anchor in a very treacherous storm.[67]

If locating a coherent and continuous sense of self is difficult for those whose illness is recognised and treated, the task is immeasurably harder for those who must cope with that task on their own. Little is written about the anguish experienced by those who live with the knowledge that their stories of self are incoherent and chaotic but who do not have an explanation of why this is so. Here White recalls Mark Freeman's description of his elderly mother, who suffers from dementia; in moments of lucidity, he reports, she remembers 'who she was' and responds to her deterioration with distress and despair: 'I want to be a person', she tells him.[68] Characterising her impaired story of self as a 'broken continuity – a continuity in discontinuity, as it were', Freeman writes that 'even amidst the chaos and debris of her life, "she" nevertheless remains, a witness to the devastation'.[69] White, pondering the wreckage of her twenties and thirties, similarly witnesses the devastation in a lament that rings throughout her diary: 'Oh, my life, my life. What a mess. What a failure' (*Diary* 2, p. 152). Her preferred term for her illness – the Beast – gestures to her sense that in its grip she lost her humanity and became a crazed, literally a caged, animal. Her preferred term for depression – accidia, or spiritual sloth – similarly underscores her conviction that a sinful, that is, bestial, nature was at the root of her troubles. Both terms foreground White's fear that bodily forces beyond her control could master her very reason or agency.

The anguish of incoherence is even more understandable if recent work on cognitive neuroscience is taken into account, work that posits that the brain possesses an innate drive to impose narrative order on the information it receives. Michael S. Gazzaniga, a psychologist well known for his split-brain studies, has argued that 'biologically, there is no such thing as a self, but only the illusion of a self created through and by narrative'.[70] Working with patients whose right and left hemispheres had been surgically severed, Gazziniga and his colleagues discovered that the left hemisphere will account for information only accessible to the right hemisphere. The left hemisphere functions as an interpreter, a 'storyteller in your head', 'whose function is to seek explanations for internal and external events and, in so doing, construct intelligible and coherent narratives about these experiences'.[71] It 'tweaks the facts, spins the story, and allows us to feel like we're in charge'.[72] Or, as Jonathan Gottschall puts it, 'The left brain is a relentless explainer, and it would rather fabricate a story than leave something unexplained'.[73] The subtitle of Gottschall's own study, *The Storytelling Animal*, sums up the power and human necessity of storytelling: *How Stories Make Us Human*.

Such findings fit comfortably with poststructuralist theories about the illusory nature of the unified self. Yet theoretical insight does not help much when the fractures of one's own psyche destroy any comfortable and secure sense of consistency in one's feelings and behaviour, when those feelings and behaviour wreck intimate relationships and render employment impossible, or when feelings and behaviour escalate into psychosis and relegation to the back wards of the asylum.[74] In this context, White's misdiagnosis of schizophrenia – a misdiagnosis that impelled her to undertake analysis – functioned as a welcome explanation for her difficulties.

Diagnosis as identity narrative

White's equation of mania and depression with bestiality highlights the issues that confront the woman who constructs an identity focused on mental illness, for to do so necessarily involves her engagement with a long-standing association of femininity with insanity in Western culture.[75] White came of age during the emergence of psychiatry and psychoanalysis, disciplines that inherited the Victorian medical conviction that

> women were more vulnerable to insanity because the instability of their reproductive systems interfered with their sexual, emotional, and rational control . . . theories of female insanity were specifically and confidently linked to the biological crises of the female life-cycle – puberty, pregnancy, childbirth, menopause – during which the mind would be weakened and the symptoms of insanity might emerge.[76]

The ideal role for the middle-class woman was thus to be a subordinate in marriage, where her mental and emotional faculties would find their best and natural expression in domestic tasks and the nurture of husband and children. This prescriptive role would enable women to stabilise their inherently unstable biology, and to defy its terms was to court insanity. Victorian doctors particularly stressed the dangers that intellectual ambition represented for women, since they believed that education and mental activity drew energy away from the reproductive organs: in the ensuing contest, the would-be intellectual woman would lose, prey to a host of nervous and physical ailments, including insanity. Even if she did not go insane, she would at best 'unsex' herself and become a freak or monster: in the words of the influential doctor Henry Maudsley, she would become 'something which having ceased to be woman is not yet man'.[77]

The linkage between female physiology, intellectual ambition and insanity persisted in twentieth-century medical discourses in Britain, shaping psychoanalysis and psychiatry as well as White's own sense of herself as a woman writer.[78] The misdiagnosis of White's illness as schizophrenia, in particular, situated White in a complex network of gendered assumptions and practices. Elaine Showalter has shown how schizophrenia succeeded hysteria as the twentieth-century 'female malady', offering a 'remarkable example of the cultural conflation of femininity and insanity'.[79] White could be considered lucky in that she was directed to psychoanalytic treatment in the 1930s, thereby avoiding institutionalisation and the by-then most common treatments for schizophrenia in British hospitals – insulin shock and electroshock, joined by lobotomy in the 1940s – all of which were prescribed more often for women than for men.[80] But she was profoundly affected by the diagnosis nonetheless. The schizophrenic woman became 'a central cultural figure for the twentieth century', Showalter observes, one associated with modernist literary movements that 'appropriated the schizophrenic woman as the symbol of linguistic, religious, and sexual breakdown and rebellion'.[81] White was familiar with such appropriations – she mentions reading one of the iconic and defining articulations of those appropriations, André Breton's 1928 surrealist novel *Nadja*[82] – but for an ambitious, supposedly schizophrenic woman writer the symbolic meanings attached to the schizophrenic woman would be far from reassuring. The linguistic incoherence that features as a prominent hallmark of schizophrenia means that in practice no one listens to what the schizophrenic says.[83] Tracing the history of dismissal accorded to the speech acts of those diagnosed with schizophrenia, Mary Elene Wood writes:

> These patients have been written into an already existing story in which their own words have meaning primarily as symptoms of an illness with a grim prognosis. Unlike those marked by almost any other diagnosis of mental illness [. . .] individuals diagnosed with schizophrenia must contend with the fact that their story-telling becomes suspect and opaque from the moment of diagnosis.[84]

In Breton's novel, Nadja embodies an array of surrealist values – contingency, unpredictability, the unrepressed unconscious, the subversion of fixed and stable identity – but she also ends up silenced and institutionalised.[85]

The diagnosis of schizophrenia often did (and does) hold out the spectre of incurable insanity and a lifetime of institutionalisation. Diagnosis itself is, as Wood points out, 'a narrative that circumscribes and predicts the future, foreshadowing the course of the particular mental illness in the form of prognosis, which is usually poor in the case of psychosis'.[86] White described the 'probable "picture" of my history' in her diary after she received the diagnosis of schizophrenia

(*Diary* 1, p. 48). Her prognosis was indeed grim: 'without treatment, I should certainly become insane again. It is by no means certain that, even with treatment . . . I can avoid insanity permanently' (*Diary* 1, p. 58). She knew all too well, as 'The House of Clouds' and *Beyond the Glass* demonstrate, the kind of treatment she could expect: incarceration in the notorious back wards of the asylum, restraints, padded cells, water treatments, forced feeding (she may not have known of the newer treatments of insulin shock and ECT). In a despairing letter to Emily Holmes Coleman in 1936, during one of the worst years of her second breakdown, White describes visiting her former cell at Bethlem, which had now become the Imperial War Museum:

> The agonies that place has seen. I thought of all those lives of horror lived in those cells – those people lost & despised, laughed at for centuries – no one even trying to understand. I am one of the lucky ones . . . But how can I believe in a kind god who lets such things happen?[87]

Her terror at the prospect of going permanently insane is reflected in the short story she wrote about this experience, 'The Surprise Visit', in which the protagonist similarly visits the Imperial War Museum, where the sight of her old cell triggers a relapse into delusion and insanity.

But White also felt relief at finding that 'I am really ill [. . .] there *is* a beast in the jungle' (*Diary* 1, p. 48). A clear-cut diagnosis gave her a way of understanding her distress and a means of appealing to others to believe in the severity of it.[88] In that same letter to Coleman, White wrote:

> As regards the mental illness, I know you think I exaggerate & think it is a joke. Everyone does except Tom & Eric [her third and second husbands, respectively]. It is not a joke though I make jokes about it when I can. Your life is tormented I know. But you are not at this moment fighting for your reason.[89]

In sharing her diagnosis with friends, White looked for understanding and compassion, but the very hopelessness and fear the term inspired could backfire, resulting in recoil rather than connection and support. The poet David Gascoyne, with whom White had a brief affair during this period, records his anxiety and apprehension about White in terms of her diagnosis, which clearly frightened him:

> It is hateful to have to say so, but I must remember that A. is a *schizophrenic*. It seems improbable that she will ever be entirely cured; her suicidal tendency is so marked that she can't take out an insurance policy on her life.[90]

He withdrew from her soon afterwards, resolving in his journal 'No more Antonias [. . .] The Marys are all very well, but give me the Marthas in the long run.'[91]

Popular misconceptions about schizophrenia, most notably that it references split or multiple personality, also shaped White's and others' sense of her illness. In fact, the term 'schizophrenia', coined by Eugen Bleuler in 1911, is formed from Greek words meaning 'split mind'; it reflects Bleuler's belief that schizophrenics separate affect from cause, thought from emotion:

> the loosening of the associations results in the opening up of wrong pathways of thought, pathways deviating from experience; and on the other hand, the patient is forced to operate with fragments of ideas. The latter abnormality leads to displacements, condensations, confusion, generalisations, clang-associations, illogical thinking and incoherence. The weakening of the logical functions results in relative predominance of the affects. Unpleasantly toned associations are repressed at their inception (blocking); whatever conflicts with the affects is split off. This mechanism leads to the logical blunders which determine (among other things) the delusions; but the most significant effect is the splitting of the psyche in accordance with the emotionally charged complexes.[92]

Bleuler's thinking reflects the impact of Freud and paved the way for psychoanalytic approaches to treating schizophrenia, although Freud himself had concluded by 1914 that those diagnosed with the illness 'are inaccessible to the influence of psychoanalysis and cannot be cured by our endeavours'.[93] In popular usage, however, the term came to stand for 'someone with two or more distinct personalities, represented iconically by the title character in Robert Louis Stevenson's 1886 novel *The Strange Case of Dr Jekyll and Mr Hyde*'.[94] This misconception, Wood observes, 'is another narrative that the diagnosed individual must contend with in telling his or her own life story'.[95] White's daughter Lyndall Hopkinson clearly subscribes to the Jekyll-and-Hyde version of schizophrenia, writing that 'those advocates of God and the devil [. . .] were forever at war in her schizophrenic brain'.[96] For White herself, the sense of possessing a 'double nature' also meant an identity perpetually at war with itself: 'If you have a double nature, you cannot expect a peaceful life', she wrote in a letter. 'After an unconscious struggle of about fifteen years and a very conscious one of five, I have managed to reach a sort of equilibrium. I have had a bad enemy in myself to fight and a real terror to overcome [. . .] I have been over the edge of something terrifying and it has inevitably altered all my ideas of what a human being is' (*The Hound and the Falcon*, p. 7). But even as she images her illness as an 'enemy' within, from whose assaults she must defend herself, she also defines herself in its terms. In one of her most definitive assertions of identity, White equates herself with schizophrenia, although she simultaneously folds into the term the oscillating mood swings that are the classic hallmarks of manic depression: 'I am a schizophrene, which in practice means that, apart from alternations between elation and accidia, I cannot with the best will in the world maintain a consistent attitude about anything for more than a few days at a time' (*The Hound and the Falcon*, p. 157).

Symptomatic (con)versions: manic depression and the paternal prohibition

The misdiagnosis of her illness as schizophrenia had far-reaching consequences for White's interpretation of herself. Psychoanalytic thinking at the time stressed that the schizophrenic had split off 'emotionally charged complexes' by repressing 'unpleasantly toned associations at their inception (blocking)'. Since White came to believe that both her writer's block and her illness had at their root her father's denunciation of her first novel when she was fifteen, this incident became the defining event in her identity narrative, 'the emotional shock in childhood which paralysed me emotionally' (*Diary* 1, p. 139). Yet, in fact, White had produced another novel while in secondary school, one her father read and discussed with her without any moralistic denunciation, although he was not as enthusiastic as White would have liked.[97]

White's attribution of her writing difficulties to her father's reaction to her convent novel came later. During analysis, White twice comments on the inception of her diary, dating its beginnings to 1921, just before her first marriage, when she began to sink into a severe depression. 'I did not begin to write notebooks until just before I married Reggie: my writing went underground as it were', White writes in the first entry (*Diary* 1, p. 140); in the second she shifts the emphasis from her writing to herself: 'It is significant that I began them just when I began to crack up – the year before I married Reggie. That was really the time when I went underground' (*Diary* 1, p. 149). The word 'underground' suggests that White, through the influence of analysis, had begun to associate her writer's block with the repression of unconscious conflicts. She would explore these conflicts in analysis, when she developed, through the promptings of her analyst, an identity narrative that 'explained' her writer's block as repressed desire for her father's pen/ penis. This identity narrative also 'explained' her schizophrenia, since the repressed rage she experienced at his denunciation of her writing – his withholding of the pen/penis, as it were –would account for the 'split' in her psyche, when part of her went 'underground'.

But the actual history of White's 'crack-up' outlines the onset of manic-depressive illness, which typically emerges in late adolescence or early adulthood. White sank into a severe depression in 1920–1, six years after she had left the Convent of the Sacred Heart. As both her diary and fictional versions of this time period attest, she began to keep a diary as a response to depression, to frightening feelings of disintegration, vacancy, emptiness and nonexistence. Like many people who are deeply depressed, White experienced tremendous guilt and self-loathing, for which she sought an explanation; by the time she came to write *The Sugar House*, she attributed her protagonist's depression to the father's denunciation of the convent novel and its author: 'Suppose he were actually to forgive her for what had outraged him in what she had written, in all innocence, at fourteen? Might that relieve the appalling guilt and self-mistrust which overcame her every time she tried to write anything that was not merely confected? In the last two months, this guilt and impotence had spread to anything she wrote at all [. . .] Only the black notebook [. . .] was exempt from the blight, simply because it was secret' (*The Sugar House*, p. 63). The word 'blight' links Clara's need to conceal her writing/herself to the title of White's first novel, *Frost in*

May, which captures brilliantly the sense of a late frost which blasts the early blossoms and destroys the possibility of fruition. White hence explains the feelings generated by depression by tracing them to what seems to be their logical cause, the father's repudiation of the daughter and her writing.[98]

A similar desire to explain the opposite pole, mania, motivates White's description of her first psychotic breakdown. She emerged from her first crippling depression when her marriage ended in 1922, and immediately started to swing into the manic state that frequently follows severe depressive episodes. Her mania escalated into psychosis within weeks, and she was hospitalised. White attributes her manic episode and resultant psychosis to the intensity of unexpected sexual desire: she had fallen deeply in love and wanted to consummate the relationship, 'but I was not ready for it and the shock drove me out of my mind' (*Diary* 1, p. 94). Once again, White explains mania and psychosis by connecting them to what seems their logical cause, the sudden release of sexual inhibition. In her fictional treatment of the onset of mania in *Beyond the Glass*, White portrays a classic manic episode: Clara does not feel the need to sleep or eat, loses weight quickly, speaks rapidly, displays grandiosity, and so forth; her manic behaviour clearly strikes family and friends as frighteningly uncharacteristic and odd. White's manic symptoms would not emerge with this kind of clarity again, although when she was in her sixties her doctor was to question her closely about signs of euphoria after she began taking antidepressants. More often, as the last chapter shows, her manic symptoms coincided with those of depression, resulting in mixed states, evidenced by irritability, agitation, anxiety, paranoia, emotional volatility, angry or even violent bursts of rage, racing thoughts (albeit with a negative cast) and sleep disturbances, as well as a heightened impulse to suicide. Given the unusual severity of her first manic episode and given its singularity in her illness pattern, White's attribution of it to the stress and shock of sexual desire makes causal sense but is not consistent with manic-depressive symptomatology. If, indeed, life events triggered the onset of her illness, they would have had to precede the onset of her severe depression in 1920–1.

White's mapping of life events on to her moods in order to explain them is understandable. Writing of the emergence of Virginia Woolf's illness, Caramagno notes that the timing of her first breakdown – it followed her mother's death when she was thirteen – became the 'emblematic' life event that explained

> her emptiness, despair, and lack of a stable self-structure [. . .] Julia's sudden death apparently triggered Virginia's first manic-depressive breakdown, but, more important [. . .] it became Woolf's metaphor for the birth of a bipolar identity [. . .] It offered a coherent story line for experiences that would otherwise seem senseless and impersonal.[99]

Because depressives 'feel guilt for which they cannot find a valid cause', Caramagno writes, they

> think back over the years and center obsessively on some past event – an unpardonable sin (to explain their hopelessness and guilt), or a traumatic experience (to explain their helplessness and life's emptiness), or the loss of a significant person (to explain their extraordinary sense of abandonment and loneliness).[100]

Her father's denunciation of her first novel became that emblematic life event for White, functioning simultaneously as unpardonable sin (she had written a novel that revealed her depravity), traumatic event (her father repudiated her as a person), and loss of a significant person (her father). The absence of a stable self-structure, an inevitable consequence of her severe affective disorder, became for White the reflection of the irrevocable damage wrought by her writing and her father's response to it: 'I often feel as if I had never been a "whole" person since that day' (*Diary* 1, p. 263).

White's monumental diary records her efforts to understand the frightening inconsistency of her moods and the motivations for her seemingly inexplicable behaviour.[101] Moods shift from a manic intensity to a 'flat' sense of 'normal' life to deep depression, a depression often infused with manic energy. Like many manic-depressives, White appreciates the intensity that colours her perceptions when in a manic phase: 'the power of the beast [. . .] was terrible and wonderful' (*The Hound and the Falcon*, p. 16), possessed of 'poetic intelligibility' (*Diary* 1, p. 131), and gave her 'the sense of continued intensity of experience. I was often agonised, miserable, and terrified, but I was never bored' (*Diary* 1, p. 136). Daily life could seem flat by comparison: 'When I live in the "real" world . . . how stale and sterile that seems. Dull jobs, dull streets, dull duties, dull conversations' (*Diary* 1, p. 122); White admits that 'Something in my nature craves for violent surprises . . . an unexpected happening, even if it is painful, sharpens my sense of life' (*Diary* 1, p. 139).[102] 'Violent surprises' externalise and provide a focus for pent-up manic energy, which otherwise threatens to explode from within: finding herself in a 'blank meaningless automatic state', White feels '*something* must happen – some kind of change, explosion, even illness' (*Diary* 2, p. 112). Without intensity, White feels as if she disappears: as she comments of her daughter Lyndall, 'her sense of not existing unless involved in some violent emotion [. . .] I understand better than she thinks' (*Diary* 2, p. 69). Non-being deepens into disintegration during phases of depression, particularly agitated depression or mixed states, and is reflected in the very syntax of White's writing, as connectivity and meaning disappear and identity becomes a list of unrelated sensations: 'depression – torment of conflicting opinions – feelings of being all bits and pieces and having no personality' (*Diary* 2, p. 197).

As White herself said of her diary, 'It is as if I kept my identity in these books' (*Diary* 1, p. 149): the diary attests to the fragmentation of that identity, since White kept one, sometimes two, notebooks for daily entries, as well as other notebooks that differ from but were written alongside the daily diary: the 'Analysis Diary', begun in 1935 to record her three-and-a-half-year Freudian analysis; two notebooks that record intense erotic affairs; and dream diaries, kept during her second analysis in the late 1940s.[103] These self-divisions are masked by the presentation of the two published volumes, in part because the published volumes are heavily edited – White's daughter, Susan Chitty, the editor of her mother's diaries, reports that they represent only a quarter of the original material – and in part because Chitty chose to standardise the volumes by developing a unified singular text out of what was, in fact, a much more heterogeneous set of manuscripts.[104] Commenting on the self-division enacted by White's manner of composition, Margaret Drabble writes:

> One of the more curious features of this volume [*Antonia White Diaries, 1926–1957*] is the way it prefigures the techniques of Doris Lessing's seminal work, *The Golden Notebook* (1962), a novel which uses this device of dividing the fragmented personality of its narrator into different-coloured notebooks.[105]

She goes on to observe that 'as with *The Golden Notebook* itself, the final effect is, oddly, not of fragmentation but of a powerful urge towards synthesis. Here was a woman who longed to be made whole.'[106]

As the diaries demonstrate, that 'powerful urge towards synthesis' develops out of White's fear of total disintegration, a fear that had its basis in her first terrifying descent into psychosis. Not only haunted by what had happened to her, White felt hunted, stalked by a relentless beast of prey that could pounce at any time; the fact that this beast lurked within only intensified her sense of imperilment. The self-divisions recorded in the diary are not celebratory anticipations of the postmodern subject, then, but rather evidence that White used her writing to shore up her tenuous hold on any sense of coherent identity at all. The notebooks in which she 'keeps her identity' function as confirmation of self:

> It is significant that I began them just when I began to crack up [. . .] They are still a sign of my distrust of myself: I look at them when I feel confused or lose my sense of identity. They are like a photograph of myself to which I refer. It is curious how, the more vain people are, the less they have a sense of identity and pore over photographs and mirrors. (*Diary* 1, p. 149)

Characteristically perceiving her need for physical confirmation that she exists at all through a moralistic lens which equates that need with vanity and egotism, White nonetheless attests here to the way writing in the notebooks became a lifeline during the initial emergence of her illness. A vocabulary of depression pervades White's diaries – words such as 'emptiness', 'incoherence', 'impotence', 'unreality', 'blankness' recur throughout – and only the act of writing seems to counter this fragmentation and disintegration into non-being.

White's search for a coherent form to encompass the Beast is thus simultaneously a search for a coherent form for her *identity* as well as for her fiction. 'One thing I have been pretty sure of for a good many years is that my job in life is to be able to give a form in writing to certain experiences', she wrote in a letter about the Beast. 'It's a kind of testimony, if you like, and difficult to make both honest and at the same time a work of art, something consistent with itself and complete and not just "reporting" or "a slice of life"' (*The Hound and the Falcon*, p. 38). To express the Beast in coherent form would confirm the identity she most longed to secure: 'If I could come to terms with the beast, real terms, I would be an artist instead of a Clever Little Thing' (*The Hound and the Falcon*, p. 16). Hence her inability to construct a fictional form for her life between the ages of 21 and 31 became for White an abiding reflection of her own incoherence. As Dunn observes, 'her true identity could only be confirmed by her writing. If she was not a writer she was nothing.'[107] Writing her story out not only explained her to herself, moreover; it was also a mode of communication and connection for a woman who felt imprisoned in her self-torment and self-loathing. In a letter to Coleman, White wrote:

> I get so much the feeling of working in a vacuum: no one among my immediate 'circle' really cares or is interested & as I always have had great difficulty in believing I could write at all I often feel like a kind of ghost.[108]

An appreciative reader, on the other hand, affirms her existence: 'anything that gives me a feeling that maybe something I've written was worth saying . . . makes me feel a little more "alive"' (*Diary* 2, p. 110).

The sense of radical incoherence at best and non-existence at worst fuels White's quest to identify organising principles (form) for both her fiction and herself. White often speaks in her letters of feeling as if fundamental springs in her had been broken: 'I don't know how one lives when all one's springs are broken & one is not allowed to die.'[109] While her misdiagnosis and subsequent analysis consolidated for White a conviction that this breakage occurred when her father repudiated her writing, that sense of having something deeply off-kilter in her personality develops out of her affective disorder and her apprehension of living without a fundamental feeling of self-integration. 'What *is* there in me that is sound and genuine?' White asks herself. 'I sometimes feel *nothing*. As if I had *no* core' (*Diary* 2, pp. 144–5). Without a core, a principle of self-organisation, White experiences deep self-distrust, afraid to 'let go' and risk exposing herself to contempt and ridicule: 'Failure is so terrible to me that I deprive myself of an enormous amount of pleasure and interest rather than expose myself to the risk of it . . . I am a very serious failure . . . because I have no control over my emotions or actions' (*Diary* 1, p. 109). 'I seem to have no true will, only compulsions', she complains (*Diary* 1, p. 117). White's distrust of herself was in fact justified: she did feel compelled to act in ways she could not explain and could not control, and these compulsions could and sometimes did have disastrous consequences.

In turning to psychoanalysis and Catholicism, White looked for structures that could impose meaning and form upon her moods and actions, that could cure her, that could shore up her claims to public identity. Psychoanalysis would encourage her to look for the intent or unconscious motivations underlying her compulsive actions, while Catholicism would instruct her to see compulsions as evidence of moral weakness: 'I *can*, with God's grace, dominate my impulses', she writes (*Diary* 2, p. 101). Charlotte Linde identifies both psycho-analysis and Catholicism as 'coherence systems' that can provide

> a means of understanding, evaluating and constructing accounts of experience. [Coherence systems] permit the speaker an extra level of distance, allowing the speaker to take a stance as his or her own expert, to step back from the account to give a deeper (or apparently more objective or truer) set of reasons than can be conveyed in a common-sense narrative. [110]

The now more knowledgeable speaker looks back on the less knowl-edgeable self, 'possessing superior knowledge of why the protagonist acts in a certain way and how the protagonist should act – knowl-edge that is inaccessible to the protagonist during the action'.[111] Such systems 'provide people with a vocabulary for creating a self'.[112]

White's adoption of these master narratives to structure her stories of self bears out Jerome Bruner's contention that eventually 'we *become* the autobiographical narratives by which we "tell about" our lives'.[113] The cultural and linguistic processes that shape our story-telling, he observes, 'achieve the power to structure perceptual experience, to organize memory, to segment and purpose-build the very "events" of a life'.[114] People become 'variants of the culture's canonical forms':

> the ways of telling and the ways of conceptualizing that go with them become so habitual that they finally become recipes for struc-turing experience itself, for laying down routes into memory, for not only guiding the life narrative up to the present but directing it into the future . . . a life as led is inseparable from a life as told – or more bluntly, a life is not 'how it was' but how it is interpreted and reinterpreted.[115]

White indeed interpreted and reinterpreted herself through the frames of psychoanalysis and Catholicism, and her layering of elements drawn from each template upon one another – the Oedipal triangle and the Holy Family, the analyst and the priest, complex and sin – supports Bruner's position that canonical cultural forms become so habitual that they become 'recipes for structuring experience'. Master narratives, moreover, tend to reinforce one another.[116] Such narratives are powerful repositories of a culture's belief systems; people are read into – and read themselves into – master narratives in order to make themselves legible: 'the master narratives of a society allow its members to understand who they are with respect to that society as well as how the world works'.[117] Sometimes actual stories, other times ensembles held together thematically, master narratives link up and confirm one another, becoming an 'interlocking, interwining web' that 'creates a plausible world view'.[118] Psychoanalysis and Catholicism worked to reinforce and confirm each other and create such an interlocking, intertwining web in White's stories of self.

It is not surprising that White's attempts to understand and to overcome what was both her illness ('schizophrenia') and her writer's block became focused on what she believed to be their source, the primal scene of paternal prohibition. Throughout her life, White would attribute her intense feelings of guilt, worthlessness, and artistic impotence to that scene, one she memorialises almost annually in her diary on its anniversaries, her birthday and Easter Sunday, which fell on the same day in 1914. Her experience of analysis in the years of her second severe breakdown, 1934–8, foregrounded this scene in White's construction of her identity narratives. That analysis, and the reconversion to Catholicism that followed, are the subject of the next chapter.

Chapter 3

Master Plots: Psychoanalysis and Catholicism

Given White's engagement with both psychoanalysis and Catholicism, it is not surprising that these discourses have received considerable attention from scholars of White's work. Both Podnieks and Valentine, for example, have explored the imbrication of psychoanalysis and modernist experimentation in White's work[1]; Podnieks describes psychoanalysis as 'the redeeming religion of the early twentieth century' and White's diary as akin to a Freudian case history in which White 'played the part of both Dora and Freud'.[2] White's relationship with Catholicism has also received considerable attention, from scholars interested in her engagement with theological issues as well as from those who focus on the parallels between White's representations of Catholicism and those of James Joyce.[3] And recently, several scholars have examined the ways in which psychoanalysis and Catholicism function together in White's work.[4] This chapter focuses specifically on how psychoanalysis and Catholicism functioned as master plots for White's identity narrative as she struggled with her illness after the publication of *Frost in May* in 1933. As I showed in Chapter 2, these models allowed White to structure her stories of self along strikingly similar lines: both privilege male authority (Freud/analyst and God/priest), both foreground family structure (oedipal complex and Holy Family) and both emphasise female inferiority (female castration complex and fallen Eve). The psychoanalytic sequence of transference (repetition, recognition and working through) parallels the Catholic sequence of sin, atonement and redemption. Affective symptoms thus become the symptoms of unconscious conflicts; unconscious conflicts in turn become sins.

White's first analysis from 1935 to 1938 and her reconversion to Catholicism in December 1940, recorded in the letters collected as *The Hound and the Falcon: The Story of a Reconversion to the Catholic Faith*, were crucial in consolidating her identity narrative as a means of coping with her sense of psychological incoherence. The first two sections of this chapter thus focus on how White adapted these two paradigms in developing her stories of self. The third section focuses on the ways in which White combined psychoanalysis and Catholicism as she continued to struggle with her illness and enduring problems with writing and identity from 1941 until her death in 1980.[5] White's identity narrative did not change significantly after 1941, although she did come to question the marginalisation of her mother in her emotional life even as she began to foreground Mary in her religious practice. White's engagement with both psychoanalysis and Catholicism, moreover, reflects the ways in which both discourses were themselves in flux during this period. This instability is particularly important in assessing White's relationship to psychoanalysis. Most scholars who discuss that relationship do so by contextualising it within Freud's writings, but White's diary suggests that she came into contact with a broad range of psychoanalytic theories, including those of Carl Jung and Melanie Klein, and that even in her first and most orthodox analysis Freud was by no means the single or even the dominant influence.

White underwent analysis three times, and different theoretical models informed each one. After two brief and apparently unproductive attempts in 1934 (with James Robb) and early 1935 (with William Brown), White entered psychoanalysis with Dennis Carroll from February 1935 until September 1938. She again entered analysis in May 1947 and continued through December 1948 with an untrained amateur, Dorothy Kingsmill, whom White credited with helping her overcome her writing difficulties and complete her second novel, *The Lost Traveller*. Her third analysis began when a Dr Galway diagnosed her as suffering from depression and on the verge of a breakdown in 1965; although he initially tried to treat White himself, eventually he felt the severity of her case warranted more intensive treatment, and in 1966 he referred her to Philippe Ployé, who saw White twice monthly for three years. Of the three, Carroll's treatment adhered most closely to orthodox Freudian lines, albeit these were strongly influenced by the work of Karl Abraham. Kingsmill's was the most eclectic and informal: a disciple of the Indian mystic

Meher Baba, Kingsmill encouraged White to record her dreams and White, in a summary of her relationship to Kingsmill, wrote that 'Where D. *did* help, was in making me see my relation to my mother' (*Diary* 1, p. 214). White found Kingsmill's 'occult background' dangerous, however, despite the 'brilliance of her analytical intuition' (*Diary* 1, p. 212); later, comparing Galway's approach to Kingsmill's, White observed that Kingsmill worked along Jungian lines but could not be easily categorised given the hybridity of her influences[6], which included, in addition to Baba, Russian mystic George Gurdjieff, Theosophy, Buddhism and the Arcane Society.[7] Both Galway and Ployé seem to have been working within the framework of object-relations theory: White praises the way in which Galway had more respect for 'aesthetic talent' than Carroll did,[8] and they discussed Kleinian theories of creativity after White read Hanna Segal's 'A Psychoanalytic Approach to Aesthetics' on his recommendation.[9] Ployé draws upon object-relations theory, specifically that of Otto Kernberg, in his published writing[10]; his specific interest in whether and how prenatal regression emerged in and impacted upon the analytical relationship reached its fullest expression in his *The Prenatal Theme in Psychotherapy*, published posthumously in 2006.

White's analyses thus reflect shifting emphases as psychoanalytic theory evolved in mid-century. The first in the 1930s reflected that decade's intense interest in female sexuality generally and the female castration complex specifically; the second, with its Jungian terminology and its emphasis on dreams and the importance of the relationship to the mother, suggests the impact that Jung and others had on shaping psychoanalysis in the 1940s; the third suggests the increasing dominance of Klein and British object-relations theory as a framework for understanding creativity.[11] Analysis was by no means White's only source of information about psychoanalysis. Psychoanalysis was a common topic of debate among intellectuals of the time, and White's friendships with Emily Holmes Coleman, Djuna Barnes, David Gascoyne and others interested in the topic provided another, if informal source. Still another source was the Dominican priest and family friend Victor White, an expert on Thomas Aquinas (a favourite of White's) and a close associate of Jung: his efforts to combine Jungian and Catholic conceptualisations resulted in a number of books, including *Soul and Psyche: An Enquiry into the Relationship of Psychotherapy and Religion* (1960), a topic he had discussed with White as early as 1949 (*Diary* 1,

p. 212). In that entry White had indicated her distrust of the 'eso-
tericism' of Jung, noting that 'Only the Freudians remain strictly
"scientific" but they are flirting heavily with drugs, shock treatment
etc.' (*Diary* 1, p. 212). She almost entered analysis with another
Catholic Jungian, Edward Thornton, in 1951, but did not, perhaps
in part because he was associated with Dorothy Kingsmill and '[a]ll
this eastern stuff' (*Diary* 1, p. 226). Many years later, while in analysis with Galway, White would reiterate her belief that a Freudian
analysis was superior to a Jungian one, which she considered less
painful and more flattering; Jung, she observed in the same entry,
was much more popular with Catholics.[12]

White's relationship with Catholicism similarly reflects cultural
and historical shifts. She had returned to the Church shortly before
Christmas in December 1940; in the letters that record her reconversion she discusses her support for theological modernism, the late
nineteenth- and early twentieth-century movement that sought to reconcile Catholic doctrine with historical and scientific developments
and that would permit Catholics to exercise individual judgement
on matters of morality.[13] In 1907 Pope Pius X issued an encyclical
condemning the movement, and leading figures such as Jesuit George
Tyrrell were excommunicated. White mentions standing by Tyrrell's
grave as a child and feeling sorry for him (*The Hound and the Falcon*,
p. 2), and her letters record her dislike of Church rigidity on a range
of issues, including sexuality and artistry. Before her reconversion she
writes that 'So much in the actual mechanics of the Church and its
extremely intolerant attitude repels me' (*The Hound and the Falcon*,
p. 2); later she explains that she lapsed from faith because 'I thought
it meant giving up everything I cared for, renouncing all human pleasure, all love of human beings, all delight in natural things and in
art and poetry unless they were directly "religious" and "edifying"'
(*The Hound and the Falcon*, p. 49). White was drawn to the more
mystical elements of Catholicism and to simplicity in faith, but at
the same time she conflated Church authority and even God Himself
with her own father and sought in the Church the unyielding 'frame'
and 'discipline' she railed against elsewhere. And despite her conviction that 'religion oversteps its function in claiming to be literally
true' and that 'religion should be a *method* of exploring the realm of
the spirit' (*The Hound and the Falcon*, p. 5), the increasing modernisation of the Church made her deeply uneasy.[14] Hence while, in the
spirit of Tyrell, she wanted to accept Catholicism as the expression

of poetic truth, her desire to secure her sense of self with literal truth would continue to vex her in the decades following her reconversion. The desire to locate the literal truth came to centre on what she called her 'Garden of Eden troubles', which I explore below.

Both her first analysis and her reconversion demonstrate the 'amazing literalness' that White would later assign to her fictional protagonist in *Beyond the Glass* (p. 95). White recasts both the female castration complex, in which the girl comes to desire her father's 'gift' of a child in lieu of her 'missing' penis, and the Incarnation, in which the Virgin becomes pregnant by God the Father, as literal rather than symbolic or metaphorical paradigms. In recasting these paradigms and assuming the role of daughter and virgin in them, White produces startlingly lurid accounts in which she highlights the paradigms' latent incestuous meanings. Tangled in White's reworking of these paradigms is the gendering of writing, the pen as metaphorical penis in the first, the Word become (masculine) Flesh in the second.[15] Tangled as well are the shadowy circumstances in which White lost her virginity to the man in her father's dressing gown and, with her father's help, aborted the male foetus that resulted. It is significant, moreover, that these lurid accounts coincide with episodes of illness, and may reflect the bold and extravagant connections characteristic of manic thinking.

Master plots, part one: analysis

When she entered analysis in the autumn of 1934, White was in a precarious state of disintegration infused by mania. As noted in Chapter 1, while she had published her first novel, *Frost in May*, to wide acclaim, her marriage was falling apart: her third husband, Tom Hopkinson, also a writer, had begun an affair with another woman, apparently in part because of feelings of competition; White had been able to finish the novel after fifteen years only with his encouragement, and his infidelity seemed to her a repetition of her father's denunciation of her first novel. White had not thought 'the Beast' would recur, and she did not identify the signs of incipient insanity until she had reached a point of crisis:

> for a long time, I did not think it was any more than tiredness, nerves and general strain. But when it came to delusions, a depression so

deep that even now I don't like to think about it and violent suicidal impulses (one very nearly successful) something had to be done.
(*The Hound and the Falcon*, p. 37)

In addition, White brought to analysis her bewilderment about the
'muddled' events of her life between the ages of twenty-one and thirty-
one, a 'very queer sexual record' (*Diary* 1, p. 274) in which she had
contracted three marriages – two annulled for nonconsummation –
had three unplanned pregnancies (one terminated by an illegal abortion), a number of unsatisfactory transient affairs, and a traumatic
incarceration for total insanity in Bethlem. Her father's sudden and
unexpected death in 1929 soon after the birth of her older daughter
Susan may also have contributed to her disintegration.

White's entrance into analysis, driven by her terror that she was
going insane again, coincided with a moment in psychoanalytic history in which the thinking about female development and sexuality, the focus of intense debate throughout the 1920s, had hardened
into a prescriptive and normative conceptualisation centred upon the
'female castration complex'.[16] Freud had by this point written his
three major essays on female sexuality, but the most influential theorisation of the female castration complex in Britain was that of Karl
Abraham, whose 1920 'Manifestations of the Female Castration
Complex' had strongly shaped Freud's thinking and who had trained
a number of first-generation British analysts, including Edward
Glover, a close associate of White's analyst Dennis Carroll.[17] As in
Freud's later formulations, Abraham posits that girls' and women's
neuroses develop out of their inability to come to terms with their
'castration' and their inevitable (sense of) inferiority. According to
Abraham, while many women are 'conscious of the fact that certain
phenomena of their mental life arise from an intense dislike of being
a woman', they are 'quite in the dark as regards the motives of such
an aversion'.[18] That aversion, Abraham claims, arises 'unequivocally'
from the disadvantage they feel when they compare 'the inferiority of
their external organs' to those of boys and men. Neurotic symptoms
develop when 'Ideas belonging to [the sense of castration] impinge
with all the force of their strong libidinal cathexis against the barriers which oppose their entry into consciousness. This struggle of
repressed material with the censorship can be demonstrated in a
great variety of neurotic symptoms.'[19]

Abraham turns first to the girl's development. Recognising a 'primary defect in her body', the girl imagines the following sequence: 'I had a penis once as boys have, but it has been taken away from me.'[20] She may cling to the phantasy that she will get one eventually, 'as though the idea of a lifelong defect were quite incomprehensible to her.'[21] She may long for the father to give her

> that part of the body she so painfully misses; for the child still has a narcissistic confidence that she could not be permanently defective, and she readily subscribes to her father that creative omnipotence which can bestow on her everything she desires.[22]

A variation of this phantasy of receiving the 'gift' of a penis develops out of defecation, whereby faeces become equated with a 'gift' that the child makes to the mother in gratitude for the latter's gift of love (that is, feeding). Since a child considers 'its faeces as part of its own body', the girl develops the phantasy that she can manufacture a penis through the act of defecation.[23] When none of these phantasies materialises, the girl 'is likely to direct an intense and lasting hostility towards those from whom she has in vain expected the gift'.[24] In the 'normal' course of development, the girl will eventually substitute for these phantasies the hope of a baby:

> Freud has shown that besides the idea of motion [faeces] and penis in the sense of a gift there is still a third idea which is identified with both of them, namely that of a child. The little girl now cherishes the hope of getting a child from her father as a substitute for the penis not granted her, and this again in the sense of a gift.[25]

This latter path is the most desirable, resulting in a 'passive' attitude towards the man who can finally 'heal' the 'wound' of castration through the 'gift' of a child. But, Abraham warns, 'frequently this normal end of development is not attained'.[26] Many factors recall to the woman her defective state. Menstruation, defloration and birth are all bloody reminders of her primary 'wound', and she may make these connections even before they occur. Hence all women manifest some signs of this psychic struggle: 'we must be prepared to find in every female person some traces of the castration complex. The individual differences are only a matter of degree'.[27] At this point

Abraham turns to women's 'neurotic transformations' as evidenced by their inability to find sexual fulfilment with men, whether that inability develops out of lack of response ('frigidity'), lack of interest or dissatisfaction with their partners. Abraham divides these 'neurotic transformations' into two broad categories: the first category encompasses those women who persist in the 'phantasy of possessing a male organ'; the second those women who 'express an unconscious refusal of the female role, and a repressed desire for revenge on the privileged male'.[28] The two categories are not mutually exclusive of one another, Abraham observes, and in fact it is difficult to distinguish between them in his subsequent elaborations.

Abraham identifies two 'abnormal' developmental paths that broadly correlate with the two categories of 'neurotic transformations'. The first is that of homosexuality, a path that includes what he terms 'repressed homosexuality', characteristic of women who do not deny their femininity but sublimate their unconscious sense of castration 'in the shape of masculine pursuits of an intellectual and professional character and other allied interests'.[29] By far the bulk of the essay elaborates the neurotic transformations manifested by women whose development follows his second abnormal path of 'archaic revenge', an unconscious desire for retaliation that leads back

> ultimately to the injustice suffered at the hands of the father. The unconscious of the adult daughter takes a late revenge for the father's omission to bestow upon her a penis [. . .] she takes it, however, not on her father in person, but on the man who in consequence of her transference of libido has assumed the father's part. The only adequate revenge for her wrong for her castration is the castration of the man.[30]

This group thus possesses two unconscious tendencies, 'a desire to take revenge on the man, and a desire to seize by force the longed-for organ, i.e. to rob him of it'.[31] The frigid woman belongs in this group, as does the woman who, unable to find relief in 'neurotic substitutes' – Abraham's example is taking pleasure in using a garden hose[32] – cherishes phantasies of Immaculate Conception, thereby relegating the 'male organ' to 'something of secondary importance and unnecessary'.[33] This group also includes women whose taste in men seems suspect. By choosing passive men, men of a homosexual character, or men with some kind of physical disability, they betray 'particularly strong feelings of inferiority; their libido prefers a mutilated man rather than one who is physically intact. For the mutilated man has also lost a limb, like themselves [. . .] such women feel an affinity to the mutilated man; they consider him a companion in distress and do not reject him with hate like the sound man'.[34] Yet another manifestation is the woman who excites a man only to fail to respond to him, thereby betraying an aggressive impulse 'to disappoint'; this type of frigid woman, Abraham writes, is 'unconsciously impelled towards violence and revenge'.[35] Overall, in fact, this 'abnormal type' of emasculating women manifests 'a sadistic-hostile attitude with the aim of possession resulting from anal motives':[36] 'These neurotics are unconsciously impelled towards violence and revenge'.[37]

It is clear from White's diary that her analyst – Dr Dennis Carroll, associated with the hard-line Freudian doctrines of the British Psycho-Analytic Society under the leadership of Edward Glover and Ernest Jones[38] – diagnosed her not only as schizophrenic but as a textbook case of this 'abnormal type' of emasculating woman. Not only was White by her own admission incapable of enjoying sex, but her choices of husbands – one impotent, one gay, and one six years younger – matched Abraham's description of the emasculating woman who chooses the 'mutilated man'. Indeed, even the man to whom she had lost her virginity had been 'mutilated', with a pronounced limp he attributed to a war injury.[39] White's status as a professional working woman and successful writer would match Abraham's description of 'repressed homosexuality' that had been sublimated by 'masculine pursuits of an intellectual and professional character'. She did not like being a mother, thus betraying her failure to overcome the castration complex. The violent outbursts she had engaged in when she discovered Hopkinson's infidelity and her anger and irritability in general – symptoms of agitated depression as well as emotional outrage – corresponded to Abraham's conviction that the emasculating woman was bent on revenge. Depression in Abraham's scheme, moreover, emerges when 'the woman's feeling of unhappiness [about castration] is wholly unrepressed',[40] and she is thus conscious of her 'intense dislike of being a woman'.[41] Here, too, White fulfilled the relevant criteria. White had always openly preferred her father to her mother, writing in her diary, 'I hated, despised and rejected all of my mother and would like to have been only my father's child' (*Diary* 1, p. 59). An only child, White was aware that her father had always wanted a son, and her choice of intellectual pursuits had been an expression of her identification with him.

Analysis focused, as might be expected, on getting White to acknowledge her unacknowledged hostility about the 'fact' of her castration and her vengeful phantasies of stealing the power (pen/penis) that her father had not given her. Through this acknowledgement, White would 'work through' her writer's block/illness by understanding that her unconscious conflicts about writing centred on her equation of it with stealing that power. Freud connects writer's block with repression and phallic inscription in 'Inhibitions, Symptoms and Anxiety', where he writes:

> As soon as writing, which entails making liquid flow out of a tube on to a piece of white paper, assumes the significance of copulation, or as soon as walking becomes a symbolic substitute for walking upon the body of mother earth, both writing and walking are stopped because they represent the performance of a forbidden sexual act.[42]

'The ego renounces these functions', Freud continues, not only to avoid a conflict with the id, but to avoid a conflict with the superego as well: inhibitions of 'professional activities' may serve as self-punishment, with the 'severe superego' forbidding 'success and gain'.[43] White's diary suggests, in fact, that she knew of the equation of writer's block with repression and phallic inscription, either through analysis or through her own reading. Within a month of entering analysis with Carroll, White reports:

> Last night dreamt someone gave me a gigantic tube of lanolin-like stuff to rub on my scorched leg . . . A great deal came out of the tube, rubbed it on burn. Hands covered with it . . . C[arroll] What did tube suggest T[ony] Oh. I suppose it's a penis . . . (*Diary* 1, p. 41)

'Great deal about faeces', she reports laconically in the first weeks of analysis (*Diary* 1, p. 39), suggesting that her analyst is exploring her desire to compensate for her 'defect'. Her constipation in the first weeks of analysis – a common metabolic change in a depressive episode – becomes linked to a refusal of 'letting go', another form of blockage and 'keeping things inside'. White, in fact, refers to analysis as 'anal lusis' (*Diary* 1, p. 154), 'lusis being the Greek word for letting go'.[44]

These early associations link writer's block to the blockage associated with repressed conflicts about castration, and White's diary throughout her analysis with Carroll records numerous entries attesting to such a conflict between (masculine) ambition and (feminine) nature, a conflict that resonates with her new understanding of herself as 'split' by schizophrenia as well as by the biological determinism of the female castration complex.[45] Several entries echo the Victorian doctor Maudsley's dictum that the intellectual woman had ceased to be a woman but was not a man either: 'I half wish I were a man yet I was meant to be a woman', reads one entry (*Diary* 1, p. 137); 'If I were more of a woman or more of a man I'd be happier', reads another (*Diary* 1, p. 89). Other entries mark White's struggle with overcoming her 'castration complex', whereby 'abnormal' and 'vengeful' phantasies of success in 'masculine' spheres of intellectual and creative activity clash with the normative female resolution of marriage and children. Hence White often castigates herself for her failed marriages, her inability to love her children, and her 'monstrous' and 'freakish' ambitions. 'I am surprised there are so few women artists', she comments in one entry. 'I suppose the production of children is a very satisfying thing to a real woman' (*Diary* 1, p. 101). 'I am such a terrible failure as a woman; as an artist I have never begun, perhaps never can begin', reads another (*Diary* 1, p. 103). Other entries stress her abnormality and monstrosity (*Diary* 1, pp. 48, 104). When an affair ends, her lover's rejection of her – 'It is rather like having an affair with a mermaid', he tells her in breaking it off – brings up her 'old fear of being a monster' (*Diary* 1, p. 99): the mermaid's divided body, in which only the upper torso is human, resonates with White's sense of herself as split and simultaneously speaks to her fear of herself as 'unsexed' by her mind and ambitions. White concludes, in fact, that artistic success for women seems to equate automatically with abnormality: 'I wonder why all women writers who are any good have been and are sexually very odd' (*Diary* 1, p. 106).[46]

Another strand in the analysis takes up White's sense of herself as a 'mutilated man', one of the centrepieces of Abraham's conceptualisation. This connection informs an entry in which White writes that 'it is very clear that a great part of my unconscious preoccupation is with the idea of myself as a mutilated man'; she explores the idea in relation to the men with whom she has been involved – 'Odd that N's broken finger had a perverse attraction for me – that I first had intercourse with a mutilated man' – before reaching the (foregone) conclusion that 'Mutilation seems to be a kind of reassurance to me in someone else' (*Diary* 1, p. 115). These reflections spring from analysis: in the same entry, White notes that 'He [Carroll] says the same characteristics appear in every man to whom I am attracted – the strong homosexual element, the fear of castration manifesting itself either in impotence or in over violent sexuality, the trait of disappointing women' (*Diary* 1, p. 114). He tells White that she 'arranged [her] life so as to disappoint and be disappointed' (*Diary* 1, p. 179): she has 'a compulsion to *disappoint*' (*Diary* 2, pp. 89, 108). White's elaboration of Carroll's prompt ties the failures of her relationships with men to the female castration complex, in which the emasculating woman experiences both humiliation and triumph when sex results not only in her dissatisfaction but that of the man as well:

> I cannot help noticing that my affairs nearly always run the same course: a violent beginning on one side or the other: reluctance on one side or the other; sexual intercourse in which one or the other is frightened, frigid, or disappointed; a period during which I consciously or compulsively knot all the strings together and try to provoke disaster; disaster which brings acute humiliation, sadness, sense of loss and failure and yet, I can see now, has elements of relief, excitement, almost triumph. (*Diary* 1, pp. 114–15)

White echoes Abraham's formulations throughout this passage. Women intent on emasculation as a type of revenge frequently develop, Abraham asserts, an 'impulse to *disappoint*': 'the woman can do this by responding to [the man's] advances up to a certain point and then refusing to give herself to him'[47]. The 'impulse to disappoint' has a tripartite sequence, in which the first stage is robbery – 'I rob you of what you have because I lack it' – the second stage is titillation and arousal – 'I rob you of nothing. I even promise you what I have to give' – and the final stage is vengeful withholding of sexual fulfilment – 'I will not give you what I have promised'.[48] This type of emasculating woman is very often frigid, Abraham writes: although consciously willing 'to assume the female role', unconsciously her object is 'the disappointment of the man, who is inclined to infer from her conscious willingness the possibility of mutual enjoyment [. . .] she has the desire to demonstrate to herself and her partner that his sexual ability is of no importance'.[49] Not only does White accede to the formulation that she chooses 'mutilated men', but the failure of her third marriage also leads her to extend this formulation to encompass her

sense of humiliation at 'being a woman without a husband – a mutilated woman as it were. Also in serious work the idea that to be an
artist involves suppression of sexual life. Not borne out by male artists' (*Diary* 1, p. 115). Whereas to be a successful *woman* requires
a husband to attest to 'normality', to be a successful *woman writer*
seems to entail the renunciation of sexuality altogether and hence of
any claim to the 'normal' resolution of the female castration complex.
White goes on to speculate about the sex lives of the great nineteenth-
century women writers – Austen, the Brontës, George Eliot, George
Sand – noting that all but Austen took men's names: 'Jane Austen the
only one that wrote *as a woman* [. . .] But *she* writes as an *unmarried
woman*' (*Diary* 1, p. 115).

Whereas White entered analysis with the belief that the chaotic
events of her twenties and the disintegration of her third marriage
were the major factors in the recurrence of her second breakdown,
analysis encouraged White to trace her troubles much further back,
to her childhood more generally and to her relationship with her
father specifically (her relationship with her mother did not constitute a significant part of this first analytic treatment). As detailed
in the introduction, White's relationship with her father was indeed
fraught, and the early stages of analysis would confirm the father's
centrality in White's 'castration complex'. Carroll's 'shaking his
bunch of keys' provoked 'convulsive horror', which White associated with the 'click' of her father's latchkey and a 'warning of disapproval' (*Diary* 1, pp. 39, 51). White's nursery and her father's study
were located in the same part of the family home, separated only by
a bathroom: White describes her childhood play in her nursery as
circumscribed by her apprehension of disturbing her father, who was
often at work in his study close by; he would storm out of his study
in a rage if she made too much noise.

Much of White's attention in analysis was directed to the sexual
energy that suffused her relationship with her father, an energy that
has led some scholars to argue that White evidences signs of sexual
abuse.[50] Yet it is clear that White's writing on this subject at this
period in her life strongly reflects her immersion in an analysis centred on the daughter's desire to receive the father's 'gift' of a penis
and her rage and resulting depression at his withholding it. To be
sure, White's relationship with her father was, in the words of her
biographer, 'unhealthily close': 'Inappropriately focused on his young

daughter, his fantasies inflamed Antonia's natural daughterly desire for her father into a complex of Electra-like proportions.'[51] Analysis contributed to that inflammation by encouraging White to envisage this relationship in the most concrete and literal terms possible: it confirms the father's centrality in the narrative White constructs of both her writer's block and her illness. The path to 'normal' femininity – the resolution of the female castration complex that would enable a woman to accept her passive heterosexual role and conceive of the man as the saviour who will heal her 'wound' with the 'gift' of a child – depends upon the daughter's substitution for her vengeful phantasies of robbing the penis by emasculating men the 'hope of getting a child from her father as a substitute for the penis not granted her, and this again in the sense of a gift'.

One of White's most startlingly explicit diary entries explores this very equation in the context of the 'shock in childhood which paralysed me emotionally' (*Diary* 1, p. 139), the father's repudiation of her after the discovery of her adolescent novel. Noting that she 'didn't feel the tremendous excitement and satisfaction in having a baby that most women seem to feel', White connects her disappointment to the fact that her first baby was both illegitimate and a girl (*Diary* 1, p. 139). As the entry continues, White speculates about what she wants to accomplish in her fiction; her musings weave together the 'fatal' first manuscript, her illegal abortion, her desire to produce a legitimate son/book, and her need for her father's permission and approval:

> I suppose I want a book in some funny way to be a male child. I can understand the extraordinary satisfaction of producing a son. A woman has not a penis but she can produce a being with a real penis. I did once, anyhow, conceive a son. I wonder if the realisation of that was what made me so extraordinarily happy and peaceful after that abortion [1924] which was in so many ways a distressing experience. It was as if after that I really recovered from insanity and collected my wits again . . . My impulse to write a novel began in the year following the beginning of menstruation. My father, as it were, killed the child. He thought of it as *conceived in sin*. Just about ten years later, I conceived a real child, about the same time of year, this time definitely 'in sin' and to my father's horrified disapproval. This time my father wishes me to go on and have the child, in very distressing circumstances, *as a punishment* [. . .] He was more willing to lend money for the abortion than for the birth

of [Susan]. If Susan had been a boy, he told me he would have found it far easier to overlook the circumstances of her birth. It was a great distress to him that all his children were girls . . . (*Diary* 1, pp. 139–40)

Here, White's thinking clearly reflects not only Abraham's influence but Freud's as well: in his 1933 lecture 'Femininity', Freud had said:

A mother is only brought unlimited satisfaction by her relation to a son: this is altogether the most perfect, the most free from ambivalence of all human relationships. A mother can transfer to her son the ambition which she has been obliged to suppress in herself, and she can expect from him the satisfaction of all that has been left over in her of her masculinity complex.[52]

By the end of this passage in her diary, White's vivid literalising of the female castration complex has led to a partially articulated fantasy of having her father's son, a fantasy underwritten by the fact that the man who fathered the baby she aborted did so while wearing her father's dressing gown. This fantasy emerges even more clearly in an entry recorded three days later, in which, once again, the metaphorical dimension of the castration complex blurs into a literal one:

Now if as it seems clear from several indications I want my father's penis or a child by him e.g. a work engendered with his loving approval. What am I fussing about?
　　I can't have his loving approval because he is DEAD
　　I couldn't have had intercourse with him anyway because presumably apart from morals
　　(a) he didn't want it
　　(b) I couldn't have endured it without mutilation. (*Diary* 1, p. 140)

White's handwriting deteriorates at this point as she launches into a tirade about her father:

Couldn't even write – filthy dirty beastly old man the way I WANTED to [. . .] I spit on your corpse [. . .] You never loved me for a second and I'm damned if I'm going to go on loving you [. . .] I was hurt and wanted your approval. THAT would have hurt you all right to know your standards meant nothing to me. (*Diary* 1, p. 140)

White continues to literalise the female castration complex here as she transforms her desire to write into the 'gift' withheld by her father's disapproval. Notably, White describes her father as not wanting inter-course: the rage that infuses the passage concerns his disapproval.

These entries detail the final stages of the female castration com-plex as well as the analysis: the daughter has now acknowledged her desire for the father and his gift as well as her rage at his withhold-ing of it. The analytic component of the process, the transference, involves the analyst himself: the analysand must 'transfer' her feel-ings about the significant authority figure in her conflict to the figure of the analyst. White's diary draws a clear picture of this process. White initially entered analysis with hostility and resistance, suspi-cious of what she called 'the high priest attitude of the psychoana-lysts' (*Diary* 1, p. 34). She viewed analysis as coercive and doctrinal, likening it to Jesus's 'reiterated' '"*I* am the way and the truth and the life" [. . .] I resent the "only way" business' (*Diary* 1, p. 34). Her attitude changed when her analyst gave her the diagnosis of insan-ity and held out the possibility that he could save her: 'I must accept analysis meekly since it is difficult for me to accept, blot myself out, become featureless, a "case"' (*Diary* 1, p. 58). White later under-lines her attitude as one of submission to the psychoanalytic 'high priest' who promised salvation: 'I *had* to submit to a pretty rigor-ous mental discipline for four years' (*Hound*, p. 10). White's atti-tude gradually grew more positive. Within weeks she would compare her analyst favourably to the confessor-saint Father Zossima in *The Brothers Karamazov*: 'I felt the confessor-saint fulfilled exactly the same function as the psycho-analyst. The psycho-analyst cuts a poor and shabby figure beside the saint but he is the best substitute an age of non-faith can produce' (*Diary* 1, p. 74). Although she notes with some amusement in her diary that 'To me it seems C[arroll] is always suggesting a sexual desire of mine for him' (*Diary* 1, p. 41), in fact White's growing attachment to her analyst evidences positive transference, the lynchpin of orthodox psychoanalysis: the analysand 'works through' repressed conflicts by repeating them in the transfer-ence. The analyst becomes a stand-in for a significant figure of the past, typically a parent. With the analyst's guidance, the analysand 'recognises' the conflict and is thereby able finally to resolve it.

Carroll indeed comes to replace White's father as the focus of her erotic phantasies. Hence while she begins analysis wishing she had '*five* fountain pens like my father instead of only two' (*Diary* 1, p. 39), by July or August, only a few months later, she buys herself a new pen 'like one of the analyst's' (*Diary* 1, p. 52). (That White herself had accepted the equation of penis=pen=writing is revealed by a late diary entry, when she left her umbrella at her analyst's office: 'I *hope* the unconscious grasps that this penis-symbol (writing power) is quite OK for me to have' [*Diary* 2, p. 137]).[53] With a pen like her analyst's, White briefly breaks her 'writing jam', a symbolic turning point that marks the shift from her father to Carroll. The subsequent loss of a notebook at this time worries White because 'I wrote something I didn't understand in it and took it up to show to Carroll. It is like losing a part of oneself' (*Diary* 1, pp. 52–3). This writing, given to Carroll in order to receive his approbation and thereby 'work through' the father's repudiation, represents

> a legitimate new beginning [. . .] I think the unconscious was at work making me lose it because I was afraid of what I had written about my father [. . .] Not only did it break the jam and lead me insensibly to begin the new book [. . .] but its pattern . . . had a significance. It was the first time I broke away from the pattern of notebook as much like my father's old ones as I could get. (*Diary* 1, p. 58)

The transference becomes more overtly sexualised in the later stages of the analysis, and Carroll's encouragement of this development is explicit: 'Carroll assures me that he is the man I want..not a man like him but himself. And that I think I cannot possibly attract him because I am too bad' (*Diary* 1, p. 151). As her divorce becomes final – concurrent with the ending of analysis – discussions concerning White's sexual feelings for Carroll take place: 'Carroll said "Do you *want* a husband?" I said "Yes" "Any particular husband?" "No" "Can you imagine what he would be like?" "Someone like you"' (*Diary* 1, p. 145). Feeling certain that 'unsuitability or even impossibility wouldn't stop me from falling in love with Carroll in the ordinary way', White entertains the 'wild fantasy' that 'Perhaps analysts really do sleep with all their patients after a certain stage and neither patient nor analyst tells' (*Diary* 1, pp. 146–7). Just before their last sessions, White declares, 'Have decided that the best Dennis [Carroll] can do for me is – *literally* – to "make an honest woman of me"' (*Diary* 1, p. 154).

Whereas the successful resolution of the transference marks the resolution of the analysand's conflict, White's transference remains unresolved: the analyst indeed substitutes for the father but the centrality of the father/analyst remains firmly fixed – and fixed, moreover, within an erotic plot that collapses the father with the husband. In fact, almost thirty years later, her third analyst will conclude that 'the transference had not been completely resolved' after White relates how she had seen 'Carroll some months after analysis was finished and was surprised to discover him clean-shaven and still more to discover that he had *always* been clean-shaven though all through 3½ years of sessions I had always seen him with a little moustache, like my father' (*Diary* 1, p. 159). In the same entry, White notes that she had always wanted to please her father as well as God. White's desire to please her analyst emerges in her production of the narrative that marks a successful 'Freudian' analysis, the narrative of the female castration complex and the daughter's acknowledgement of her desire for the father's gift. And, just as White equates her writer's block and her failures in 'normal' heterosexual relationships with her father's disapproval of her writing/sexuality, so she turns to Carroll, the analyst/father figure, for his approval: 'Still need to get my man approved [. . .] Trying hard to get C[arroll]'s "permission". Obviously really my own. Must SOMEHOW get my own permission about writing and making money. . .' (*Diary* 1, p. 130). White ends her analysis with Carroll convinced that her illness has its roots in her castration complex.

Carroll seems to have viewed the analysis as a success, not only because White had acknowledged her repressed anger about her 'castration' but because she had been able to enjoy sex several times and had now moved back into the family home and assumed her maternal responsibilities. He congratulated White on the fact that 'something very sweet and womanly is beginning to appear in you'.[54] But numerous diary entries suggest that White still suffered from crippling depression as analysis drew to a close, and that she herself felt that, 'sex having cleared [. . .] but temporarily drive demon into money and writing' (*Diary* 1, p. 130). Furthermore, Carroll's misreadings of both her compulsive overspending and her weight fluctuations – the first Carroll associates with faeces, revenge phantasies and desires for power; the second he ascribes to White's feeling it 'safer to have things *inside*' (*Diary* 1, p. 145) – are wildly off the mark, since both are symptoms of manic-depressive disorder and not signs of psychological conflicts. White herself will conclude, soon after completing analysis, that 'Extravagance is I am sure a symptom of anxiety with me' (*Diary* 1, p. 169); she will later build on this insight by connecting nervous energy to over-spending: 'When I am not working well, I begin to spend money' (*Diary* 1, p. 223).[55] In 1949 she admits, 'The money thing, never properly worked out after Carroll' (*Diary* 1, p. 207). Similarly, near the end of analysis White charts the fluctuations in her weight, which demonstrate a clear connection between mania and weight loss on the one hand and between depression and weight gain on the other (*Diary* 1, pp. 144, 151).[56] She observes that 'I am getting very fat very fast again but believe it is psychological', only to accede to Carroll's interpretation that she wants to keep things inside (*Diary* 1, p. 145).

White's desire to please Carroll by producing the 'correct' psychoanalytic narrative and by acceding to his readings of her symptoms prevents her from fully trusting her own insights. In *The Hound and the Falcon*, White will credit analysis with saving her mind and her life, describing analysis as a 'slow, dull, patient process of unravelling threads which have got tangled' (*The Hound and the Falcon*, p. 37). Yet without Carroll's authoritative presence to provide 'complete security' (*Diary* 1, p. 147), White's drive to understand her illness compels her to turn to another patriarchal paradigm. Hence, while White records her conviction that 'I could not live by the rule of the Catholic Church. But the morality of which Carroll made me conscious is one that I can at least attempt to live up to' (*Diary* 1, p. 162), she also records a contradictory conviction that analysis erases the beauty of poetry and religion:

> Can all these be explained away by anything so apparently boring and trivial as the desire to have a penis or the fear of losing one or the desire to appropriate and damage someone else's? . . . I come back and back to 'Suppose the Catholic religion *is* true after all, and I shall have no peace until I submit to God'.[57]

White identifies Catholicism as the source of principles of coherence and a peace that will free her from fragmentation, disintegration and bipolarity.

Master plots, part two: Catholicism

White's return to Catholicism, detailed in *The Hound and the Falcon*, suggests a dramatic reconciliation with her faith but in fact her diary reveals that, as her analysis grew to a close and her third marriage ended – both in September 1938 – familiar patterns of unsettling mood shifts signalled that she had not been 'cured' by analysis: 'Chaos is come again so I must see where I've gone wrong [. . .] Too much preoccupied with self" (*Diary* 1, p. 160). Her diary records moods that shift between feelings of languor, heaviness and emptiness, and 'nervous energy [. . .] some of that must have been released by analysis' (*Diary* 1, pp. 156, 166). Stress intensified her moods: unemployed, with two daughters to raise on her own, White struggled with feeling 'fearfully humiliated not having [a husband]' and the prospect of what she was expected to do:

> What I should be doing is making a home for my children and without the impulse of love I cannot see it as anything but a mutilated and dreary life to centre my life round them, least of all be left to look after children without a man. (*Diary* 1, pp. 159, 148)

But White now interprets symptoms of her illness as symptoms of unconscious conflicts. Hence, in an entry that records compulsive eating in response to feelings of '*emptiness*. . .like annihilation [. . .] complete numbness of mind and extreme depression' (*Diary* 1, p. 169), White observes that 'If some of the trouble comes from having my father inside me, I should get him out' (*Diary* 1, p. 168). Another entry of the same time notes, 'I discovered in analysis that the main cause of my own melancholy and paralysis was . . . repressed rage . . . what I feel when I begin to write is a complete *lack* of power. My mind seems to go to pieces' (*Diary* 1, p. 170). While she had entered analysis in 1935 with an expression of faith – 'If I can hold on, I really do believe . . . that I shall have learnt a new language and that at last I may have a base on which to build' (*Diary* 1, p. 73) – analysis did not provide the coherence of self she had hoped to find. Within a year of completing analysis, an entry in the 'Analysis Diary' begins 'Still waiting for revelation: key to unlock' (*Diary* 1, p. 168).

A month before completing analysis, in fact, an entry reveals White's fear that without the structure of analysis she will be without a coherent source of external support for her internal chaos:

> I am so weak that I doubt if I can behave as an ordinarily decent human being without the support of a religion [. . .] It may be an illusion to rely on God, yet it makes it more possible not to lean on human beings. (*Diary* 1, p. 148)

Wishing she could accept 'chaos and contradiction in the external world' as well as in herself, White admits, 'I have this craving to find order in it' (*Diary* 1, p. 148). The desire for a stable core or 'centre' becomes a dominant theme: unable to find satisfaction in centring her life upon her children, White longs for 'a *working* centre of my own [. . .] it is vital for me to find my own centre and live from it' (*Diary* 1, p. 164). The practise of her religion initially provides a way for White to organise her moods, although it does little to dispel her writer's block: 'Practically, religion has been of great value to me, giving me a centre, helping me to deal a little with my immense egotism – but all the time curbing and calming rather than giving me incentive' (*Diary* 1, pp. 178–9). Another diary entry makes explicit the role the Church initially plays in providing a coherent structure that helps her to cope with internal chaos: 'The old troubles persist: the old symptoms. I have had them now for 24 years [. . .] Yet in one thing I do know where I stand: my religion. That is my centre' (*Diary* 1, p. 183).

White often employs the language of form to image what she hoped to find in her return to Catholicism. '[T]o be a Christian may be to be an artist with one's nature – composing and disciplining its elements', she writes (*Diary* 1, pp. 163–4). In an entry that lists her fears and desires as she nears the end of analysis, White includes a desire to escape a claustrophobic self-enclosure – 'something outside myself, not my own reflection in a glass' – and then continues, 'I wish I could pray . . . So that even if my life seemed to me utterly frustrated and meaningless, I would at least be able to accept it and know that I was not opposing the creator's design' (*Diary* 1, pp. 116–17). Above all, these entries record White's ongoing search for a solution to her 'unquiet mind' and her sense that her inner torment is somehow indicative of innate corruption.[58] Wondering whether

her feelings are 'genuinely religious' or just 'another projection of my father and my conscience, shelving of responsibility', White connects her 'unquiet mind' to her refusal to submit to God in an entry that attests both to her desire for a calmer mind and her association of manic-depressive symptoms with lack of self-control:

> I so often feel if I try to make my own life I am opposing God's will and shall be punished even in this life by never having a peaceful mind. All the Catholic teaching is the necessity of denying oneself, giving up one's own will to the will of God. Yet I know neither my own will or God's will. I seem to have no true will: only compulsions. (*Diary* 1: 117)

The quest for a peaceful mind is paramount.

The Hound and the Falcon, her series of letters written to a former Jesuit novitiate in 1940–1, provides perhaps the clearest and most succinct account of the events White identified as crucially significant in the narrative she had constructed of herself through analysis, even as she was in the process of returning to the Church and incorporating another and in many respects similar paradigm into this narrative. In fact, this correspondence is so intimate and revealing that White would later confuse it with her diary (*Diary* 2, p. 99). As she remarks in her 'Foreword' to *The Hound and the Falcon*, her diary at the time of her reconversion says 'disappointingly little about what had been my most intense preoccupation. Everything vital [. . .] had gone into my correspondence with "Peter"' (*The Hound and the Falcon*, p. xviii). The sheer scope of the material suggests the intensity of White's preoccupation: 'The typescript of these letters, all written in the space of less than a year, in the intervals of a full-time job in the BBC and against the background of the London blitz, amounted to over eighty thousand words – more than the average length of a novel' (*The Hound and the Falcon*, p. xx).

White's obsession with creating a logical and sequential order for her life story emerges on multiple occasions in *The Hound and the Falcon*, where she provides not only two separate summaries of crucial and defining events but a chronological timeline from her birth until October 1940, when she began to correspond with Peter (*The Hound and the Falcon*, pp. 52–4). The first 'bald synopsis' or 'outline of this queer and funny story' attributes her breakdown to 'being married three times between 20 and 30' (*The Hound and the Falcon*, pp. 24–6) and White briefly discusses each marriage in turn. The second synopsis, developed in an 'imaginary' letter to Cyril Connolly in which she explains her return to the Church, develops her life story within the framework of Catholicism. Here, White begins her narrative with her father's conversion to Catholicism when she was seven and recounts her life through her third divorce and her 'reconversion' (*The Hound and the Falcon*, pp. 153–60). Both accounts highlight the centrality of analysis in helping her stabilise herself (*The Hound and the Falcon*, pp. 37, 159). At the end of this second synopsis, White constructs two readings of her life, one developed through a psychoanalytic frame, the other through a Catholic frame. She explicitly identifies the importance of the interpretative act and also the choice of interpretative frame in creating a coherent life story: 'The facts are simple but a modern psychologist and a Catholic would give entirely different and equally coherent interpretations of them', she remarks (*The Hound and the Falcon*, p. 153). These two competing interpretations are stunning in their ordering of the 'simple facts' and her use of master narratives as framing devices, and so I quote them in full:

> The psychologists would presumably say that Catholicism was one of the factors in my life with which I had failed to come to terms, as I had failed to come to terms with money, sex, and writing. Obviously the Catholic Church would be very much mixed up for me with my father, who was directly responsible for my becoming a Catholic in the first place. Analysis had convinced me without any shadow of doubt that my ambivalent attitude of unconscious love and hate towards him was one of the prime factors of my neurosis. Therefore I would naturally project into my attitude towards the Church, particularly such a very authoritative Church, the same mixture of love and hate, submissiveness and rebellion. In rebelling against him I would naturally rebel against the Church too, and also feel guilty about it [. . .] having finished a fairly successful analysis and discharged quantities of aggression and fear, I was free to approach the Church, like everything else, more rationally. Having disentangled myself at least partially from my fantastic notions of my father, and though he was dead, 'forgiven' him and reconciled myself to him, reconciliation with the Church became a possibility. I could return to my religion disinfected of my morbid fears about it

and acceptance of the Catholic way of life, so satisfactory to many neurotics, might be as practical a sublimation as I could hope to find. The return to the Church might, on the other hand, be a regression in face of a conflict too difficult to sustain alone or it might be yet another stage in the cure – a situation to be faced and dealt with, in spite of squirming and repugnance, just like the other situations which I had been forced to face up to. (*The Hound and the Falcon*, pp. 160–1)

White's brilliant reading of her 'reconversion' demonstrates her thorough mastery of psychoanalytic paradigms. She follows it with a second interpretation that demonstrates a similar mastery of Catholic paradigms:

How would the Catholics describe the process? Something like this, I imagine. Through my father's courageous conversion to Catholicism I was given the great grace of being received into the Church and being educated as a Catholic. But, through my own perversity, I was not humble and submissive enough to the divine will and the Church's authority and eventually, through love of my own will, unchecked curiosity, self-indulgence and association with infidels, I renounced my faith. After long years of wandering, in the course of which I suffered a great deal, partly as the result of my sins, and during which in a blundering way I did grope after what truth I could assimilate, God took pity on me and gave me the great grace of returning to the Church. The doubts from which I still suffer so constantly are partly the result of my obstinacy and the intemperate habit of mind I cultivated during my 'apostasy', partly an affliction from which many whole-hearted and devoted Catholics, even saints, have suffered and do suffer. They may also be attributed to the devil. The only way to deal with them is to brush them aside and pray incessantly for faith. The truths of faith are not contrary to reason, but transcend reason, and reason cannot dispel them. (*The Hound and the Falcon*, p. 161)

White refuses to privilege either version: 'It is quite possible that both these interpretations are correct in their own realm and not mutually exclusive' (*The Hound and the Falcon*, p. 153). She attributes the disparity between the two accounts to the different 'idioms' or 'languages' used to construct them, a concept she develops throughout *The Hound and the Falcon*. She stresses her own multilingualism even as she points to the gulf that opens up between speakers of different languages: whereas 'I can talk to Catholics in their language and I can talk to [. . .] the 'intelligentsia' in [theirs] [. . .] so far I have not found anyone who understands both languages' (*The Hound and the Falcon*, p. 152). Similarly, she likens 'the great artists, the great scientists and the great saints' to 'three nations speaking different languages and sometimes quarrelling like children because the object they are contemplating is not the *word "hund"*, *"chien"* or dog but some object validly labelled all three' (*The Hound and the Falcon*, p. 119). In winding down her correspondence with 'Peter', she alludes to their inability to bridge their linguistic gulf – 'we belong to different species and don't speak the same language' (*The Hound and the Falcon*, p. 145) – in a letter in which she concludes that '[w]e live in too much of a tower of Babel world [. . .] for there to be a universal language' (*The Hound and the Falcon*, p. 145).

Yet, because *The Hound and the Falcon* documents White's reconversion to Catholicism, it also documents her uneasiness with her multilingualism and her yearning to speak a single language of identity, the 'universal language' she hoped to find through faith (*The Hound and the Falcon*, p. 145). That uneasiness predates her reconversion – 'All my life I shall see things in the Catholic idiom', she writes in 1936, during a critical year of her second breakdown (*Diary 1*, p. 74) – and her first letter to 'Peter', written prior to her return, stresses that 'the pull of the Church is very strong. It is like one's native language and, though one may have become denationalised, one cannot help reverting to it and even thinking in its terms' (*The Hound and the Falcon*, p. 1). In this state of exile White longs 'to be part of something as one may long for a language and a *fatherland*' (*The Hound and the Falcon*, p. 9; emphasis added).[59] Her return to Catholicism enables her to revert to her 'natural language' (*The Hound and the Falcon*, p. 100), and this reversion in turn serves to still the clamour issuing from the Tower of Babel and the uproar created by the 'quarrelling' of the artists, scientists, and saints: 'One can learn one language and the rudiments of another but it's no good mixing them up in a hideous Esperanto. And the Church, thank God, is a language and not Esperanto' (*The Hound and the Falcon*, p. 119). The clamour and the quarrelling, significantly, speak to the confusion of voices that White herself hears in the competing versions she constructs of herself.

In an attempt to silence the babble of Esperanto and limit herself to speaking in a Catholic idiom, White hopes to incorporate a 'discipline' that promises 'clarity and detachment' and 'self-knowledge without despair or presumption', a self-knowledge, in other words, which promises a path out of bipolarity, since despair points to depression and presumption to mania. White images this structural self-knowledge as the grammar of religious practice: 'The Catholic Church is, as it were, our grammar of this language and, without a grammar, the language would be useless' (*The Hound and the Falcon*, p. 109). That grammar not only provides a logical structure for the expression of Catholic doctrine, then; it also provides a logical structure for the expression of White herself. 'I don't say there can't be other languages and methods', she acknowledges, 'but this is the language I know and everything I feel and need can, I think, be expressed in it' (*The Hound and the Falcon*, p. 44). Insisting that she needs a 'way of life', 'something which can be *lived* as well as *thought*' (*The Hound and the Falcon*, pp. 159, 44), White locates in the practice of Catholicism the 'grammar' that she hopes will give her a means of self-integration:

> The great merit of the Church is that it does *organise all one's impulses and give one a method both of disciplining and expressing them.* Anybody who loves form as I do is not horrified by having limits imposed on them because the limit is the artist's greatest boon. (*The Hound and the Falcon*, p. 44; emphasis added)

The form developed through 'method' and 'discipline' – the grammar of the Catholic idiom – thus appeals to White precisely because its ordering principles constitute for her a seductive ideal of coherence in which the cacophony of multiple languages of self ceases: 'I think I can [cultivate what mind I have] much more productively with a background of some sort of harmony and organisation of all the rest of one's nature' (*The Hound and the Falcon*, p. 45).

Even as she struggles to adhere to a single Catholic idiom in *The Hound and the Falcon*, White cannot entirely silence her tendencies to construct her identity in a psychoanalytic idiom, in part because she considered her analysis crucial in saving her from insanity:

> It was remarkably successful in removing the agonising obsessions and fears and making me capable of managing my life at least reasonably

tolerably [. . .] I can never be grateful enough either to the analyst himself or to Freud who laid the foundations of analysis. (*The Hound and
the Falcon*, p. 159)

In this interim text, as White moves from a psychoanalytic reading of
herself to a Catholic one, she plays down differences between the two
paradigms, drawing, for example, parallels between the 'true saint'
and the 'neurotic case': both articulate 'passion, madness and all the
emotional states', although for the former these are 'transcripts of
the spiritual life' and for the latter 'psycho-pathological' (*The Hound
and the Falcon*, p. 92). In her diary she perceptively observes that
'Both the Church and Freud are right about the profound importance of the sex instinct' (*Diary* 1, p. 176). Above all, White down-
plays the differences between Freud and religion. Freud appreciates
religion 'as the most important of human creations and activities',
White remarks, and his 'investigations into the actual workings of
human psychology [. . .] back up doctrines which seem to many to
be mere myths, such as the fall of man particularly, in the most astonishing way' (*The Hound and the Falcon*, p. 93). White even employs
psychoanalytic terms to address the Church's refusal to consider new
historical developments which have brought tenets of faith like the
Fall of Man into question: 'How can she cure us if she won't even
listen to our symptoms?' (*The Hound and the Falcon*, p. 140).

In claiming that Freud's 'investigations' back up the story of the
Fall of Man, White seems to link the Freudian unconscious, the
repository of instincts and aggression, to Original Sin, the doctrine
that all human beings are born with natures irrevocably flawed by
Adam's sin against God's commands. This doctrine holds that primitive man (old Adam) survives in every human being: all are born
weak, prone to ignorance, sin, and suffering; and they must struggle
to attain what Adam lost for mankind through his rebellion against
God, the Divine Gifts, living at one with God by living by His Will
rather than one's own. Although it is unclear what White had read
of Freud – or indeed, whether she had read any of his works on
religion at all – Freud's views do indeed accord with this reading of
human nature as prone to an instinctual aggression that, as civilization proceeds, must be curbed by submission to (ideally) an authoritative paternal authority. In *The Future of an Illusion*, for example,
Freud speaks of religion as an illusion, 'perhaps the most important

item in the psychical inventory of a civilization'.[60] And in *Moses and Monotheism*, Freud argues that the transformation of God into an abstraction, the 'mental labour of monotheism', paved the way for human achievements in mathematics, science, literature and law by encouraging abstract models of thought.[61] This abstract, albeit personified, model of God the Father enabled human beings to bring 'humane order to life'.[62]

But the Freudian unconscious and the doctrine of Original Sin differ in one key respect in White's formulations. Whereas Freud and his representative, the analyst, identify the symptom as indicative of the clash between instincts and superego, God the Father and his representative, the priest, identify the sin as indicative of human corruption and depravity. White often mentions her discomfort with the doctrine of the Atonement, which 'often seems to me an insult to God and man, a beastly legal profit-and-loss notion' (*The Hound and the Falcon*, p. 113) and she repeatedly expresses her preference for considering 'justice, honesty and kindness as human ideals instead of demanding divine sanctions for them' (*The Hound and the Falcon*, p. 112). Freud 'doesn't demand your assent to his theories', she writes, whereas '[t]he Church is dogmatic all right and asks you to believe her dogmas on pain of loss of salvation' (*The Hound and the Falcon*, p. 123). Structuring the self through the 'grammar' of Catholicism hence requires submission to a punitive paternal authority – an authority White constructs in the figure of her own father writ large.[63] White admits at the time of her return to the Church that 'God the Father was my great stumbling block' (*The Hound and the Falcon*, p. 102); and her descriptions of that stumbling block increasingly merge her own punitive and disapproving father with the spiritual one. Just as White 'was terrified that God would demand too much of me and I would fail' (*The Hound and the Falcon*, p. 49), so she remembers her father's demands as requiring her to be '*impossibly* good, in behaviour, in work, in everything' (*Diary* 2, p. 132). White draws a clear equation between her father – 'I felt that he only loved me when he was *pleased* with me. I was extremely afraid of his displeasure' – and God the Father – 'The way God is "put over" to me in the Christian religion is so *much* the idea of an omnipotent being who only loves you when you *please* him and is exceedingly angry with you when you don't and, if you are not careful, will punish you not only in this world but eternally in the next' (*Diary* 2, p. 159). This 'eternal, eternal, more and more insoluble problem and conflict' leads White to assert that 'much in Catholicism is *repellent* to me [. . .] most of all this insistence on sin, Christ's atonement, the angry Father who will condemn to hell those who are not "saved"' (*Diary* 2, p. 197).

The 'insistence on sin' in particular motivates White to examine her profound sense of guilt, which she always attributes to her father, whose disapproval she still feels, who still arouses a sense of guilt in her, and who 'had all the weight of religion behind him' (*Diary* 2, p. 203). But it is clear that White's feelings of guilt and depravity develop from depressed moods, in which White writes that she feels 'corrupt and poisoned right through' (*The Hound and the Falcon*, p. 112), the 'whole mind not only disintegrating but putrefying' (*The Hound and the Falcon*, p. 159). If in analysis White attributed guilt to unconscious conflicts, as a Catholic she finds herself tormented 'by the awful old fear that it is my fault if I can't see [the light of faith] . . . that I'm fundamentally perverted. This is a very bad state if I want to preserve the sanity I've built up with considerable labour and pain' (*The Hound and the Falcon*, p. 130). White identifies her 'Garden of Eden troubles' as her conflicted feelings about the doctrine of Original Sin, which assigns her sense of guilt to her innate human depravity (*Diary* 2, p. 201).[64] But White's personal version of the story of the Fall of Man is a revision in which Original Sin does not originate with Adam, but with Eve: 'It is a profound truth that makes Eve the *Channel* of the fall and the Church's defects may be due to her femaleness. A woman is more corruptible, I believe, than a man because of the slower rhythm of her life, as still water breeds scum. And haven't you often noticed, in men, that it is their female side that betrays and corrupts them? It is not for nothing that in no religion is God imagined as female' (*The Hound and the Falcon*, p. 86). In imagining Eve as the 'channel' of human corruption, White suggests an innate female depravity connected to female sexuality.[65] In a manic inflation of her own depravity some years later, White will record entries in which she tries to convince herself that she is not herself fallen Eve, the source of all human depravity: 'To be "NOT GUILTY" . . . doesn't mean I have a beautiful nature or am not liable at any moment to behave disgracefully. It simply means that I am not responsible for the Fall of Man [. . .] Somehow the unconscious has to accept the "NOT

GUILTY" verdict' (*Diary* 1, p. 216).[66] To accept that verdict would mean toppling her father from his pedestal: returning once again to the primal scene of paternal prohibition, White finds that 'since he pronounced me guilty, I must remain under sentence forever [. . .] I've gone on unconsciously trying to justify him all these years. Is that because a father can become such an idol, such a representative of God on earth, that the most painful things are more bearable than admitting he might be wrong? Because..*if one's father is fallible, there is no security anywhere*' (*Diary* 1, p. 216, emphasis added). The need to identify a principle of security returns White once again to the need to confirm an unshakeable foundation for coherence and identity.

The Virgin Mary is, of course, the corollary to fallen Eve, the conduit not of sin but of salvation. But White's versioning of the Holy Family is again a singular one that incorporates elements drawn from her own personal history. Hence, when White discusses the Holy Family, she imagines Joseph as a husband who has to step aside and allow his wife's impregnation by God the Father: 'I thought of this man, the support of the Holy Family yet always "below" Our Lord and Our Lady, unknown and holding back always from this beautiful girl he had married as a man and not as a saint' (*The Hound and the Falcon*, p. 66). White depicts the marriage of Joseph and Mary as a *mariage blanc*, her term for an unconsummated marriage. White's sense of Joseph as the husband who is no husband, who must allow the Father precedence, resonates with her own unconsummated marriages – marriages that left her father central in her psychic life and that left her *virgo intacta* after the first. White writes very little about Mary and even less about Jesus at this stage of her reconversion, but a remark about Mary seems telling: 'No rationalising can be as beautiful as the Virgin pregnant with God' (*The Hound and the Falcon*, p. 83). White cannot explain why she finds this image so appealing, but it anticipates the Ritual Rape Dream discussed in the introduction. In the same mood of manic inflation in which White tries to convince herself that she is not responsible for the Fall of Man, she transcribes a graphic account of undergoing 'the ritual of symbolic rape by my own father': she is carried into a church and laid naked on the altar, awaking at the moment of penetration.[67] A dream of reconciliation with her father, the dream also literalises the Incarnation of Christ, just as White had literalised the female castration complex in analysis. In composing an identity narrative in the Catholic idiom, then, White swings between the depressive pole of despair – she is fallen Eve and hence the channel of human depravity – and the manic pole of presumption – she is Virgin Mother and hence the channel of human redemption. White herself remarked her tendency to see herself as 'sub-human or super-human, never as just "human" and I would prefer to be called a devil to an ordinary human being' (*Diary* 1, p. 153). And just as White's entries on the female castration complex link her desire to engender a book/son with her father's loving approval to the denounced first novel and baby boy, both 'conceived in sin' and both aborted, so her dream of the Ritual Rape links her desire for his approval to the scene of writing: White has finally been forgiven for her Original Sin, the adolescent novel that revealed her depravity and that created a permanent barrier between them.[68]

One of White's rare poems, 'Sed Tantum Dic Verbo', written around the same time as the Ritual Rape Dream, similarly links paternal penetration to the engendering of writing in the context of the Incarnation: the speaker explicitly invites God to 'Plunge Thy divining-rod, the two-edged sword. / Strike to my source; cleave, one me with the Word'.[69] Here White echoes Luke 2: 35, a verse in which Simeon, having celebrated the birth of the Divine Saviour, cautions Mary about the sorrow and pain that lie ahead for her: 'And thine own heart a sword shall pierce that out of many hearts thoughts may be revealed'.[70] Standard Biblical commentary interprets this verse as a testimonial to the way in which 'our deepest wounding becomes the channel through which the most profound grace flows'[71]. Other allusions foreground the power of God's Word, which is sharper, quicker and more powerful than a two-edged sword (Hebrews 4: 12), and capable of healing the terminally ill (Matthew 8: 8; the congregation typically voices this line before receiving Communion in the Catholic service). White's poem again demonstrates her propensity to literalise symbolic abstractions, whereby the speaker longs for the Word to become Flesh. Sandra Chait observes that this transference of incestuous desire from father to God the Father entangles the profane and the sacred, thereby creating 'a religious discourse articulated on a sexual unconscious' and, simultaneously, a sexual discourse that 'revealed its yearnings as spiritual'.[72]

Master plots, part three: psychoanalysis and Catholicism

White's second analysis with Dorothy Kingsmill began in early summer of 1947, following a spring of what Chitty characterises as 'religious mania' (*Diary* 1, p. 184), and ended in December 1948 after the
completion of *The Lost Traveller*, White's first completed novel since
Frost in May. White began work with Kingsmill after the latter told
White she could 'release' her writing: 'Her reward, she said, would be
the birth of "the real Antonia"' (*Diary* 1, p. 213). But this analysis
was, by all accounts, extremely unorthodox and even unprofessional:
Kingsmill also analysed numerous members of White's circle at the
same time that she was seeing White; she moved into White's cottage,
which created later difficulties when she did not want to move out; and
she accepted no payment for her services, which created a power imbal-
ance between them (*Diary* 1, pp. 209–15). Indeed, Kingsmill rejected
the terms 'analyst' and 'patient', preferring to see their work together
as a partnership; and White in hindsight would view an 'impersonal'
professionalism between analyst and analysand as key to protecting
both.[73] Their work together consisted in the copious analysis of White's
dreams – White kept voluminous 'dream diaries' at this time – and in
Kingsmill's 'handing' White over to the Indian mystic Meher Baba.[74]

Diary entries suggest that White was highly unstable during these
years. Her 'religious mania' in the spring of 1947, when she was erotically involved with a woman who was herself unstable, affected her
daughter Susan, whose own illness began to emerge during this period.
In August 1947 White had a 'bad analytical crisis but D[orothy] was
. . . ill with a sort of nervous breakdown' that Kingsmill later attributed to dealing with White's 'shadow side' (*Diary* 1, pp. 214, 213),
a Jungian term for 'the primitive, uncontrolled, and animal part of
ourselves'[75]; White's mental state alternated 'between extreme nervous tension & jitters & complete lethargy'.[76] In January 1948 'an
extraordinary session' at White's cottage frightened both of them, in
which Kingsmill 'went so deep that I was babbling in a kind of trance'
(*Diary* 1, p. 214). White was 'terribly depressed' for several weeks
afterwards, and Hopkinson reports that her mother slept a great deal
as well as lying down 'in a peculiar state between sleeping and waking in the daytime'.[77] White was in a 'low physical state as well', with
'headaches, sore mouth, stomach upsets, and night fevers'.[78] White
nonetheless announced in February 1948 that Kingsmill had 'cured'

her (*Diary* 1, p. 194). She felt 'remarkably well during the early summer of '48', which may indicate mania or hypomania, but shortly 'had the severest of all crises, during which D[orothy] said she could do nothing but wait and warned the caretaker here that I might have an accident' (*Diary* 1, p. 214). In retrospect, White believed she had been 'in considerable danger' that summer:

> There were times when I really was not normal: I was in semi-cataleptic states and doing very peculiar things under the influence of Baba. I think what saved my sanity was Lyndall's coming here and my having to nurse her through tonsillitis. (*Diary* 1, p. 214)

Chitty notes that her mother 'looked awful' during this time: 'Her face was grey, her hair was dull, her body swollen. At times she felt like imitating Domina [White's cat] and jumping out of the window. And then she would be suddenly ecstatic. She felt "new centres coming alive".'[79]

Hopkinson suggests that Kingsmill's 'analysis' may have contributed to her mother's instability. White herself acknowledged that 'My own unsolved mystery is Baba . . . Should I have "contacted" him if it hadn't been for D.? . . . She certainly talked about him a good deal, quoted letters etc. And she did say she had asked him to "contact" me' (*Diary* 1, p. 210). After her February 'cure', White had 'become very conscious of Baba's presence', Hopkinson writes: 'Over the next months he often appeared in her dreams or had "mental conversations" with her as she lay in one of her drowsy states'.[80] Hopkinson felt that White was undergoing a religious crisis, brought on in part by writing about Catholicism in *The Lost Traveller*, but also by efforts to interpret Baba's messages and by increasing turmoil 'over whether Baba represented God or some figment of her imagination'.[81] By August, Hopkinson reports that White's conflicts about what faith meant resulted in nightmares, headaches, insomnia and daytime lethargy, all symptoms of a mixed episode. The situation came to a head when Hopkinson arrived home with tonsillitis: she found her mother 'lying on her back with her eyes open, staring at the ceiling', apparently in a 'semi-trance having a mental colloquy with Baba. He had been "telling" her that he was going to test her obedience to him' by having her eat a turd from the cat's litterbox.

> After a battle in her mind – was it the will of God or of the devil that she should do this? She had just decided she must fight down disgust and force herself to get up and perform this act, when I had burst into her room and flung myself on her mercy.[82]

Kingsmill's work with White on dream analysis was more productive, based on Jungian principles that differ considerably from the more orthodox Freudian ones that framed White's first analysis. For Freud, the dream develops from unconscious conflict and the repression of forbidden, often libidinal and lawless, wishes; it is disguised by the operations of the unconscious and, through the techniques of free association and analytical interpretation, the analyst and analysand together uncover the latent content that lies concealed behind the manifest content. Often the dream relates to the past, particularly to childhood and sexual development, and the task of analysis is to identify the repressed material that informs the analysand's conflict. For Jung, on the other hand, the dream develops as a form of compensation: it draws attention to psychic imbalances, to parts of the psyche that have been ignored and that need to be brought into consciousness and integrated into the personality. The dream does not disguise meaning but rather expresses it: it has a direct relationship to the dreamer's present circumstances, and 'presents itself as an actuality which becomes the more strikingly actual the more we try to repress it'.[83] Jung denounces the Freudian concept of the '"infantile-perverse-criminal" unconscious' that makes a 'dangerous monster out of the unconscious, that really very natural thing'.[84] The unconscious is not a 'demonic monster', he writes, although it does become dangerous

> when we practise repressions. But as soon as the patient begins to assimilate the contents that were previously unconscious, the danger from the side of the unconscious diminishes. As the process of assimilation goes on, it puts an end to the dissociation of the personality and to the anxiety that attends and inspires the separation of the two realms of the psyche.[85]

Jung's model of the unconscious encompasses both a 'personal unconscious' – a repository of forgotten or repressed memories and conflicts – and a 'collective unconscious' – an inborn or inherited repository of archetypes and mythic patterns that have developed over the course of human history. Significant dreams develop when the images in the personal unconscious become attached to archetypes in the collective unconscious such as the anima, the animus and the shadow. Jung dismisses the 'hard and fast sexual "symbols"' of the Freudian school, instead conceptualising the symbol as 'the announcement of something unknown, hard to recognise and not to be fully determined'.[86] Whereas Freudian 'so-called phallic symbols' represent 'the *membrum virile* and nothing else', for example, in other cultures the phallus as ritualistic symbol is not simply the penis but

> the creative *mana*, the power of healing and fertility [. . .] Its equivalents in mythology and in dreams are the bull, the ass, the pomegranate, the *yoni*, the he-goat, the lightning, the horse's hoof, the dance, the magical cohabitation in the furrow, and the menstrual fluid, to mention only a few of many. That which underlies all of these images – and sexuality itself – is an archetypal content that is hard to grasp.[87]

The sheer volume of dreams White produced during this 'analysis' – up to thirty pages a week in special notebooks that also contained drawings by White in which 'D. finds all sorts of clues'[88] – speaks to Jung's belief that a single dream typically did not provide enough information about the psychic compensation it expressed. Instead:

> [a] series of dreams makes a more satisfactory basis for interpretation than a single dream, for the theme which the unconscious is presenting becomes clearer, the important images are underlined by repetition, and mistakes in interpretation are corrected by the next dream.[89]

Jung thus encouraged analysands to record their dreams carefully, and even to illustrate them:

> It is better to approach the work naïvely, for one is less likely to falsify the picture. The expressions of the unconscious are often most primitive, and their power is lost if there is too great an attempt to fit them into aesthetic concepts.[90]

The work of recording dreams and representing them in other media enables the analysand to develop independence in understanding the unconscious:

> He makes real the fantasies that are activating him, and so he knows better what they are. Even the mere painting of a picture can have an effect, curing a wretched mood, or bringing a release of tension [. . .] dreams become, not only sources of information, but also of creative power.[91]

By giving 'form to his inner life', the analysand discovers 'himself in a new sense, for his ego now appears as an object actuated by the life forces within':

> [Such discoveries] shift the centre of gravity of the personality [. . .] as though the ego were the earth, and it suddenly discovered that the sun (or the self) was the centre of the planetary orbits and of the earth's orbit as well.[92]

Jungian analysis aims, then, to challenge the analysand's overvaluation of rationality, will and consciousness and to establish trust and self-confidence in 'the depths of our own psychic life'.[93]

This aspect of Kingsmill's analysis seems to have had a salutary effect on White, for not only did she complete *The Lost Traveller* by the end of 1948 but, in a burst of productivity, she completed *The Sugar House* and *Beyond the Glass* over the next several years as well. It is finally unclear, however, whether this analysis freed White's ability to write – and publish – fiction, and if it did, how it did so. It is possible that the emphasis on giving voice to dreams did indeed have the effect Jung claimed it did of releasing the imagination: White credited Kingsmill with helping her see her relation to her mother (*Diary* 1, p. 214), and in her last analysis White would consider whether her 'writing side' really came from her 'imaginative, intuitive' mother, connecting her 'jam on writing' to 'criticising too soon' and a terror 'of getting carried away. Because of my mother's "cuckoo" side, which is in me too. I am *afraid to let go*' (*Diary* 2, p. 159). Kingsmill not only gave analytic 'permission' for White 'to let go' but she also provided a non-judgemental space in which White felt total acceptance. 'I find – and this is something I have never found with any human being – that there does not seem to be any thought or experience, or even crazy speculation, that I have which does not find some response in you', White wrote to Kingsmill in a letter.[94] Hence, when the two fell out over a disagreement about White's cottage, Kingsmill seriously undermined White's confidence by telling her she was '"depraved", and she must "withdraw from me and my situation"' (*Diary* 1, p. 217). Entries over the next several years attest to White's need for reinforcement from a trusted other who could inspire her with confidence in herself:

If someone can give me confidence I can sometimes do better than I thought possible [. . .] I am always looking for someone I can trust completely. Over and over again I think I have found this, only to be let down. Obviously – and for good reason. I don't trust myself. (*Diary* 1, p. 227)

The holistic focus of this analysis may also have been salutary. In contrast to the biological determinism that structured White's analysis with Carroll, the Jungian focus on integrating and balancing contradictory and incompatible elements in the psyche gave White a vocabulary for discussing her 'masculine' and 'feminine' traits that did not tie them to normative roles or to biological sex. In a 1951 discussion with Edward Thornton, another amateur Jungian analyst, White identifies her 'own trouble' as 'obviously concerned with this animus, my male side', which Thornton defines as 'the unconscious male side of women which can become diabolical' (*Diary* 1, p. 224). While the Jungian concepts of 'animus' and 'anima' are indubitably based on gender stereotypes – masculine thought versus feminine emotion and the like – they enabled White to recast her relationship to her father in terms of fantasy and projection rather than sexual desire and biological destiny. According to Jung, a woman's animus develops from inherited images of masculinity in the collective unconscious, her own experiences of masculinity garnered from her contact with the men in her life, and 'the latent masculine principle in herself'.[95] The father is the source and embodiment of the 'animus image', and 'this combination seems to exercise a profound and lasting fascination over her mind, so that instead of thinking and acting for herself she continually quotes father and does things in father's way, even late into life'.[96] In addition, Jung identifies as a 'peculiarity' of the animus 'its tendency to be expressed as a group of men':

The animus is rather like an assembly of fathers or dignitaries of some kind who lay down incontestable, 'rational', *ex cathedra* judgements [. . .] This critical judgment is sometimes turned on the woman herself as an over-active conscience, giving her feelings of inferiority and stifling initiative.[97]

Given White's conflation of her father with a punitive God the Father, this understanding of the animus may have been helpful.

When personified in dreams, archetypes such as the animus 'present an opportunity to understand something of what has hitherto been unconscious'.[98] Other people 'can be seen as they are, instead of figures on whom we have draped our fancies and endowed with every possible and impossible characteristic, i.e. on whom we have projected ourselves'.[99] Hence White can admit, using Jungian terminology, that her father had never meant to become the terrifying imago and psychic obstacle he had become in her mind.[100]

This second analysis also allowed White to reconcile psychoanalysis and Catholicism, a reconciliation White brought to the design of *The Lost Traveller*, which she was in the process of writing. Jung specifically defines neurosis as a spiritual crisis that neither traditional religion nor classic Freudian psychoanalysis can address, the former because 'our religious truths have somehow or other grown empty', the latter because it 'holds the position that the basic problem is that of repressed sexuality, and that philosophical or religious doubts only mask the true state of affairs'.[101] Jung, by contrast, sees the causes of a neurosis as a combination of present and past conditions: 'A man is not tubercular because he was infected twenty years ago with bacilli but because foci of infection are still active today. The questions when and how the infection took place are quite irrelevant to his present condition.'[102] Jung posits that neurosis is 'an inner cleavage – the state of being at war with oneself [. . .] the intuition or the knowledge that they consist of two persons in opposition to one another. The conflict may be between the sensual and the spiritual man, or between the ego and the shadow [. . .] A neurosis is a dissociation of personality.'[103] The psychotherapist takes on the role of the priest in order to convert the 'destructive forces' into 'healing forces' by enabling the archetypes of the collective unconscious 'to come to independent life and serve as spiritual guides for the personality'.[104] This transformation occurs when themes appear in dreams or fantasies whose source springs from psychic depths unknown to the analysand:

> This spontaneous activity of the psyche often becomes so intense that visionary pictures are seen or inner voices heard [. . .] From this point forward a light shines through his confusion; he can reconcile himself with the warfare within and so come to bridge the morbid split in his nature upon a higher level.[105]

In contrast to Freud, then, Jung viewed the healing of psychic conflict as a religious problem.[106] Indeed, he faults Freud for limiting psycho-analysis to 'the task of making conscious the shadow-side and the evil within us', thus bringing back into action 'the civil war that was latent' but then abandoning the analysand to deal with that war as best s/he could.[107] 'Freud has unfortunately overlooked the fact that man has never yet been able single-handed to hold his own against the powers of darkness – that is, of the unconscious', Jung comments. 'Man has always stood in need of the spiritual help which each individual's own religion held out to him. The opening up of the unconscious always means the outbreak of intense spiritual suffering.'[108] Although Jung goes on to criticise traditional religion and clergy for failing to respond to modern spiritual crises, he does perceive Catholicism as succeeding more fully than Protestantism in doing so:

> It is quite clear to me that, in its healing effects, no creed is as closely akin to psychoanalysis as Catholicism. The symbols of the Catholic liturgy offer the unconscious such a wealth of possibilities for expres-sion that they act as an incomparable diet for the psyche.[109]

Jung's sense of analysis as effecting a spiritual transformation sounds very similar to the concept of Sanctifying Grace, and White may have explored this connection through her close friendship with the Dominican priest Victor White, who was working directly with Jung at this time.[110] Father Victor had immersed himself in Jung's writings after suffering an emotional breakdown and spiritual crisis in 1939, and the two men struck up a working correspondence after the war: Father Victor had embarked on an 'ambitious bridge-building proj-ect' to bring Jungian analysis and Catholicism together as a means of reaching those in spiritual crisis for whom the Church no longer held meaning, while Jung found in Father White 'a living dictionary of Catholic tradition' from whom he hoped to learn the intricacies of Catholic symbolism.[111] In his letters to Jung, Father Victor describes his use of Jung's psychology both in the classroom and in his pastoral counselling; he also expresses concern that he is practising a form of analysis.[112] Jung and Father Victor also discussed George Tyrell in their letters: they agreed that the spiritual transformation Jung ascribed to the activation of archetypes in the collective unconscious closely resembled ideas Tyrell had formulated earlier in the century, when he had been declared a heretic and excommunicated.[113] White had discovered Tyrell's writings through her correspondence with 'Peter' when she reconverted to Catholicism, and Father Victor's appreciation of Tyrell constitutes another potential point of intellectual commonality between the two.

Even after White ended analysis with Kingsmill in 1948, then, Father Victor may have been someone with whom she continued to explore Jungian ideas. She records a discussion between them in 1949, for example, in which Father Victor describes psyche and soul as indistinguishable (*Diary* 1, p. 212). Jungian ideas clearly reshaped White's attitude towards her first analysis, for she observes that Carroll turned her from a Catholic and pagan into a Protestant and that Freudian thinking goes wrong by conditioning analysands to a world of material success.[114] Following the debacle of her analysis with Kingsmill, White describes how each analysis has helped her but how each has also driven her deeper into the Church in a reaction against the analyst's beliefs.[115] The Church is sane and concrete by comparison with analysis, she comments, and Christ the only safe place for a transference.[116] And, in a state of emotional confusion following her break with Kingsmill, White describes how she holds on to Our Lady and St Thomas Aquinas.[117] This reconciliation of analysis and Catholicism, effected throughout the late 1940s and early 1950s, informs the three novels completed during this period, and I take up this subject in the next chapter.

White's last analysis in the mid-1960s was influenced by yet another set of psychoanalytic paradigms. Through Galway, the NHS doctor who took White on in a kind of informal analysis in 1965, White learnt about Kleinian theories of creativity, although she never mentions Klein explicitly and apparently did not know that Klein's theorisations shaped Galway's interpretations. Once again, White had entered analysis because of intensifying symptoms of illness and an inability to make progress with her writing: in late February 1965 she describes 'familiar' states of mind in which she feels 'stale, listless, poisoned all through' (*Diary* 2, p. 120). Although at times energetic, instead of having 'tried to get on with the book [Clara IV]', she has had an 'orgy – an expensive one too – of getting the flat improved [. . .] It's the old thing – this compulsive spending that I seem unable to control' (*Diary* 2, p. 120). At the suggestion of Malcolm Muggeridge, White began writing her autobiography later that spring, but by summer she was rereading her old notebooks and recording that she had 'made

NO progress in all these 25 years since my return [to the Church]' (*Diary* 2, p. 129). Other entries record despair, exhaustion and a sense of paralysis. By the time she sought treatment for swollen eyes in late September 1965, she had reached a point where she could not read or write; she also records her sense of loneliness and her fear that her money is running out.[118]

Galway seems to have recognised White as bipolar for, in treating her with antidepressants, he monitored her closely for signs of excitement in an effort to avoid White's getting into 'an excited manic state' (*Diary* 2, p. 136); he thinks it better for her to be 'depressed than euphoric', for example, although ideally she would be neither (*Diary* 2, p. 140).[119] At the same time, Galway, like White's other analysts, suggested that she was 'split', although Galway interprets this split from a perspective that is distinctly Kleinian: 'He says there is a whole area of myself that has got split off and which I think of as bad, destructive terrifying etc. . . . he thinks the trouble goes very far back indeed, to pre-conscious stage, actually babyhood', White reports (*Diary* 2, p. 132). Believing that Galway's views represent 'an established axiom, at any rate in the Freudian school', White admits that she finds 'hard to swallow in psycho-analytical theory [. . .] the idea that the baby has violent destructive phantasies about its parents [. . .] since it has no verbal thoughts' (*Diary* 2, p. 139). In that entry, White also records that she is rereading Hanna Segal's 'A Psychoanalytic Approach to Aesthetics', a classic elaboration of Melanie Klein's theorisation of creativity as developing out of the need to make reparation to the mother for destructive, sadistic phantasies of attacking her in phantasy; White even copies sections of Segal's essay into her diary.[120] In brief, Segal argues that:

> [art is] really a re-creation of a once loved and once whole, but now lost and ruined object, a ruined internal world and self. It is when the world within us is destroyed, when it is dead and loveless, when our loved ones are in fragments and we ourselves in helpless despair – it is then we must recreate our world anew, reassemble the pieces, infuse life into dead fragments, re-create life.[121]

The 'inability to acknowledge and overcome depressive anxiety must lead to inhibitions in artistic expression', Segal adds.[122]

White's unpublished diary indicates that she discussed with Galway the difference between depression as a mood and the 'depressive position', Klein's term for the guilt and depressive despair that develops from the phantasied destruction of internalised objects: the infant is 'beset with terrifying anxieties involving the containment of aggression' and, in retreat from them, finds in idealisation 'a refuge from persecutory anxiety and murderous rage' and in grandiosity a '"manic" defense against the depressive anxiety inherent in feeling small, helpless, and abjectly dependent upon another'.[123] Galway thought White's fear of her aggression and rage played a role in her depression and inhibited her creativity:[124] until she could allow destructive phantasies expression and restore the destroyed internal objects as an act of reparation, writing would remain impossible and she herself would remain depressed and guilty.[125] Following Klein, he told White that she had a tendency to sentimentalise ('idealise') her internalised objects to render them acceptable to herself and to deny her own powers of destruction. Therefore her book had 'gone dead': she had cut off her destructive power because, on the one hand, she felt it corrupt and dangerous, both to others and to herself, and because, on the other, she feared that if she gave way to accessing this area of herself she would succumb to its fascination and get carried away in insanity.[126] White ponders Galway's interpretations and Segal's essay for several months, wondering if insanity, in which everything is expressed in images that seem more real than reality, is the same state as infantile phantasy.[127] She also ponders the role of depression and mourning in creative work, noting that if they are not fully experienced the work remains superficial.[128] Finally, she considers her relationship to her dead parents, noting that she did mourn her mother when she died, but not her father.[129] In Kleinian theory, significantly, the failure to mourn results in depressive illness, paranoia and/or mania.[130] Klein observes that those who fail to experience mourning 'may escape from an outbreak of manic-depressive illness or paranoia only by a severe restriction of their emotional life which impoverishes their whole personality'.[131] Both the manic-depressive and the person who cannot mourn 'have been unable in early childhood to establish their internal "good" objects and to feel secure in their inner world'.[132]

A poignant passage about her father in her unfinished autobiography suggests White's reworking of these analytic paradigms. Recalling a blissful outing with her father when she was four, when the two gorged themselves on cream cakes, White imagines herself from a child's perspective, wanting to store up generative memories of her father and feed herself with them when 'life was grey and my father severe':

> I had not had time to take in all the happiness of the afternoon any more than I had had room inside me to take in all the cream cakes I had been offered. How delightful it would be if I could shut away this lovable, approachable Daddy somewhere inside me so that he would be there whenever I wanted him. When he was cross and Olympianly aloof, all I would have to do would be to open this secret cupboard inside me and get him out, as I got my favourite toys out of the toy cupboard. And in another cupboard inside me, I would store all the Appenrodt cream pastries to which I had been legally entitled but had not been able to eat at the time and get them out when I was hungry and there was nothing for tea at home but thick bread and butter and seed cake. ('Autobiography', p. 276)

This passage concludes a chapter in which White's father had deprived her of a half-sovereign given to her by one of his pupils, leaving her with a 'bitter sense of injustice', the seeds of a 'money complex', and a conviction that the more she wanted something the more unlikely it would be for her to get it ('Autobiography', p. 270). It also follows several chapters in which White depicts the process by which she came to fear her father's disapproval, memorialised most vividly in a scene in which she scribbled on the dining-room walls and he threatened to beat her on her exposed bottom. White here imagines – from a perspective seventy-two years later – a 'lovable, approachable Daddy', an internalised 'good object' whose restoration will alleviate her anxiety, guilt and inhibitions. Characteristically, she transforms the Kleinian 'good mother' into a 'good father'.

Initially, Galway's treatment – a combination of antidepressants and talk therapy – had positive results: White notes that the antidepressants have had a calming effect and that she has been able to work productively on her autobiography. But soon depression returned, with its attendant inertia and paralysis; despite changing her drug in November 1965 the depression did not lift, and in January 1966 Galway referred her to Philippe Ployé.[133] White began treatment with Ployé the following month and continued until February 1969, when Ployé discontinued their sessions together because his in-patient workload had become too onerous for him to continue seeing White on an out-patient basis (*Diary* 2, p. 203). Like Galway, Ployé employed a Kleinian approach to analysis, although Ployé's own theoretical interests centred on how prenatal experience affected both postnatal life and the encounter between analyst and analysand. At their first meeting, Ployé told White he planned to focus on the mother rather than the father, as 'analysis had probably coped with that', and that he thought 'trouble may have started pre-natally' (*Diary* 2, p. 142). A dream of White's, in which she descended into a swimming bath containing a submarine and refrained from stepping on a stopcock that could potentially cut off the air supply to the people inside, elicited from Ployé the interpretation that White had experienced 'a pre-natal trauma that at some time in the womb the supply to the foetus through the umbilical cord had been cut off – "a matter of life and death" he said, which would cause acute anxiety' (*Diary* 2, p. 183). He also suggested that White's imaginative side came from her mother (*Diary* 2, p. 159), and eventually White came to see the conflict between art and religion as one that reflected her own internal conflict between mother and father.[134] Overall, however, while White liked Ployé and found him both intelligent and kind, she struggled with crippling depression throughout the years of her work with him; shortly before their sessions came to an end and in despair over her writing, she acknowledged that 'Ployé seems unable to help at all' (*Diary* 2, p. 195).

These last years of analysis also coincided with a return of White's 'Garden of Eden' troubles. These came to centre on the question of whether the story of Adam and Eve and the expulsion from the Garden represented literal or metaphorical truth: if the story were not true, then the entire edifice of Catholic dogma, built upon the concept of Original Sin and the crucifixion as Christ's sacrifice of Himself to the Father as an act of redemption for fallen humanity, crumbled for White.[135] The impetus for White's ruminations came from an article in a Catholic periodical in which the author pointed out that the idea of inherited sin does not occur in the Gospels, and yet Catholic theology is built entirely on that idea; further, the author argues that evolutionary theory calls into question the story of Adam and Eve and the doctrine of Original Sin.[136] White's worry over this issue speaks to her worry about the changes in the Church: she had returned to the Church in part as a way of structuring her psychic incoherence, and thus ideas that brought its structural stability into question were deeply troubling for her. White's worry over this issue, which confused some priests to whom she spoke, also makes sense in the context of her pervasive feelings of guilt, an outgrowth of her almost constant state of depression.

White found no consolation or sense of stability in either analysis or religion in these last decades. Her diary of this period makes for bleak reading: in entry after entry, White records her states of inertia and paralysis, her pervasive sense of guilt and inner corruption, her inability to think or concentrate, her belief that her life has been a failure. Many entries simply catalogue her faults and shortcomings. And in entry after entry, White returns to the 'themes' that have dominated her life: her conflicts about religion, her father, her writing, herself. When Ployé broke off his treatment, White reported that 'He made it obvious that he didn't feel that the treatment was finished – when I said "It is like an unfinished story" he agreed' (*Diary* 2, p. 203). The similarly unfinished fictional story of self is the subject of the next chapter.

Chapter 4

An Unfinished Story: White's Fictions of the Self

White's four published novels, taken together, trace the fractured development of a would-be woman writer from childhood to early adulthood. Fractures characterise the composition and publication history of the four novels as well as the protagonist's development: *Frost in May* took more than fifteen years for White to complete and *The Lost Traveller* took seventeen more; the next two instalments followed in quick succession, but then White found herself unable to continue, thwarted by the crippling writer's block that made it impossible for her to construct a coherent account of her protagonist's movement into adulthood and artistry. Thus the published sequence constitutes a narrative of failed artistic development, a narrative that the title of the first novel in the series, *Frost in May*, seems to predict. Given that the novels are strongly autobiographical, it is not surprising that the fractures that seam the series have typically been glossed over or ignored altogether, for the scaffolding of White's own life story holds them together. Indeed, in rereading *Frost in May* in 1962, White remarked that 'all the themes of my life are there – my father and religion' (*Diary* 2, p. 67); those themes, amplified and elaborated, carry over into the succeeding novels and thereby impose considerable coherence on the storyline. As Jeanne Flood observes, '*Frost in May* is to the Batchelor novels what an overture is to an opera, for the later novels work out themes announced but not developed in the first novel'.[1] The fractures that characterise both composition and publication history, however, constitute important sites that reveal the evolution of White's identity narratives and the subsequent changes in her fictional conceptualisations of illness,

Catholicism and the father-daughter relationship as well as family dynamics more generally. This chapter focuses on the ways in which White's fictions record that evolution and those changes. It focuses on the ways in which the plot of *The Lost Traveller* relies on Catholic and psychoanalytic frames to shape the representation of family dynamics. It then focuses on the ways in which White's dominant storyline in *The Sugar House* and *Beyond the Glass* functions as a palimpsest that only partially overwrites a narrative of the onset of manic-depressive illness, a narrative that has hitherto gone unremarked, concealed by the explicit identification of the father and the Catholic Church as the agents responsible for the daughter's inability to progress into adulthood and artistry.

That the fractures in the sequence have been unremarked is not surprising. When Virago reissued the three novels that succeeded *Frost in May*, they appeared with an influential introduction based on an interview publisher Carmen Callil conducted with White. That introduction stressed the continuity of the sequence, despite the fact that White flagged the differences as significant. White explained that she changed her protagonist's name from Nanda Grey to Clara Batchelor because 'I wanted *The Lost Traveller* to be a *real* novel – *Frost in May* was so much my own life. So I changed her name'.[2] Callil continues, 'In every other respect this novel begins where *Frost in May* ends',[3] a view most commentators on White have accepted with little question,[4] and in fact White herself stated in the same interview, 'Of course Clara is a continuation of Nanda'.[5] But when White began writing *The Lost Traveller* in the 1930s she had not planned to continue the story of *Frost in May*'s protagonist. Instead, White's diary in the 1930s reveals her struggle to move away from the autobiographical dimensions of her fiction writing, in part because she believed that her inability to 'invent' (her term) was a sign of her limited artistic talent and that less reliance on her life story as scaffolding for her fiction would be a sign of her return to psychological health.[6] As a result, *The Lost Traveller* is the 'most inventive' of White's novels, one that shifts between the protagonist's perspective and that of her parents, and that diverges in several significant ways both from biographical fact and from the plot of *Frost in May*.[7] Nor did White initially plan to write more instalments of Nanda/Clara's life story during the composition of *The Lost Traveller*. White explained that when she finished the latter she 'thought of it as just being one book, and then suddenly I felt I wanted to write another one about my first marriage'.[8] In that instalment and the next, White returned the narrative perspective to Clara, finding that perceiving relationships 'through the eyes of one person, as in *Frost in May* – I think that suited me much better'.[9] In returning to Clara's perspective in the final two novels, White also adhered more closely to the identity narratives she had consolidated through psychoanalysis and Catholicism. In constructing the final two novels, White deliberately imposed more coherence on the sequence through narrative flashbacks and sustained patterns of imagery.

The compositional history of the quartet, then, is not quite as straightforward as Callil suggests. *The Lost Traveller* marks a transitional moment in White's quartet, shifting the locus of Clara's difficulties from Catholicism to the family, a shift indicated by White's working title for the novel, *Family Circle*.[10] The alteration of the protagonist's name underscores that shift: the name 'Nanda' references Henry James' protagonist in *The Awkward Age* (*The Hound and the Falcon*, p. 37), whereas 'Nanda became Clara because my father had a great passion for Meredith and a particular passion for Clara Middleton (heroine of *The Egoist*)'.[11] In *The Awkward Age*, Nanda rejects her mother's irresponsible and morally corrupt social circle and chooses to become a surrogate daughter to Mr Longdon, who wants to protect Nanda from her mother's corrupting influence and see her safely into marriage. In *Frost in May*, Nanda similarly perceives her mother as frivolous and irresponsible; her embrace of Catholicism functions in part as a repudiation of her mother's values and her identification with her father's. In *The Lost Traveller*, by contrast, White presents a far more complicated picture of family dynamics, in which the father's erotic and narcissistic investment in his daughter complicates her growth to adulthood. At the same time, White presents a much more sympathetic portrait of Isabel, Clara's mother, who, although she retains the childish and frivolous traits of her earlier incarnation in *Frost in May*, now possesses an attractive spontaneity in emotion and behaviour as well as genuine compassion and love for her daughter. Uncritical and accepting of Clara in a way that Claude, Clara's father, never is, Isabel nonetheless struggles with her awareness that Claude's opinions and actions carry far more weight with her daughter than do her own. *The Lost Traveller* and the subsequent two instalments trace Clara's growing appreciation of her mother's emotional support, but they also show that this late flowering of the mother–daughter relationship does little to change powerful, long-established family dynamics.

White's decision to return to the fictionalising of her own life in the third instalment shifted the focus from family dynamics to mental illness, for White described the writing of *The Sugar House* as an opportunity to work through the period leading up to her first serious breakdown:

> What I have got to face and interpret now is all that queer, horrid Chelsea time leading up to the asylum – a time which seems particularly unreal and fantastic [. . .] of course, I am in a much better position to understand it now: at the time I had not the least idea what it was all about. (*Diary* 1, p. 235)

She completed this instalment and the next with unusual rapidity, as if 'facing and interpreting' the 'queer, horrid Chelsea time' and giving expression to what had seemed 'unreal' and 'fantastic' released her from the grip of experiences that had by this point haunted her for thirty years. Her belief that she was in a better position to understand the period that led up to her breakdown suggests furthermore that White now viewed it through the dual lenses of psychoanalysis and Catholicism. Indeed, so successful was White in conceptualising Clara's psychic distress as a tangle of Catholic and oedipal conflicts that most interpretations of the series determine that the father's incestuous desires, informed by patriarchal authority and buttressed by the authority of God the Father and the Catholic Church, created unbearable conflicts about writing and sexuality that eventually drove both protagonist and author psychotically insane.[12]

As compelling and artistically crafted as that explanation is, it rationalises what White also conveys in her final two instalments of Clara's story, the unmistakable onset of manic-depressive illness, beginning with a severe episode of depression in the second half of *The Sugar House* and rapidly building up to a psychotic and prolonged manic episode in *Beyond the Glass*. Further complicating White's portrayal of manic depression is her (mis)understanding of schizophrenia. In conceptualising Clara's psychic distress, White portrays a process by which Clara's vexed relationship to her father creates a split in her psyche. In order to conform to her father's expectations and stave off his anger and disapproval, she adopts a false and outwardly compliant mask, behind which her anxieties about her worth as a woman and writer seethe without expression. White conveys this splitting through a complex patterning of mirrors, glass and windows, imagery then associated with schizophrenia that speaks to Clara's sense of nonexistence, invisibility and estrangement.

Frost in May: an overview of the themes

Thematically, White's sequence coalesces around a set of related conflicts, all of which develop from the protagonist's vexed relationship with her father and with the Catholic Church.[13] *Frost in May* inaugurates this web of conflicts, opening with nine-year-old Nanda Grey in transit to the Convent of the Five Wounds, a Roman Catholic girl's school outside Lippington Village on the outskirts of London. A conversation between her father and an Irishwoman who is also a passenger in the omnibus reveals that Nanda is a recent convert to Catholicism, having followed in her father's footsteps only a year earlier. This conversation also sets the groundwork for what will become dominant leitmotifs, the sacrifice of the daughter's sexuality to the father and conversion as a form of coercion.[14] By suggesting that Nanda may have a vocation and become a nun later on, the Irishwoman makes this link explicit: 'And wouldn't it be a beautiful thing now if she was to offer her life to God as a thanksgiving for the great blessing of your own conversion, sir?' (*Frost in May*, p. 15). Notably, Nanda's father is as pleased with the idea as Nanda is dismayed, even though 'she had absorbed enough of the Catholic point of view to see how very appropriate such a sacrifice would be' (*Frost in May*, p. 15). Already at nine Nanda is anxious to please by conforming to others' expectations; she 'was one of those children who cannot help behaving well' (*Frost in May*, p. 17). This habit of conformity masks an internal core of rebellion that becomes ever more insistent as Nanda grows older and as she increasingly struggles to preserve a sense of autonomy. Indeed, the nuns, expert in surveillance tactics, deliberately set out to shatter this autonomous core, which in their view evidences a potentially dangerous propensity to set up her own 'conceited little judgement against the wisdom of the Church, which is the wisdom of God himself' (*Frost in May*, p. 49). As Mother Francis observes, '"The trouble with your faults is that they don't show. You're obstinate, you're independent, and if a child of nine can be said to have spiritual pride, spiritual pride is your ruling vice"' (*Frost in May*, p. 49). Nanda finds herself 'growing a hard little protective shell' in response to these assaults on her sense of self (*Frost in May*, p. 49).

From this foundational conflict between autonomy and (patriarchal) authority springs a number of related conflicts. First, Nanda never feels that she really belongs at the convent, for many of the other students come from long-established Catholic and aristocratic families and move in the highest circles of European diplomacy. Nanda is hence at a double disadvantage. As a recent convert, she bears an anxious relationship to doctrine, whereas her schoolmates take their faith for granted as an inherent aspect of their lives: Catholicism, her friend Léonie tells her, is in the blood, a nationality, not a religion (*Frost in May*, p. 122). But Nanda does not feel as if she belongs to the world outside the convent either, and in the succeeding volumes Clara repeatedly experiences herself as an outsider.[15] Second, the Catholic codes of female chastity and purity equate ignorance with innocence. Nanda vaguely understands the importance of her 'mysterious possession. . .her Purity', but she does not know what it is (*Frost in May*, p. 68). This ignorance informs the disaster that befalls Nanda at the novel's conclusion, for any reference to sexuality, no matter how inadvertent or innocent, is taken as a sign of innate depravity and impurity. In the succeeding volumes, this sense of innate depravity and guilt infuses not only sexuality but also writing and other forms of self-expression. Third, this repressive code of purity requires the suppression of all sensual pleasure. The girls are constantly encouraged to mortify their senses through, for example, eating food that disgusts them (*Frost in May*, pp. 27, 62). The convent teaching holds that self-denial and mortification should be a source of pleasure, and sensual pleasure – in one's own body, in the bodies of others, in the natural world and particularly in literature – becomes deeply suspect.[16] Hence a divide opens up between the demands and delights of artistry and the mortification of the senses required by Catholicism.

This repression of sensual pleasure has a profound effect on Nanda and seeds the ground for her eventual rebellion. Nanda explicitly wonders why God has made the world so attractive if everything in it is a potential source of sinful sensual pleasure, and her own passionate responses, particularly to literature and music, form a stark contrast to her lukewarm responses to religious experiences. Nanda is well aware of the fact that she ought to respond more passionately to the latter. At her First Communion, which she has repeatedly been told is supposed to be the happiest day and greatest moment of her life, Nanda feels 'numb and stupid' and compares herself unfavourably to the other girls, who look 'gay or recollected or content' or even, in one girl's case, ecstatic and 'dazed with happiness' (*Frost in May*, pp. 83–5):

> With all her efforts, all her devotion, there was something wrong with her. Perhaps a convert could never ring quite true. Perhaps real Catholics were right always to mistrust and despise them a little. For weeks she had been preparing herself, laying stick on stick and coal on coal, and now, at the supreme moment, she had not caught fire. Her First Communion was a failure. (*Frost in May*, pp. 84–5)

By contrast, reading a Francis Thompson poem fills her with rapture and excitement; Nanda feels 'intoxicated by the mere rush of words': 'Something was happening to her, something that had not happened when she made her First Communion [. . .] This new feeling, whatever it was, had nothing to do with God' (*Frost in May*, pp. 103–4). As Nanda moves into adolescence, she tries dutifully to persuade herself 'that her love of beauty was connected to God', but 'some small, clear irritating voice assured her that it was an independent growth', and she acknowledges that 'only very rarely and by extreme concentration could she ever obtain from any religious exercise the pure delight that poetry or music aroused without the least effort on her part' (*Frost in May*, p. 157). She realises that the Saints' feelings about God parallel her own 'extreme delight' when she listens to her friends reading poetry or singing (*Frost in May*, p. 158). This awareness highlights her sense of difference and exclusion from 'cradle Catholics' and also heightens her guilty conviction of her perversity.

The split that her education opens up between art and religion eventually finds expression in Nanda's own character, for the 'small, clear irritating voice' emanates from her developing sense of autonomy, which from the beginning of the novel she has had to protect from the nuns' vigorous and relentless character assaults. When a good-natured but dim-witted student is expelled for the irreverent artistic act of drawing caricatures of the nuns, a 'hot sense of injustice' impels Nanda to challenge the Mistress of Discipline and to condemn the nuns as uncharitable (*Frost in May*, pp. 154–5). This incident becomes a turning point, leaving a 'definite mark' on Nanda:

'A small core of rebelliousness which had been growing secretly for four years seemed to have hardened inside her' (*Frost in May*, p. 156). Yet 'Outwardly her conduct was perfectly respectable' (*Frost in May*, p. 156): Nanda complies with the demands made upon her and defensively protects this autonomous and heretical core. Indeed, she tries 'to mould herself into the proper shape of a young Catholic girl' and believes that her inability to share the Catholic suspicion of aesthetic and sensual pleasure is 'entirely due to a perverse and worldly nature' (*Frost in May*, p. 126). Only to her friend Léonie does she voice her rebellion. When the former is thrown out of a play for enjoying acting in it too much, Nanda exclaims:

> 'When I got so excited about the play the other night it hadn't anything to do with you or Rosario or God or anything. It was just the thing itself. I don't want poetry and pictures and things to be messages from God. I don't mind their being that as well, if you like, but not only that [. . .] I want them to be complete in themselves.' (*Frost in May*, p. 170)

Nanda's first attempt at writing a novel encapsulates the conflict between art and religion: 'she knew that religion must play a large part in it, but feared that too much piety would conflict with a really exciting plot' (*Frost in May*, p. 158). Her decision to 'describe a brilliant, wicked, worldly society, preferably composed of painters, musicians and peers, and to let all her characters be sensationally converted in the last chapter' results in disaster when the Mistress of Discipline discovers and confiscates the unfinished manuscript before Nanda has had a chance to complete it (*Frost in May*, p. 158). Despite the fact that Nanda's knowledge of depravity is extremely limited – the most 'depraved' scene is one in which her heroine receives 'a kiss of burning passion upon her scarlet mouth' (*Frost in May*, p. 202) – her parents are called in and she is expelled. This fictional scene, of course, memorialises White's own experience of expulsion from Roehampton in 1914. Mr Grey's denunciation and repudiation finally shatters the autonomous self that Nanda has been protecting for years: 'one sentence of her father's had torn right through every protective covering and shamed her to the very marrow. If he had stripped her and beaten her, she would not have felt more utterly humiliated' (*Frost in May*, p. 217). The Mistress of Discipline who comforts the sobbing Nanda in the wake of her father's repudiation celebrates the shattering of Nanda's 'hard little core of self-will and self-love':

> 'Every will must be broken completely and re-set before it can be at one with God's will [. . .] Real love is a hard taskmaster, and the love of God the hardest taskmaster of all. I am only acting as God's instrument in this. I had to break your will before your whole nature was deformed.' (*Frost in May*, p. 219)

Nanda must nonetheless leave the convent, the nun adds, not only because the nuns have nothing left to teach her, but also because Nanda is a 'germ-carrier' who could infect the other students (*Frost in May*, p. 220).

Frost in May thus introduces the web of conflicts that carry over into the succeeding novels of the sequence. The father's desire to convert his daughter extends beyond religion to encompass a coercive desire to turn her into what he wants her to be.[17] Increasingly, that coercion centres on her sexuality, which in turn is tied to writing: the father's and the Church's insistence on female innocence precludes the protagonist's self-expression and autonomy. The father's inappropriate eroticising of the father-daughter relationship further confuses the daughter, as she becomes first an adolescent (in *The Lost Traveller*) and then a young woman (in *The Sugar House* and *Beyond the Glass*). The shattering of Nanda's will creates difficulties as well, for, in the succeeding volumes, Clara is unable to make decisions for herself and is vulnerable to the persuasion and stronger wills of others. For that reason the convent remains a seductive world of order and routine, where the 'cold, clear atmosphere' smooths away 'the discomfort and bewilderment' of life outside and where 'everything had a sharper outline than in the comfortable, shapeless, scrambling life outside' (*Frost in May*, p. 190). As Penny Brown observes, Nanda's appreciation of the convent routine develops out of her sense that it is 'safer because it is restricted and tightly controlled'; Nanda is thus 'in danger of becoming institutionalised'.[18] Yet, paradoxically, the convent structure creates the order and routine in which Nanda can define that sense of self in the first place. This paradoxical relationship to the convent reflects Nanda's relationship to Catholicism itself, for Nanda admits that she could never

> break away without a sense of mutilation [. . .Catholicism] had grown into every fibre of her nature; she could not eat or sleep or

read or play without relating every action to her secret life as a Christian and a Catholic. She rejoiced in it and rebelled against it. (*Frost in May*, p. 136)

In the succeeding novels, Clara's relationship to institutional structures will remain powerfully ambivalent: she will long for limitations and clear-cut boundaries, only to rebel at her entrapment within them.

If White had not 'continued' Nanda's story, the ending of *Frost in May* would read very differently from how it does in the context of the entire quartet. Nanda's sense that 'the whole world had fallen away and left her stranded in this one spot alone for ever and ever with her father and those awful words' and that 'nothing for her would ever be the same' would read as the overwrought reaction of a young girl, a reaction, in fact, articulated by the Mistress of Discipline: '"Life's not all over at fourteen, my dear"' (*Frost in May*, pp. 216, 221). It is only from the perspective of the later novels – written many years later and after two decades of almost constant illness – that this scene acquires the resonance of permanent lifelong damage to the daughter's sense of self and artistic potential. In fact, White did not link the father's repudiation of the protagonist's writing to her subsequent writer's block until *The Sugar House*, begun in 1951 and published in 1952, nineteen years after the publication of *Frost in May*. This linkage reflects the identity narrative about her illness that she had consolidated in the intervening years. It is significant, then, that *The Lost Traveller* revises the scene of rupture between father and daughter: Clara leaves the convent because her father can no longer afford to send her there, not because she has been expelled. Nor is writing the site of psychological conflict in *The Lost Traveller*: instead, Clara engages in literary efforts without stress and shares her efforts freely with a like-minded friend. White's second novel, begun as she embarked on her lengthy analysis in the 1930s, shifts the site of difficulty with the father explicitly to the daughter's emergent sexuality.

The Lost Traveller: the seductive father and the oedipal victor

Less formally controlled than any of White's other novels, *The Lost Traveller* evidences its long gestation and the changing conceptualisations she brought to its composition. In its earliest stages, just prior to beginning her lengthy analysis with Carroll in 1935, White defines its central subject as the 'relation of a father and daughter; the hopeless impossibility of an adjustment between two people so different when one person will not allow for differences' (*Diary* 1, p. 34). This entry reveals that White planned to revise the scene that would become the emblematic event of her identity narrative, her father's condemnation of her first novel and concomitant repudiation of her as a daughter. Noting that she could not 'repeat a situation indefinitely', White searched for another incident that would 'consolidate the profound guilt about a fear of sex in the father which reacts on the child' and 'produce the first dislocation in the relationship which makes the light go out for the child':

> Therefore we must disentangle the essence of the 'book' incident and transplant it. That, it seems to me, is what 'inventing' incident means. The essences of situations one can only perceive clearly in one's own experience, but, having perceived them clearly, one can embody them in another form. 'Truth' in fiction depends on this. If the thing is rightly perceived, it will convince in whatever actual incident you choose to embody it. The mere recounting of an 'actual' incident will not do it. Hence the failure of the 'actual' incident in *Frost*. (*Diary* 1, p. 35)

In defining the 'actual incident' as a failure that did not capture the essence of the conflict between father and daughter, White shifts the central conflict to the daughter's sexuality, not her writing about sexuality. At this point White envisioned the 'essence' of the conflict embodied in the father's furious reaction to his seeing the daughter kiss a boy, 'a fearful scene followed by an almost amorous reconciliation' (*Diary* 1, p. 35). She also posits that 'the first part should be entirely devoted to getting *him*. I am sick to death of E[ircnc] and her convent education. Let that rest. I want *him*. His life is finished: can be examined. I will *not* be afraid of him any more. It is a pure accident that we were father and child. I have a *right* to look at him, yes, sexually too' (*Diary* 1, p. 35).

White apparently put the book aside during the next several years, as she struggled to regain her mental stability. In 1937 she mentions that she has begun 'to think about the father and daughter book again'; the entry continues with White connecting the book to both Carroll and her 'cure' as well as her feeling that Carroll now represented both 'harsh' father and sometimes 'satisfactory', sometimes 'recalcitrant', lover to her.[19] Just a few weeks later, White records that it has been two-and-a-half years since she wrote the first chapter, and that she now wants to expand her initial conception to encompass the figure of the mother as well as that of the father: 'My father's life is over. I can see it in some sort of perspective. I want the gradual disintegration of my mother's life through him to be one of the main things in the book. She takes refuge in a dream because his own solution does not fit her nature' (*Diary* 1, p. 88). The word 'solution' suggests that White had come to believe that her father took refuge in Catholicism as a way of containing his guilt and fear of sexuality, a conceptualisation White explores in detail in the novel.

White's sense that marriage had caused her mother's disintegration and subsequent escape into fantasy also finds expression in the final form of the novel. White had been horrified by her mother's retreat into a fantasy world as she aged, but after her mother's death in December 1939 White found that she mourned her mother far more deeply than she had her father. In an entry recorded in 1941 White describes her belated appreciation for her mother's sympathy, tolerance and unconditional love (*Diary* 1, p. 174). This changing conceptualisation of the mother is reflected in the novel: whereas the first chapter centres on Isabel's childishness, her character assumes more weight as the novel progresses, and a new-found firmness and confidence in her judgement play a crucial role in the final chapters.

White thus shifted her initial and exclusive focus on the father–daughter relationship to family dynamics more generally. 'We only managed a semblance of family life at the cottage', she recalls. 'In London it was conspiracies of twos: my father and mother, myself and my father or myself and my mother. We were not a family' (*Diary* 1, p. 135); the book hence needs to reveal the 'interaction of 3 characters on each other' (*Diary* 1, p. 162). White wanted to explore in particular the unconscious motivations that underpin those interactions. 'Before the theory of unconscious all motives had to be explicable', she muses in that same entry. '[. . .] we now know most people are ignorant of their own motives or give entirely wrong reasons for them' (*Diary* 1, p. 162). At the same time, White wanted to explore the ways in which Catholicism shaped both family dynamics and unconscious motivations. Here her immersion in analysis dovetailed with her conflicts about the Church. In a long entry in 1941, White traces the history of her relationship to Catholicism, admitting that her 'chief difficulties about the Church centre round her attitude to sex' and that her lapse from and return to Catholicism bracket her sexual life:

> I have always had an either/or attitude about sex and the spiritual life [. . .] Both the Church and Freud are right about the profound importance of the sex instinct – probably the Church's extreme attitude about sex which so often seems unreasonable is due to the fact that, indulged for its own sake, it takes away spiritual force. (*Diary* 1, p. 176)

Although White does not elaborate here on the similarities between Catholic and Freudian understandings of sexuality, *The Hound and the Falcon* letters, written during the same period, demonstrate White's familiarity with Freud's view that religion plays a crucial role in curbing instinctual aggression by demanding submission to an authoritative paternal authority.

Parental sexuality, the unconscious motivations underpinning sexuality, the ways in which Catholic teachings shape sexuality and family dynamics – all inform *The Lost Traveller*, but, because it has been studied primarily as just one instalment of Nanda/Clara's development, White's ambitious plan for the novel has been overlooked. To be sure, the incestuous dimensions of the father–daughter relationship have drawn critical attention, but even here the complexities White embedded in the representation of the father's sexuality and his conversion to Catholicism have not been fully appreciated.[20] In part, this critical oversight reflects the novel's shifting priorities: White's decision to incorporate Isabel's 'disintegration' in marriage came after her initial plans to focus on the father–daughter relationship, and the portions of the novel centred on Isabel's sexuality are neither as compelling nor as convincing as those centred on Claude's. But the focus on father–daughter incest also reflects the fact that the two later instalments deliberately represent conflicts about writing and sexuality as having their origins in Nanda/Clara's relationship to her father. The novel's focus on a range of transgressive sexualities – incest, marital infidelity, homosexuality – has been subsumed by the

overarching explanation White crafted to account for the protagonist's mental illness.

The Lost Traveller's treatment of sexual transgression and particularly the proliferation of gay subtexts that White embeds in her characterisation of Claude complicate a straightforward heteronormative
reading of his incestuous desire for his daughter. Key to White's characterisation of the father's incestuous eroticism is her own sense that
'I obviously represented both son and daughter to my father: in a
sense animus and anima' (*Diary* 1, p. 224). Claude's eroticisation of
the father–daughter relationship speaks to both aspects: on the one
hand he acts as the seductive father who wants to turn his daughter into his romantic partner; on the other hand his most erotically
charged evening with his daughter is one that replicates his own most
erotically charged experiences with another man. White thus queers
the scene of paternal seduction and locates it within the framework
of literary decadence to uncover Claude's deeply repressed and repudiated homosexuality.[21] In a diary entry recorded soon after the novel's publication, White noted that her father was not 'unsympathetic'
to her writing but rather jealous of her talent and conflicted about its
homosexual associations: 'he certainly saw [writing] in some way as
"unrespectable" and I think this ties up with Wilde and his homosexual side' (*Diary* 1, p. 220). Claude's sexual conflicts not only inform
his relationship with his daughter, moreover, but his relationship
with his wife as well, and Isabel's visible misery in the marriage adds
to Clara's difficulties as she navigates the treacherous geography of
female adolescence.

The 'essence' of the sexual conflict between father and daughter crystallises around two scenes that capture White's early plan to
record the father's reaction to witnessing his daughter's first kiss, a
kiss that provokes 'a fearful scene followed by an almost amorous
reconciliation' (*Diary* 1, p. 35). Claude becomes insanely jealous
when, unbeknown to Clara, he watches a young farmer kiss her. In 'an
access of rage' and with his face 'distorted; his eyes narrowed as if the
flesh round them was swelling and silting them up', he berates her for
'[k]issing and giggling like a common servant girl. How that young oaf
dared to touch you. The swine' (*The Lost Traveller*, p. 77). When she
tries to defend the innocence of the encounter, he responds by attrib-
uting men's advances to women's implicit invitation: '"A young man
doesn't . . . unless he is a scoundrel . . . if the girl doesn't lead him on.

I've no right to blame [him]. You were fair game"' (*The Lost Traveller*, p. 77). Claude's final words equate innocence with perfection: 'I thought you were an innocent child [. . .] I wanted one thing in my life to be perfect' (*The Lost Traveller*, p. 77). These last words he utters 'as if to himself': White thereby underscores the narcissistic dimensions of Claude's reaction, his demand that Clara embody a sexless ideal in order to suit his needs. He walks away in a posture of defeat and (phallic) deflation, moving slowly and with his head, 'which he usually carried so stiffly erect [. . .] sunk forward' (*The Lost Traveller*, p. 78). For her part, the 'girl in the glass' Clara had glimpsed earlier, a girl of new-found maturity, comes to the fore:

> Some part of herself seemed to have broken loose and to judge differently from the rest. Had he beaten her, the original Clara could not have felt more humiliated. But someone else [. . .] was it the girl in the glass? [. . .] had the strangest sense of triumph. (*The Lost Traveller*, p. 78)

This scene carries resonances of the Fall, for 'a tainted mist seemed to come over the day' (*The Lost Traveller*, p. 77); it is, in fact, a moment of sexual awakening, and later Clara will date her desire 'to be thought of as a girl rather than "almost as good as a boy"' to the moment 'Blaze had kissed her in the orchard' (*The Lost Traveller*, p. 160). This scene also marks the emergence of an explicit split in the protagonist's personality, one that builds on the split between the autonomous core and outward compliance in *Frost in May* and which widens as the series continues.

The 'amorous reconciliation' with her father soon follows. On a magical evening, Claude escorts his daughter to her first opera, a performance of Wagner's *Tannhäuser*, while Isabel remains behind, still recovering from an emergency hysterectomy. Clara regains her sense that she and her father are 'fellow conspirators', and finds it impossible to reconcile this courtly man with 'the father who had paralysed her with terror' earlier (*The Lost Traveller*, pp. 101, 102). The barriers of both age and relationship fall away: he forgets she is 'a child', and she realises 'he was probably not so very old after all' (*The Lost Traveller*, pp. 105, 102). The two lose themselves in the 'intoxication' of the performance and drown in 'sensuous, easy music'; when the lights come up they 'blinked at each other as if waking from the same rapturous dream' (*The Lost Traveller*, p. 105). Yet the harmony of the evening results from Clara's mirroring of her father. Claude basks in his daughter's unconditional and flattering approval: telling her father he looks 'magnificent', Clara 'gaz[es] at him with admiration [. . .] Never, she thought, had she seen him looking so young and handsome' (*The Lost Traveller*, p. 101). Similarly, as Claude expounds his interpretation of the sexual politics of the opera,

> Clara listened with parted lips and shining eyes, as he talked on. She felt she was being initiated into a new world and *abandoned herself* completely to this extraordinary, transformed father. She thought with his mind, heard with his ears, until both his talk and the music he had just heard seemed a revelation of something at once subtle, exciting and profound. (*The Lost Traveller*, p. 105, emphasis added)

This 'abandonment' carries the suggestion of erotic abandonment and, indeed, over the romantic dinner for two that follows, the couple conduct a charged conversation in which the father elicits and endorses his daughter's oedipal desires:

> 'I was toying with a wild notion I sometimes have.'
> 'Tell me.'
> 'Well, now and then, I try to fancy how it would be if you and I were not father and daughter.'
> She took it up eagerly.
> 'Oh, I've often thought that too.'
> '*Have* you? That's remarkably interesting.'
> 'Of course I don't mean I want anyone else for a father. But just that now and then . . .'
> 'We could forget,' he nodded. 'Exactly. Sometimes the idea is so vivid to me that it is almost like a memory. We meet, you and I, in a lonely tower. I don't know why a tower. And by some spell, we have forgotten our own identities. We talk without any self-consciousness.'
> (*The Lost Traveller* 113)

As most commentators on White have noted, this moment is one in which the father breaches the incest barrier, albeit in fantasy and at an emotional level.[22] Yet the 'tower' of their encounter is one in which father and daughter are immured in a masculine and phallic economy that elides feminine difference.[23] At the end of the evening, 'he kissed her goodnight, more lingeringly than he had done for many months, stroking her hair, while she tried to tell him what a wonderful evening it had been' (*The Lost Traveller* 115). Claude then sends his 'Cinderella' off to bed, an allusion that gestures back to his courtly behaviour at the evening's outset, when he presents his daughter with flowers and accompanies her to the opera in a hired car, complete with liveried chauffeur, that he refers to as her 'carriage'. These acts cloak Claude's phallic fantasy with the accoutrements of heterosexual romance.

Perceiving the incestuous dimensions of the father–daughter relationship solely within the frame of heterosexuality erases the complicated tensions White has embedded in her representation of the father's desire. To be sure, the novel opens with Claude's memory of his conversion, which takes place when he is suddenly overcome by a fantasy of raping a woman who kneels next to him at church. That chapter ends with explicit references to Claude's banishing thoughts of his daughter:

> Innocent images, yet suddenly he forced himself to check them. There is a point at which a dream, while still sweet, becomes menacing. He made himself inhabit the cool, scentless black and white chapel, for, in another second, he might have been kneeling in a different church. (*The Lost Traveller*, p. 29)

Other passages underscore the ways in which Clara resembles Claude's ideal of 'golden-haired women' (*The Lost Traveller*, pp. 5, 93). Such passages support a straightforward reading of the father's incestuous desire, whereby he reacts jealously to other men and treats his daughter as his romantic companion.

But the '*Tannhäuser* evening' brings other facets of Claude's desire into focus and, in fact, Claude's unconscious conflicts about sexuality power this 'amorous reconciliation'. His choice of Wagner's *Tannhäuser* for his fifteen-year-old daughter's 'initiation' into opera is a case in point. Ostensibly a staging of the battle between profane and sacred love and the redemptive power of the latter, *Tannhäuser* follows the eponymous hero's journey from damnation to salvation through the loving, self-sacrificing intercession of the saintly, virginal Elizabeth as well as that of his close friend Wolfram, who, himself in love with Elizabeth, defers to his friend's priority in her affections. Tim Ashley writes that the opera reflected the moral and sexual conflicts of the late Victorian period more than any other of Wagner's operas, and 'appealed above all to those who were – or felt – outlawed by their sexuality'.[24] The opera promotes a vision of 'sexuality and spirituality as antithetical yet mutually dependent' by bringing 'the sacred and the profane into disturbing proximity [. . .] by allowing flesh and spirit to speak the same thematic language'.[25] The lengthy opening scene celebrates the erotic excesses of Venus and her lover Tannhäuser in the 'Venusberg Music' that Ashley characterises as 'one of the most extreme depictions of sex attempted in music'.[26] Championed by Baudelaire, who praised the Venusberg Music for its depiction of 'frenzied love, immense, chaotic, elevated to the level of a counter-religion', the opera became associated with literary and artistic decadence, and Swinburne, Beardsley, Huysmans and Wilde all created works in reference to it.[27] *Tannhäuser* features, for example, in Wilde's *The Picture of Dorian Gray*, where Dorian describes the Venusberg Music as 'a presentation of the tragedy of his own soul'.[28]

Claude's interpretation of the opera – '"Every man [. . .] is both Wolfram and Tannhäuser. But women are different. They are either Venus or Elizabeth"' (*The Lost Traveller*, p. 105) – seems to sidestep the transgressive context of the opera and its associations with literary decadence by speaking instead to conservative and conventional divisions between men and women, and between good women and bad. Yet his topics of conversation during the romantic dinner for two that follows centre upon his nostalgic memories of his now-dead Cambridge friend Larry O'Sullivan, who not only introduced him to *Tannhäuser* but to Wagner in general and to the works of Pater, Wilde and Meredith, writers associated with literary decadence. It transpires, moreover, that the restaurant he has chosen is one where O'Sullivan always brought him, one that he has seldom visited since O'Sullivan's death and never with his wife. A 'romantic figure' who 'stood for everything [Claude] never had', O'Sullivan had 'the gift of turning life into a fine art' (*The Lost Traveller*, p. 112); Claude describes how his worldly friend infused him with his passion for sensual delights: '"everything came through him"' (*The Lost Traveller*, p. 114). Indeed, *The Egoist* – the novel that inspires Clara's name – contains for Claude a portrait of O'Sullivan: he was Horace de Cray '"with a dash of Lord Henry Wotton"' (*The Lost Traveller*, p. 114).[29]

De Cray is an unconventional and transgressive figure in *The Egoist*; Lord Henry is the older and more sophisticated man who sets Dorian Gray on his path to perdition. During dinner Claude even quotes Lord Henry's notorious advice to the youthful Dorian, '"The only way to overcome a temptation is to yield to it"' (*The Lost Traveller*, p. 111). Another anecdote stresses the manner in which O'Sullivan, a born Catholic, wore his religion lightly: after inadvertently eating meat on a Friday, O'Sullivan claimed the meal was well worth a bit of Purgatory, a sentiment that echoes the decadent position that sensual excess is well worth the price of damnation. Claude pulls back from such implications: regaining his 'old manner' of paternal authority, he assures Clara that '"No doubt [Catholicism] went deeper than he admitted. I'm sure he made a good end"' (*The Lost Traveller*, p. 112). But a few moments after sharing his fantasy of immuring himself with his daughter in a tower, he returns to the subject of his dead friend's Catholicism:

> 'Odd that the Catholic faith should have been the one thing he never tried to communicate to me.' He seemed to have forgotten all about Clara and to be talking to himself. 'Well, perhaps, not so odd,' he said with a peculiar smile and added 'It was a comfort to me that Wilde died a Catholic.' (*The Lost Traveller*, p. 114)

Claude's 'peculiar' smile, his lapse into reverie, his linking of O'Sullivan and Wilde as hedonistic sinners who died good Catholics – in fact the entire tenor of the conversation – all point to Claude's youthful immersion in literary decadence and homoerotism at least, if not actual homosexuality. His youthful predilections thus cast new light both on his conversion to Catholicism and on his 'amorous reconciliation' with his daughter. The link between decadence and Catholicism was well known; as Ellis Hanson points out, 'No other literary movement can claim so many converts to Rome.'[30] Hanson accounts for the seeming paradox that many homosexual writers and artists sought refuge in a church that condemned homosexuality by noting that the Church combines the sensual and the spiritual, the pagan and the Christian, the spirit and the flesh in a highly aestheticised manner that foregrounds and intensifies desire, thereby reflecting the very principles that undergird the decadent movement.[31] The attitudes of both Church and decadence towards sexuality, moreover, are similar: Hanson observes that there is 'no such thing as good sex in decadent literature'; instead, shame, remorse and disgust are the attendant emotions.[32] Finally, the Church offered solace and comfort as well as 'a powerful language through which to cope with guilt, shame and sorrow'.[33] Within this context, Claude's conversion conforms to a familiar narrative of literary decadence; indeed, it bears similarities to that of Oscar Wilde, who first began to flirt with the idea of conversion to Catholicism while an undergraduate at Oxford.[34] Claude similarly becomes 'fascinated' by Catholicism while a Cambridge undergraduate: 'It had fascinated him then by the very things which gave it such a sinister aura in the eyes of his family. Intoxicated with Wilde and Pater, it had glittered for him with decadent splendours' (*The Lost Traveller*, p. 21).[35]

White thus depicts Claude as a deeply repressed man who harnesses his uncertainty about his masculinity through an 'obstinate will' which he uses to control himself '[w]ith all his might [. . .] as if forcing himself into a tight jacket' (*The Lost Traveller*, pp. 2–3). His youthful flirtation with Catholicism gives way to a more mature and studious approach, but his actual conversion takes place at the moment he realises the depths, force and brutality of his sexual fantasies. Prior to this moment, he has studied Church teachings, but while '[h]is mind was satisfied, his heart remained cold'; he feels 'suspended [. . .] convinced in his reason but impotent to act' (*The Lost Traveller*, p. 22). Kneeling at a church one evening, he is suddenly aroused by the sight of the woman next to him taking off her gloves: an impression of 'deliberately exposed nakedness' and the fact that she resembles his wife provoke 'the demons of his imagination' to leap on her, 'stripping her, using her with a cold brutality of lust' (*The Lost Traveller*, p. 22). Not only does this rape fantasy gesture towards Isabel's dissatisfaction in her marriage – an oft-repeated family narrative concerns his drunken assault on his wife early on in their marriage – but it also gestures towards the way in which women often intuit male sexual aggression: 'He was not looking at her, but as if she had guessed his thoughts, he felt her shift further away' (*The Lost Traveller*, pp. 22–3). A profound sense of guilt overwhelms Claude, who feels he has grasped 'the meaning of evil' for the first time in his life:

> He was conscious of something corrupt in the depths of his nature; something at once frigid, impure and violent. Hitherto he had thought of sin mainly in terms of lust and rage but the quality of this had a

peculiar malignancy that tainted the very source of the spirit. He felt
as if he were isolated from every human contact; locked in a dark cell
that was both icy and suffocating. (*The Lost Traveller*, p. 23)

As he continues to kneel in the Church, the red light emanating from
the sanctuary lamp becomes 'the one point of contact with the world
of sanity and hope', and with 'some faculty never awakened before'
he feels the 'intense personal presence' of Christ: 'Christ was the
key that could unlock his prison of frozen isolation and the key was
his for a single act of faith' (*The Lost Traveller*, p. 23). He remains
'minutely faithful' but never again experiences 'that direct touch on
his soul' (*The Lost Traveller*, p. 24).

Claude's conversion, then, hinges on his repudiation of his sexual
fantasies and his desire to control them. Notably, Christ is the 'key' to
unlocking his spiritual 'impotence', terms that, given White's familiarity with psychoanalysis, carry highly charged phallic connotations.[36]
In fact, White consistently suggests that Claude's deepest and most
passionate relationships are with men: he reverences his father, not
his mother; he longs for a son and considers his students beloved sur-
rogates; the most passionate relationship in his life was with Larry
O'Sullivan, his 'greatest friend': 'No one could ever take his place',
he tells Clara during their fateful dinner (*The Lost Traveller*, p. 112).
Photographs of his father, Larry and his students even have pride of
place in his study, a masculine preserve where he tutors young men
in the classics. Claude's conversion to Catholicism thus does not set
him on a path of humility and compassion for others, but functions
as a form of defensive repression and a bulwark for his authoritarian and domineering impulses. Tellingly, he recalls the moment of his
conversion as he prays for his dead father, a former alcoholic whose
business failures and public scenes deeply mortified Claude as a child.
Until the age of eight Claude had admired his father as a 'powerful, all-wise being' but had then become aware of the mockery and
ridicule directed at him (*The Lost Traveller*, p. 25). Vowing that his
'father was not to be laughed at', Claude sets out to grow up and
work hard 'so that he could look after his father and make everyone
respect him' (*The Lost Traveller*, p. 27). He succeeds: after he establishes himself as an adult he makes his father retire from all work,
and '[g]radually he became exactly what Claude had always dreamt
he should be, an extremely distinguished-looking old man, known

and respected throughout the neighbourhood' (*The Lost Traveller*, p. 28). This image of masculine authority is, however, a hollow and constructed one. It is not surprising, then, that on the day of his father's death his 'shell' cracks, exposing a 'long-forgotten Claude, dreamy, uncertain and awkward', who fears 'that one day he might lose all control of his mind' (*The Lost Traveller*, p. 2).[37] He enters the church to pray soon after.

Tangled in Claude's erotic investment in his daughter is a deeply repressed identification with her that speaks not only to his heterosexual desire but to his homosexual desire as well. As the *Tannhäuser* evening makes clear, Clara occupies the same position in relation to Claude that Claude had once occupied in relation to O'Sullivan, and just as O'Sullivan had initiated Claude into the sensual pleasures of aesthetic decadence, so Claude initiates Clara in turn. Claude's rage over the kiss he witnessed and his wish that one thing in his life be perfect – a wish he utters aloud but as if speaking to himself – captures not only heterosexual jealousy but also a narcissistic fantasy that Clara represents an unsullied version of himself before he indulged in sensual pleasures with a more experienced, older man. The guilt about and fear of sexuality that White identified as a crucial element of her working plan for the father's character thus has two dimensions: a flight to Catholicism as a refuge from illicit sexuality and also a demand that Clara's purity function as a form of redemption for his own sexuality. *Tannhäuser* speaks to both elements, opening with an explicit exploration of sensual decadence, and closing with the saintly Elizabeth's sacrifice of her life to redeem the soul of the fallen man. The references to Oscar Wilde's *Dorian Gray* that punctuate the *Tannhäuser* night link Claude to Lord Henry Wotton, whose worldly views astound the beautiful and innocent Dorian, while the dinner itself alludes to a dinner Lord Henry has with Dorian: Clara responds, like Dorian, with 'strangely bright' eyes and 'lips parted in frightened pleasure'.[38] And Claude resembles Lord Henry, who revels in his ability to influence Dorian:

> To project one's soul into some gracious form and let it tarry there for a moment; to hear one's own intellectual views echoed back to one with all the added music of passion and youth; to convey one's temperament into another as though it were a subtle fluid or a strange perfume: there was a real joy in that.

More ominously, 'to influence a person is to give him one's own soul'.[39]

Clara, in a sense, inherits her father's unconscious conflicts about sexuality and gender through her father's narcissistic identifications with her. The 'tainted mist' that contaminates the atmosphere in the orchard following Claude's witnessing of Clara's first kiss emanates from Claude's own sense that his sexual urges possess 'a peculiar malignancy that tainted the very source of the spirit' (*The Lost Traveller*, pp. 77, 23). This unconscious transmission encompasses Claude's relationship with his own father. Like Clara, Claude is his father's only surviving child, but his father has never reciprocated his son's 'incurable love', responding to him only with gratitude and 'cool detachment' (*The Lost Traveller*, pp. 25, 28). Instead, Claude's father has harboured special affection for Clara, who 'had revived in him the one passionate affection he had ever felt, which had been neither for [his wife] nor Claude but for his first child, a girl, who had lived eighteen months and died the day before his son was born' (*The Lost Traveller*, p. 28). Claude's narcissistic identification with Clara enables Claude not only to imagine himself reflected in the daughter who shares his intellectual interests, but enables him to experience himself as the beloved object of an adoring father/older man. (Notably, Claude's fusion of Clara with the girl he imagined assaulting in the church follows on his memory of his father's preference for his sister/his daughter.) These shifting identifications anticipate contemporary critical and psychoanalytic accounts of the fluidity and indeterminacy of sexuality and its power to exceed or resist the constraints of conventional gender roles. Acknowledging the 'materiality and historical contingency of the experiences of fathering and being a daughter', Adrienne Harris describes the designations of 'father' and 'daughter' as 'placeholders, not as essentials': 'How is meaning and power pulled into or emanated out of the particular circumstances of being a daughter or a father, given that daughters may be boys or girls, and fathers housed in many different sites?' she asks.[40] Drawing upon the work of Haydée Faimberg, Harris observes that 'oedipal triangles are actually multigenerational. One is bound into many imaginary father–daughter scenes, all read through the fantasies and longings of the parental figures', a process that Faimberg terms a 'telescoping of generations'.[41]

Isabel's bitter revelations about her illness – she has had an emergency hysterectomy after a series of disastrous pregnancies imposed on her by Claude because he wants a son – further roil Clara's confused feelings about her father. To the startled Clara, Isabel discloses a long history of sexual suffering: the brutality of the wedding night ('"I knew nothing. Absolutely nothing. Never, never shall I forget the appalling shock, the dreadful disillusion"' [p. 101]); the horror of childbirth ('"when a woman has a child she goes down to the gates of hell"' [p. 101]); the Catholic ban on contraception ('"making us have babies whether we want them or not"' [p. 122]); Claude's insistence on sex despite the danger pregnancy represents to Isabel ('"even the best of men is selfish when it comes to *that*"' [p. 123]); and, perhaps most startling of all, Claude's disappointment at Clara's birth ('"for your sake it would have been a good thing if Daddy had had his way and you'd been a boy"' [p. 119]). Isabel makes clear that she considers sex a brutal imposition, describing it as a 'torment' inflicted upon women in the name of love (*The Lost Traveller*, p. 122). Her descriptions resonate with those detailed by Freud in '"Civilized" Sexuality Morality and Modern Nervous Illness', his powerful 1908 critique of the constraints that cripple female sexuality and desire in the interests of social conventions and norms.[42] Like the women described by Freud, Isabel's education in ideals of feminine purity and refinement means she recoils from sexuality, which she considers disgusting. Freud also provides a plausible explanation for Claude's apparently brutal approach to sex. Through the operations of the oedipal complex and the resultant incest barrier, men develop a split between tenderness and sensuality: tender feelings attach to those women who recall the maternal imago, whereas sensuality is directed at those who do not. This psychic division results in a form of 'psychic impotence' for men, who cannot fully enjoy sex with their respectable wives: instead, their performance is 'capricious, easily upset, often clumsily carried out, and not very pleasurable. Above all [. . .] it avoids all association with feelings of tenderness.'[43] Claude's homoeroticism and the brutality of his fantasies in the church – fantasies directed at a woman who reminds him of his wife – suggest this division between tenderness and sensuality. In this context it is significant that one of the earliest, most painful and most influential sexual encounters that Isabel repeatedly references is one that occurred soon after their marriage, when Claude came home drunk after dinner with some old Cambridge friends: although White does not provide details, the implication is that he assaulted Isabel (*The Lost Traveller*, p. 100).

The extensive and nuanced portrait of the parents' sexuality that White develops in *The Lost Traveller* contextualises Clara's conflicts about sexuality in general and feminine gender identity in particular. An acknowledged 'Daddy's girl' who takes after her father's side of the family, shares her father's intellectual interests and views her mother with contempt, Clara has always overvalued her father's approval and dismissed her mother as trivial and irrelevant. Her intellectual ambitions align her further with her father, a classics master, and distinguish her further from her mother, a reader of trashy romance novels. Even Clara's physical appearance speaks to this gendered division, for Clara's body and face combine 'elements of lightness and heaviness' that clash, preventing the development of her mother's 'sleek, harmonious shape' (*The Lost Traveller*, p. 37). Squarely built like her father but with her mother's slender arms and legs, 'she seemed to have the body of one person and the limbs of another', and her features, such as her 'high masculine forehead and her small feminine ears', 'contradicted each other' (*The Lost Traveller*, p. 37). Clara has always wanted to be a boy and longed for brothers; 'As a small girl she had despised other small girls and her friends had all been boys' (*The Lost Traveller*, p. 160). Even during her years at the convent school, she had been 'the only female member of a secret gang of boys' (*The Lost Traveller*, p. 160). Like her father, she appreciates her mother's beauty but is repulsed by the biological bond that ties her indissolubly to her mother's female flesh. When she learns the facts of life from her friend Patsy, 'What shocked her most was the confirmation of her terrified suspicion that she had once been a part of her mother. She thought she would not have minded quite so much if her mother had been [Patsy's]' (*The Lost Traveller*, p. 165).

Both her first kiss and the *Tannhäuser* night make Clara reconsider her aversion to femininity (*The Lost Traveller*, pp. 160, 120), but both experiences also instil doubt, guilt and discomfort: her father's denunciation 'taints' the former, and she recalls him as 'wonderful, yet faintly disquieting' in her memories of the latter (*The Lost Traveller*, p. 126). Her mother's shocking revelations add further disquiet, for Clara had thought children were the result of 'love': 'Now her mother seemed to be implying that a man in some way forced a woman to have a child because he "loved" her and that it caused her extreme suffering' (*The Lost Traveller*, p. 122). On the threshold of adulthood, aware of 'a new creature growing up inside her, something still unformed and skinless that could not be exposed to the light', Clara now realises 'for the first time that her father and mother had had a life before she existed and that all those dull relatives whom she could never imagine otherwise than middle-aged had once been young and capable of feeling' (*The Lost Traveller*, pp. 35, 94). En route to their country home, Clara considers her parents in a new light:

> [Her mother] looked older than Clara had ever seen her and there was something frightened and reproachful in her expression. Had she told the truth when she said that men were cruel to the women they loved? Once more she studied her father's absorbed face. No one could be frightened of him tonight, yet how often in his presence she had felt a panic out of all proportion to anything, however harsh, he might have said or done. What was he really in himself? (*The Lost Traveller*, p. 126)

Isabel's unhappiness introduces deep doubt about the possibility of marriage as a vocational choice. But the other two choices open to Clara – nun and schoolmistress – also implicitly incorporate choices about sexuality, for both require celibacy. Her friendships with Patsy Cohen and Ruth Phillips point up the self-division Clara experiences between (female) body and mind, since the former, spontaneous and uninhibited, feels completely comfortable with her body and sexuality ('Life presented no abstract problems to her' [*The Lost Traveller*, p. 164]) and the latter is single-minded in her commitment to higher education, work and spinsterhood. The life of the convent seems to appeal to Clara simply because it provides regulation, structure and clarity, whereas she has felt anchorless and without direction since leaving it behind (*The Lost Traveller*, pp. 178–9). Her sojourn as a governess at Maryhall, an aristocratic Catholic manor overseen by the saintly Lady Cressett, seems to offer a compromise, marriage as a stable structure and secular vocation.

Clara fits the profile of what Christine C. Kieffer calls the 'oedipal victor', 'the girl whose company is preferred by the father and who receives greater admiration than the mother'.[44] Kieffer distinguishes between two types of 'Daddy's girls', 'the doted upon "princess," who is hyperfeminine and sometimes hypersexual but remains an incompetent little girl, and the "heroine," who attains competence at the expense of sexuality'.[45] The oedipal victor conforms to the latter category. As a child, this type of daughter functions as an extension of her father: 'He may share confidences with the daughter that he withholds from her mother, crediting her greater intellect, but in actuality, because of his perception that she is more like him – an idealized woman he has created.'[46] Her 'active attempts to be like him' thus supply him with an idealised version of himself. But as the daughter enters adolescence, her developing autonomy and independence threaten to shatter the flattering reflection she has provided:

> When the daughter starts to demand recognition of herself as a similar though independent person, the narcissistically vulnerable father may react with astonishment and then outrage [. . .] The narcissistic father may either actively thwart the daughter's autonomous strivings [. . .] or simply withdraw.[47]

In particular, the narcissistic father finds his daughter's emergent sexuality deeply threatening. Kieffer writes that the seductive father:

> may subtly or even flagrantly encourage his daughter's erotic feelings toward him and often attempts to control other aspects of her life as well. Most seductive fathers view their daughters' burgeoning sexual interest in male peers as a threat to their exclusive position, and many project their disavowed erotic feelings onto potential suitors, characterizing them all as potential roués from whom their daughters need protection.[48]

The father's preference also affects the mother–daughter relationship and the daughter's subsequent sense of her own femininity. Kieffer notes that the 'mother's role in this type of family constellation is a denigrated one [. . .] Such mothers are often depressed and ineffectual as well as hyperfeminine.'[49] For that reason, the oedipal victor may find it difficult to identify with her mother. The daughter's emotional intimacy with the father may, moreover, create tension between mother and daughter: the former may feel resentment, the latter guilt. While the oedipal victor may develop relationships in which she, too, is devalued and denigrated – thereby achieving identification with the mother while punishing herself for her 'victory' with her father – she may

> phobically reject the denigrated maternal role and thus be unable to attain marriage and motherhood – or, if she does achieve them, she may feel humiliated by these roles and thus not enjoy them. Indeed, her very femininity may be experienced as a humiliation.[50]

Ronald Britten differentiates between two versions of the oedipal victor in what he terms the 'Athene–Antigone complex', whereby the 'daughter derives her significance by being the reincarnation' of the father's power: the Athene identifies herself as the incarnation of his ideas, whereas the Antigone identifies herself as his handmaiden, guardian and caretaker.[51] A version of the 'masculinity complex' identified by Abraham and Freud in the 1920s and 1930s, the Athene lives 'in triumphant denial, by phallic identification, of being an ordinary woman': she chooses a life 'devoted to "nun-like" service', her sexuality 'sacrificed in an act of [. . .] renunciation'.[52]

Clara never accepts her father's authority and the sacrifice of her sexuality wholeheartedly, however. In his study – which indeed features a plaster cast of Athene – she feels trapped and under interrogation: the 'high padded sides' of the armchair 'hedged her in like a prisoner's dock; the light overhead poured mercilessly down on her face' (*The Lost Traveller*, p. 41). But Claude disappears from much of the second half of the novel, a disappearance the novel attributes to the outbreak of the First World War: he accepts a commission in the Officers' Training Corps, where he feels like 'a man among men' for the first time since his marriage and where his youth 'revive[s] through his intense sympathy with his subalterns' (*The Lost Traveller*, p. 172). He gradually becomes 'so preoccupied with the fate of his pupils that he was almost indifferent to his family' and 'no longer seemed to want [Clara's] intimacy', for 'he was far less concerned about his one daughter than his twenty or thirty vicarious sons' (*The Lost Traveller*, pp. 171–2). Accordingly, the second half of the novel alternates between sections that focus on Clara's explorations of her three vocational paths – schoolmistress, wife, nun – and those that focus on Isabel's deepening relationship with one of Claude's secondary-school colleagues, Reynaud Callaghan. This relationship in particular reflects White's decision to provide a more balanced

account of the parents' marriage generally and the mother's subjectivity specifically, but it is far sketchier and less convincing than
White's detailed analysis of Claude's sexuality. It does, however, lay
the foundation for a more empathic mother–daughter relationship at
the novel's close, in which Isabel asserts her new-found authority on
behalf of her daughter.

Isabel's role in the novel's structure is crucial in understanding
White's linkage of Catholicism and psychoanalysis in the concluding
sections. Isabel's relationship to Callaghan begins as little more than
a flirtation, whereby Isabel amuses herself by impersonating various
literary heroines with the men she meets while selling flags for the
war effort. Callaghan punctures this world of fantasy when he forces
her to acknowledge the emptiness of her life, quoting to her from
Yeats's play *The Land of Heart's Desire* – '"Faeries, come take me
out of this dull house/ Let me have all the freedom I have lost"' – to
which he adds, 'For it is a dull house, isn't it? Own up now' (*The
Lost Traveller*, p. 188).[53] Callaghan thus recognises Isabel's misery
and intuitively grasps its source; furthermore, he casts himself as the
man who can rectify the situation: '"You're starving for love and
understanding. I could make you so happy [. . .] There's a whole side
of you that's never had a chance. I'm the only person that even cares
about it"' (*The Lost Traveller*, pp. 190–1). Her study of the Yeats
play seems to awaken Isabel from her 'dream of the troubadour and
the imprisoned queen': for the first time in her life she experiences
physical desire instead of 'romantic attachments and greedy private
fancies' (*The Lost Traveller*, p. 210). But when she proposes to leave
Claude for Callaghan, a glimpse of a 'tawdry holy picture of the
Sacred Heart' effects her transformation: Callaghan reminds her that
their shared Catholic faith would make an illicit union '"one more
torment between us"' (*The Lost Traveller*, p. 272). White thus situates Isabel's renunciation within the frame of Catholic devotion: she
sacrifices her personal claim to human happiness in keeping with the
faith that posits as its central claim Christ's love and compassion for
suffering humanity.[54]

The death of Charles Cressett, Clara's ten-year-old charge, in a
freak accident ties the various threads of the novel together. As Flood
has shown, Claude's irrational angry reaction to the letter from Clara
announcing the terrible news – he identifies with the boy's father
and tells Isabel that, if he were Sir George Cressett, he would have

Clara up for manslaughter – makes clear that 'he sees her as the murderer of his own son'.[55] Clara's real crime, Flood explains, 'is the conversion of Claude's son into herself. Clara's crime is being alive, being a woman, being herself. Because she is who she is, she has destroyed the son she should have been. Simply in being herself, she is guilty of murder.'[56] His incestuous desire for Clara is thus 'linked in the novel to his contradictory wish that she were a boy'.[57] White herself acknowledged in her diary that Charles's death represented 'something about the male side of myself and destroying it' (*Diary* 1, p. 225), but she goes on to connect it to the illegal abortion she had arranged with her father's support: 'The death of Charles must symbolise something. Clara feels guilty though it is not really her fault. I think the abortion of the first child: a son, is worrying me' (*Diary* 1, p. 225). Charles's death also destroys Claude's fantasy that Clara is his romantic partner, for it is certainly incestuous desire that fuels his jealous outburst against her, in which he connects her supposed responsibility for the little boy's death to the earlier scene in the novel when he saw Blaze kiss her in the orchard: '"There was some young man or other about. Instead of looking after the boy, she was fooling about with *him*. As a result the boy breaks his neck"' (*The Lost Traveller*, p. 261). At still another level, Charles's death exposes Claude's narcissistic view of Clara as a conduit of his own masculinity. His fury at her 'possessed him as completely as his grief had done on the day of his father's death', for she has destroyed his dream that she will marry 'some young Catholic squire' and 'hav[e] a country house of her own. Since he could never have a son, he had begun to look forward to the idea of a grandson. Now Clara had disgraced herself and destroyed the whole fabric of his dream. If Charles Cressett had been that grandson, he could hardly have felt more bitterly towards her' (*The Lost Traveller*, p. 273).

Clara's guilt propels her into an engagement to Archie, the young officer present at Charles's death, and functions as a form of atonement, both to Lady Cressett and to her father. Lady Cressett accepts Charles's death as God's will, but she also suggests that it may have been God's way of bringing Archie and Clara together; she further counsels the doctrine of feminine self-sacrifice that she herself practises (*The Lost Traveller*, p. 285). By marrying Archie, Clara will also restore her father's dream and possibly produce in time Claude's longed-for (grand)son. It is Isabel, newly empowered by her renunciation of Callaghan, who intervenes to free Clara from the expectations of others. Significantly, Isabel's return to the family home after breaking off with Callaghan interrupts Claude's sexual assault of Patsy Cohen, who has come to plead on Clara's behalf: Patsy clearly substitutes here as a surrogate for Clara and the scene definitively confirms Claude's transgressive desire for his daughter. Isabel's interruption symbolically enacts the mother's intervention in the dyad: in short, she saves the daughter from the father's desire. The power dynamics between the parents shift radically: whereas Claude had determined he needed to take 'a firm line with Isabel' and 'force her to realise what he was suffering' before his assault of Patsy, he cedes all authority to Isabel afterwards: '"I will go absolutely by what you say"' (*The Lost Traveller*, pp. 274, 280). Isabel's intervention with Clara is similarly effective. Urging Clara to break off the unwanted engagement, she explains that Clara cannot marry just to fulfil her father's dreams: '"you'll find one day that you can't make people you care for happy just by giving them what they imagine they want"', she tells Clara (*The Lost Traveller*, p. 311). The novel closes with Clara voicing an appreciation of her mother, as if she can see her for the first time 'as a real person' (*The Lost Traveller*, p. 314).

Like *Frost in May*, *The Lost Traveller*'s conclusion would read very differently if White had not decided to 'continue' Clara's story. In contrast to all other instalments in the sequence, *The Lost Traveller* ends with Clara freed from her father's domination and the expectations of others through her union with a newly empowered and confident mother.[58] The novel thus ends with a revisionary, female-centred vision of Catholic and psychoanalytic paradigms. White stages Isabel's intervention as a deliberate parallel to the opening of the novel: Isabel finds Clara in the chapel of Our Lady of Sorrows, the same chapel in which Claude prays for his dead father in the novel's opening chapters. Claude's memory of the fantasies of sexual assault that led to his conversion includes his sense that the woman who inspired them intuited his aggression: 'as if she had guessed his thoughts, he felt her shift further away from him' (*The Lost Traveller*, p. 23). Clara, similarly, 'shifted further away' when she feels someone on the bench beside her, but Isabel only moves closer and draws her into a comforting embrace (*The Lost Traveller*, p. 309). Claude's conversion occurs when he feels the 'direct touch' of Christ, whose 'key' unlocks 'his prison of frozen isolation': this imagined male touch and his memory of his dead father stand in stark contrast to the warm, living and embodied embrace of mother and daughter. Our Lady of Sorrows provides a female counterpart to the emblems of the Sacred Heart of Jesus that recur throughout the novel: in both devotions, the emphasis is on compassion for the suffering of others. Whereas Claude's conversion springs from guilt and repression and confirms an illusion of male authority, Isabel liberates Clara from Claude's coercion – his conversion of her from who she is to who he wants her to be – as she assumes a vital female authority on behalf of her daughter.

White's invocations of Our Lady of Sorrows and the Sacred Heart also enable her to yoke Catholic mystical traditions to the psycho-analytic concept of the unconscious. Much of the book concerns the ways in which family members really don't know each other at all: as Claude jokingly remarks, '"A woman can be married to a man for sixteen years and know nothing of his innermost life"', to which Isabel responds, '"Women can have their secrets too"' (*The Lost Traveller*, pp. 125–6). To capture this hidden life, White centres a sig-nificant number of sections upon one character, whose experiences remain unknown and unspoken of to the others. Sexuality plays a major role in these unshared and private experiences, and, in fact, the 'invented' aspects of the novel all centre upon unconscious or barely conscious sexual desires. These include Claude's lustful fantasies in church and his assault of Patsy; Isabel's all-but-consummated affair with Callaghan; and Clara's 'murder' of her father's son.[59] Neither Claude nor Isabel confess their sexual lapses to the other, although each is 'aware of something unspoken in the other' (*The Lost Trav-eller*, p. 281); Isabel, similarly, withholds from Clara the reasons she has become 'real': her 'strange, transfiguring smile' adds some-thing to her face that 'Clara had never seen and could not fathom' (*The Lost Traveller*, p. 314). White's 'inventions' literally flesh out the nature of the characters' tangled desires and gloss both dyadic (parent/child; husband/wife) and triadic (father/mother/child) inter-actions, but the information thus revealed remains opaque to the characters themselves. White's epigraph, taken from St Augustine's *Expositions on the Psalms*, points to this opacity as an inevitable facet of human life: 'In the sojourning of this carnal life each man carries his own heart and every heart is closed to every other heart'

(*The Lost Traveller*, np.). This sentence follows St Augustine's contention that 'Every man is a stranger in this life, in which you see that
we are girt round with flesh, through which flesh the heart cannot be
seen'. St Augustine goes on to warn against judging and condemning others, since only at the Second Coming will God make manifest
'the thoughts of the heart'.[60] With knowledge of others permanently
sealed off, only compassion, forgiveness, tolerance and acceptance
make human intimacy possible.

The Lost Traveller thus encompasses unconscious desire and the
lawlessness of sexuality within the context of Christian teachings on
compassion, mercy and forgiveness. It thereby marks a significant
shift in White's depiction of Catholic teachings about sexuality in
general and female sexuality in particular. Whereas *Frost in May*
depicts the nuns as enforcing a rigid and puritanical code in which
all sexual matters, particularly those embedded in literary representations, represent contamination and impurity, *The Lost Traveller*
depicts sexual lapses as potential vehicles for grace and spiritual
growth. As Philip O'Mara points out:

> Every major character must yield, relying only on religious convic-
> tion, to a divine law that seems unrelentingly harsh. Blessings of a
> manifest kind [. . .] result from such decisions, but only when they
> are made with a deep sense of their human cost, in blind, unex-
> pectant faith. Through this unhappy, almost unbelieving submission
> each character comes into conformity with the hidden movements
> of Providence.[61]

Claude's assault of Patsy and Isabel's flight to Callaghan paradoxically render the Batchelor marriage stronger and more equitable.
'Both partners grow in love and faith, neither fully aware of the danger that their marriage had been in from the other; in these novels, even consolations appear as an aspect of the obscurity of faith',
O'Mara observes.[62] Isabel's accession to real passion through her
illicit affair similarly heals the rift between mother and daughter and
enables Isabel to exert a powerful counterforce to Claude's dominance and control of Clara. Had the novel remained a standalone,
White's revisionary and subversive conceptualisation of a Catholic
unconscious would leave Clara on the threshold of an autonomous
identity based on defining her own desires.

Writing out madness: *The Sugar House and Beyond the Glass*

White would call *The Lost Traveller* a 'transition book' and a 'freak' as she began to plot out *The Sugar House* in 1951 (*Diary* 1, p. 235). Now fully committed to fictionalising her own experience, she found it 'a great pity that I did not make *The Lost Traveller* a proper sequel to *Frost*' (*Diary* 1, p. 235). Because *The Lost Traveller* ends with Clara prepared to call off her engagement to Archie, White lamented that 'practically all I have done so far – about 50,000 words – has really been undoing what I did in *The Traveller* and getting the marriage on again' (*Diary* 1, p. 235). To be sure, the family dynamics established in *The Lost Traveller* persist: Clara still fears her father's disapproval above all else, and Claude continues to upbraid Clara for what he perceives as lapses in behaviour and judgement. Isabel, similarly, retains her role as empathic emotional support, intuiting Clara's unspoken feelings and intervening with Claude on her behalf, although Clara has returned to treating her mother with dismissive contempt. These long-established patterns now underpin Clara's deepening psychic distress, and, significantly, White ties that distress not only to family dysfunction and sexual conflict but to the act of writing: in *The Sugar House*, White returns to the 'primal scene' of her own identity narrative, the father's repudiation of the daughter's adolescent novel as the seed of her mental illness and her writer's block. White does not explicitly discuss her decision to revive this explanation of her protagonist's departure from the convent school, despite the fact that it contradicts the explanation developed in *The Lost Traveller*. Yet her decision to do so indicates that White now conceives of the novels as instalments of a single protagonist's story and that Clara truly has become 'a continuation of Nanda'.[63]

In order to fictionalise the story of her first breakdown, White had to tie it to what she considered the precipitating event – that is, the repudiated convent novel and *Frost in May*. The final two novels of White's sequence thus contain two plots: a manifest plot that continues the storyline in which the protagonist's split between compliance to patriarchal authority and needs for self-expression create unbearable conflicts resulting in psychotic breakdown; and a second, latent plot, which charts with almost clinical accuracy the onset of bipolar disorder, when the pattern is one that begins with an episode of depression followed by an episode of mania. This section discusses the latent plot, while the following section will demonstrate how White maps her identity narrative of illness on to the latent plot.

From the outset, *The Sugar House* stresses Clara's psychic instability, a peculiar sense of 'doubleness' that Clara attributes to Charles's death. '"I don't believe I've ever been quite real since. Not a whole person. As if some part of me died when Charles did"', she tells Archie (*The Sugar House*, p. 76). These feelings of splitting, deathliness and unreality, which White assigns to narrative events and psychological conflicts, also delineate the increasing chaos of mood swings that destabilise any sense of self-coherence. Clara even compares herself to a chameleon, telling Charles's mother that '"I change all the time according to where I am and the people I'm with"' and explaining her sudden divergent trains of thought as a chameleon's '"automatic reflex. They have nervous breakdowns, don't they, if you change their backgrounds suddenly?"' (*The Sugar House*, p. 110). The image of the chameleon aptly captures Clara's sense that her behaviour is highly reactive to her environment rather than motivated by consistent internal cues. 'The amphibious, mercurial, many-personed, and highly responsive nature of both the artistic and manic-depressive temperaments is at the core of what they are all about', Jamison observes. 'Not without reason does the word "chameleon" permeate the descriptions of the artistic personality [. . .] Implicit to both chameleonic and manic-depressive temperaments is the coexistence, within one body or mind, of multiple selves'.[64] But Clara's chameleon-like nature cannot adjust to the new background of marriage to Archie: she sleepwalks through the ceremony in a dream-like state she compares to a 'trance', feeling her will completely 'paralysed' (*The Sugar House*, p. 119). Her wedding day seems 'glittering' and 'unreal', and Clara watches herself playing the 'unrehearsed part' of the bride with 'surprising ease', changing into her going-away clothes with 'the sense of dressing for another act in a play' (*The Sugar House*, p. 121).

White depicts Clara's descent into depression with clinical accuracy. With 'no definite occupation, [Clara] could not establish any order in her life [. . .] Day by day she grew more inert and apathetic, weighed down by a sense of guilt but too listless to pull herself together' (*The Sugar House*, p. 152). She becomes 'incapable of writing anything, even the simplest letter', for her mind is 'fuddled and inert'; she tortures herself by comparing herself to the productive artists she imagines living around her (*The Sugar House*, p. 153). Despite her loneliness, she deliberately cuts herself off socially:

> She did not know what obscure impulse drove her to isolate herself in this way but, once she had formed the habit, she could not break it. The more she was alone, the more she became convinced of her own emptiness. (*The Sugar House*, p. 153)

Indeed, she doubts 'whether she existed at all. Once this sense of non-existence was so acute that she ran up from the basement to the sitting-room full of mirrors almost expecting to find nothing reflected in them' (*The Sugar House*, p. 154). In the early stages of depression, Clara can still sometimes stave off her sense of 'paralysed drifting' and a conviction that her life is 'irretrievably broken' (*The Sugar House*, p. 155). But as her depression deepens, so does her conviction that she is 'inwardly corrupt' and 'a kind of monster. Not a real person at all' (*The Sugar House*, p. 174). She castigates herself as 'an absolute, utter sham'; a disappointment to family and friends; and a corrupting influence responsible for Archie's dissipation (*The Sugar House*, p. 175). As she reaches crisis point, Clara feels 'overwhelmed by that sense of being utterly cut off from life, gasping for air inside a bell jar' (*The Sugar House*, p. 211). A large gulp of whisky momentarily arrests the 'creeping paralysis [. . .] She could actually feel it move some steps away, as a circle of wolves is said to do when the menaced traveller throws a firebrand at them' (*The Sugar House*, p. 211). But she finds that, when the whisky wears off:

> The oppression had returned in full force. Each anxiety was like an actual weight on her diaphragm pinning her down on the rumpled bed: the bills, Archie's drinking, her own impotence to write, the impossibility of going either backwards or forwards in any direction. But more crushing than any of these was an overall sense of guilt, not localised, as if all these were a punishment for some mysterious sin she could not remember having committed. (*The Sugar House*, p. 212)

Paralysis and inertia, self-recriminations, ruminative patterns of thought, inability to concentrate and pervasive guilt: all are classic signs of depression. Clara also manifests physical signs. She no longer troubles about her appearance, instead 'slouching about for days in the same crumpled frock', with a 'vacancy in her expression' and 'a dulled look as if there were a film of dust all over her skin and hair' (*The Sugar House*, pp. 154–5). The disorder and untidiness of the house mirrors her mood, for Clara thinks she looks as 'battered' as the stained and dusty sitting room, and she compares the 'tawdry and unkempt' house to 'an actress with last-night's make-up still on her face' (*The Sugar House*, pp. 208–9). She begins to put on weight and, as depression tightens its iron grip, she desperately tries to resist the aimless activities of the 'terrible days':

> The paralysed lethargy she had managed to fend off for the last weeks began to creep over her. At all costs, the day which had begun so hopefully must not turn into one of those terrible ones when she wandered aimlessly about the house, stopping now and then to stare for long spells at an old newspaper whose meaning she could not take in, smoking cigarettes, mechanically combing her hair and eating, if she ate at all, with a strange compulsive greed; stuffing herself with anything she could find; sponge cakes, chocolates, old heels of bread and cheese, like a ravenous child. (*The Sugar House*, p. 209)

Family and friends also remark on her 'black mood', her irritability and a 'queer look' which makes her seem ill – but not 'just ordinary illness' (*The Sugar House*, pp. 186, 249). Her father, too, registers this physical transformation, telling his wife that Clara looks like '"some stranger twice her age"' (*Beyond the Glass*, p. 18). Asked to elaborate, he explains that he is '"not referring merely to her looks. Though goodness knows she was slatternly and unkempt enough. No, it was something in her expression. A kind of distortion . . . rigidity"' (*Beyond the Glass*, p. 18).

Clara's physical transformation literally mirrors her psychic splitting as her own reflection becomes that of an alien, menacing stranger who can control her and pull her into a world on the other side of the looking glass:

> Like herself, the other had fair, wildly disordered hair and wore a creased tussore dress but its face was almost recognisable. The eyes were dull and parched between the reddened lids; a pocket of shadow, dark as a bruise, lay under each. The features were rigid and distorted as if they had been melted down and reset in a coarser mould. (*Beyond the Glass*, p. 30)

The rigidity and distortion Clara and her father identify resonate with the psychiatrist Karl Jaspers' description of schizophrenics, whose personalities 'have something about them, which baffles our understanding in a peculiar way; there is something queer, cold, inaccessible, rigid, and petrified there [. . .] when faced with such people we feel a gulf which defies description'.[65] What White depicts is Clara's alienation from *herself* as her sense of depersonalisation intensifies. Hence when the phone rings, her mind goes blank: 'If someone had asked "Who is that speaking?" she could not have replied. But at the sound of Archie's voice she recovered her identity' (*Beyond the Glass*, p. 31).

Clara's sense of depersonalisation and estrangement may reference the 'praecox feeling' that the schizophrenic supposedly inspires in others: according to Jaspers, 'we find ourselves astounded and shaken in the presence of alien secrets' when in the schizophrenic's company.[66] What White captures is Clara's sense of panic as she inspires the praecox feeling in others and then witnesses the confirmation of her own estrangement. At the family's country home, for example, Clara stands outside in the dark with her parents, gazing into the lighted room where her aunts sit, unaware that the others are outside.[67] Clara initially relishes a sense of her singularity, savouring 'this sense of being apart' and feeling 'neither old nor young, as if some part of herself were as unchangeable as the rest was amorphous and unpredictable. That part seemed to have no other desire than to stand outside watching, observing, registering' (*Beyond the Glass*, p. 64). Almost immediately, however, her mood shifts, and she experiences an 'overpowering', 'overwhelming' and 'violent' 'longing not be to be alone but to be loved, to share her whole life, her whole being with someone else' (*Beyond the Glass*, p. 64). Tapping on the glass to alert her aunts to her presence and seeing the fright register on their faces, Clara experiences

> a third sensation [. . .] a touch of pure panic. She had an instantaneous vision of herself as someone forever outside, forever looking in through glass at the bright human world which had no place for her and where the mere sight of her produced terror. (*Beyond the Glass*, p. 65)

These violent shifts in mood and this feeling of being cut off, even from those closest to her, similarly informs the scene in which Clara must identify Archie through a glass door in her solicitor's office, and her 'imagination went off on one of its crazy tangents' (*Beyond the Glass*, p. 77).

White's initial characterisation of Clara references schizophrenia, but the prelude to psychosis also references the manic and depressive symptoms of both mood states. Several times Clara experiences 'sudden switches from listlessness to activity' (*Beyond the Glass*, p. 38), but in general she feels 'an increasing sense of unreality, as if her existence had been broken off like the reel of a film' and she finds she can neither think nor act decisively (*Beyond the Glass*, pp. 84, 78). Prior events seem to have happened to someone else: they are 'unconnected with real life, a scene she had once acted in a play' (*Beyond the Glass*, p. 38). Neither 'happy nor unhappy, merely indifferent', she falls back into the rhythm of her parents' routine and finds that routine enough to keep her from lapsing into the 'drifting apathy' of her last weeks in the Sugar House (*Beyond the Glass*, p. 78). This mood of 'indifference' is, however, marked by her inability to concentrate on anything:

> Now her mind dissolved at the mere threat of having to form any opinion. She could barely manage to take in what [her father] was saying, let alone make an intelligible reply. Sometimes a phrase would lodge in her brain and go on repeating itself like a record when the needle sticks, distracting her from hearing what followed. Sometimes a word such as 'Consequences', 'Unemployment' or 'Inflation' would slowly write itself on the air as if traced in smoke and her eyes would follow each stroke, intent only on the shaping of each letter. (*Beyond the Glass*, p. 79)

Eventually she comes to view her state of 'blank inertia' as a 'deadness of the soul', as if 'something in her had died and already exhaled a faint odour of corruption' (*Beyond the Glass*, p. 114). She welcomes this deadness, for not feeling anything is better than the agonised record of depression recorded in her private black notebook:

> If that was what it meant to be alive, nullity was better [. . .] A decree of nullity would be merely the outward confirmation of the inward fact. It was she herself who was null and void [. . .] there would be no more violent feelings, either of pleasure or pain. Null and void. Null and void. (*Beyond the Glass*, p. 121)

Prodromes, 'mild and often transitory and indistinct manic symptoms'[68], occur in this interim stage between episodes. Clara twice suffers from blinding headaches during her legal ordeals (*Beyond the Glass*, p. 80). Other symptoms include uncontrollable flights of thought, when Clara finds it 'extraordinarily difficult to control her thoughts as well as her movements. At one minute her mind was an utter blank; the next it was off on some irrelevant, even frivolous tangent' (*Beyond the Glass*, p. 70). Such examples abound (*Beyond the Glass*, pp. 77, 102, 112, 113). She feels compelled to act out reckless behaviours, simply in order to break through her 'tranced immobility' (*Beyond the Glass*, p. 84). She thus almost acts upon an 'insane desire' to break into the Sugar House, stopped only when she sees the owner come out through the front door (*Beyond the Glass*, p. 83); shortly thereafter she starts to act on an impulse to seek out Marcus Grundy:

> Her sudden longing to see Gundry was as crazy as the other. But to want anything again was so intoxicating that she could no more control the want than she had been able, all these months, to force her will into any channel [. . .] what was left of her reason kept saying 'This is absurd'. (*Beyond the Glass*, p. 85)

Her fortuitous meeting with an old friend interrupts this compulsive act: as her friend remarks when she tells him what she was about to do, '"No risk. Hence no excitement. One of your few flaws is that you have a craving for dramatic situations in ordinary life"' (*Beyond the Glass*, p. 98).

White depicts here the manic energy underpinning Clara's depression and the increasing strain she experiences as she tries to keep the volcanic forces of explosion under control. As Clara's mood escalates into mania, classic symptoms emerge. As noted in Chapter 1, mania develops rapidly in comparison to depression: it can develop over several weeks or even several days. Clara passes through the stages of hypomania and acute mania into delirious mania over a period of three weeks (*Beyond the Glass*, p. 142). The 'switch' into hypomania occurs when she meets Richard Crayshaw at a party: she feels 'the strangest sensation. It was as if the whole of her past self had suddenly dropped away and she were a perfectly simply, perfectly free creature' (*Beyond the Glass*, p. 130). The switch, textually explained by the couple's ability to communicate telepathically, bears resemblance to the 'manic alert', a term for a rapid switch into recognisable hypomania:

> She felt as if she were simultaneously asleep and awake. Far from being unaware of what was going on around her, her senses were more alert than usual. Even in the dimness of the smoky, crowded room, she noticed details of faces and dresses with a peculiar sharpness. Scraps of conversation came to her clearly through the general soft babel; she found she could follow several threads of disjointed talk at the same time, just as she could distinguish the separate layers of scent, tobacco, smoke, hot wax, alcohol and human flesh which made up the smell of the room. She was almost more conscious of all these small, vivid new experiences than of the man she was dancing with. *Yet she knew that they came to her only through him.* If she lost contact with him, this miraculous enhancement of life would vanish. Though she was so acutely aware of what was going on around her, the two of them seemed to be moving invisibly in another dimension. (*Beyond the Glass*, p. 131; emphasis added)

Although attributed to the impact of meeting Richard, mania follows upon Clara's depressive episode and prodromal symptoms. Entering into sudden, intense and often excessive romantic involvement is typical of the hypomanic stage, as is the hyperacuity of the senses. Clara feels herself caught up in a 'tranced tension' she compares to a spinning top in which others become 'strands' in 'a web of heightened perception' (*Beyond the Glass*, p. 132). She brims with self-confidence and assurance: although normally terrified of water and walking on slippery surfaces, for example, she walks confidently on a slimy waterside path in high-heeled shoes 'as surely as on a carpet. She knew, with absolute certainty that, as long as she was with him, nothing could ever frighten her again' (*Beyond the Glass*, p. 135).

As she did with depression in *The Sugar House*, White represents Clara's escalating mania with clinical accuracy. Believing that 'everyone and everything about her was in a conspiracy to make her happy', Clara describes a 'happiness that was of a different order from anything she had known or even imagined', a 'magical power that transformed, not merely herself but every person she met, everything she saw and heard and touched':

The strange sense of heightened perception she had felt when she danced with [Richard] had now become her permanent state [. . .] until now, she had never even begun to know what it meant to be alive [. . .] the most trivial words and objects seemed to be charged with extraordinary significance as if she were living in a fairy-tale where everything had its own language and conveyed a secret meaning. At first she had moments of doubt that the spell might break and she would find herself back in the old dull world. But soon each day not only confirmed but increased her sense that everything had become flawlessly, effortlessly right. No activity, physical or mental any longer presented any difficulty. The flesh she had put on during those months with Archie disappeared so quickly that every morning she arose with a lighter body. Soon her clothes hung loose on her but she did not trouble to take them in. She knew that, whenever she wanted to, she could discard all her present ones and become possessed of delightful new ones, perfect to the last detail, as effortlessly as a snake sloughing its skin. Her mind worked with astonishing speed and clarity. She was full of plans and projects [. . .] She did not tell [Richard] that soon she would be making a great deal of money [. . .] she did not yet know exactly how she was going to make her fortune. That would be revealed to her when the time came. She was also convinced that, in due course, she would write a very wonderful book. She had only to convey this dazzling new intensity of vision to make it unlike any book written before. (*Beyond the Glass*, pp. 142–3)

This passage reads like a textbook description of hypomanic thinking. Symptoms of hypomania include euphoric or sometimes irritable mood, flight of ideas, grandiosity and increased energy. Euphoric, ebullient, over-confident, Clara imagines herself living in an enchanted world where nothing can ever go wrong and where all her projects and plans are bound to materialise. As one description details, 'Self-esteem and self-confidence are greatly increased. Inflated with their own grandiosity, patients may boast of fabulous achievements and lay out plans for even grander conquests in the future'[69]. Hence Clara imagines not just that she will write a book, but that she will write a 'very wonderful' one unlike any other. She will make a fortune when the means are made known to her through a miraculous revelation. Clothes will magically materialise, perfectly designed as if a second skin.

Physical symptoms also abound, particularly the classic symptoms of decreased sleep and appetite. Clara rapidly loses weight, and hails a discovery

> so obvious that she wondered she had not discovered it before. Sleep was a sheer waste of time if one were really alive. Night after night she would lie awake [. . .] content simply to feel this high pulse of life throbbing through her. She would get up and dress, as refreshed and clear-eyed as if she had had nine hours of sleep. (*Beyond the Glass*, p. 144)

She also discovers that it was 'hardly necessary to eat. Her appetite had almost vanished yet everyone kept saying how amazingly well she looked' (*Beyond the Glass*, p. 144). Clara imagines that her decreased need for sleep and food means she has hit upon 'the secret of life', 'remarkable discoveries' that she should impart to the world (*Beyond the Glass*, p. 144). Hypomanic patients imagine that 'if only the rest of the world could feel as they do and see as clearly as they do, then the rest of the world would be sure to join them'.[70] Further, the hypomanic mood is 'infectious' and 'those around them often get caught up in the spirit'.[71] So it is with Clara, who notes that her 'new clarity of perception affected her relations with other people': her new-found 'charm' works not only with family and friends but with '[p]eople in shops, bus conductors, waiters [. . .] They smiled at her in a special way as if they knew her secret and were grateful to her for being so happy' (*Beyond the Glass*, pp. 143–4). Her happiness is

> like a sparkling fountain [. . .] that overflowed into every detail of her daily life [. . .] She brimmed with affection for everyone; she would have liked to stop strangers in the street and tell them she loved them. She found herself planning wild schemes of benevolence. (*Beyond the Glass*, p. 144)

Pressured speech is one of the hallmarks of hypomania and one of the first symptoms likely to strike other people as uncharacteristic and troubling. In the early stages of hypomania, Clara finds it 'difficult sometimes not to burst out singing or laughing from sheer ecstatic joy' (*Beyond the Glass*, p. 144), but as her control begins to break down she speaks to her parents in an 'eager rush', feeling a 'sense of triumph to see how absorbed they were by her words even if they did not quite understand them' (*Beyond the Glass*, pp. 147, 148). Here Clara begins to ascend into acute mania, describing to her parents her delusional belief that the photographs of dead soldiers in her father's study were 'looking at her and smiling at her as if they were glad to know she was going to marry a soldier': '"They've forgiven me. They've told me so"', she tells them (*Beyond the Glass*, pp. 145, 148). Her parents recognise that something is wrong, although Clara does not register their concern (*Beyond the Glass*, p. 148). They urge her to get more rest, her mother drawing attention to Clara's bright eyes, flushed cheeks and lack of appetite. Richard, too, asks her if she is feverish; he remarks as well her weight loss and lack of appetite. Taking her hand, he remarks that it is '"Burning hot. It's as if you were on fire inside. I look at you sometimes and it's as if you were melting away"' (*Beyond the Glass*, p. 154).[72] Clara shrugs off everyone's concern, for '[h]ypomanic patients rarely recognize that anything is wrong with them, and though their judgement is obviously impaired they have no insight into that condition'.[73] When her mother, running her hand over Clara's hair, exclaims that '"it's all electric like a cat's fur. Darling, you mustn't get over-excited [. . .] you'll burn yourself out"', Clara responds, '"I can't burn out"' (*Beyond the Glass*, p. 148).

Burn out, of course, she does. Clara escalates from acute to delirious mania in the following four days, and others begin to register their bewilderment, even fear at her extravagant behaviour. At this point Clara's mania is all too evident, and White captures the rush of a mind in overdrive. Hence Clara's 'dazzling joy [. . .] soared up to a new peak of exultation' in which she feels she and Richard 'kindled all these fires as they raced through the countryside like a torch, scattering sparks of life to the left and right, leaving a trail of glory. It was difficult not to sing aloud as they sped along [. . .] But she had to keep her wild exhilaration secret' (*Beyond the Glass*, p. 156). A flock of skylarks elicits Clara's conviction that they are 'writing music in the sky' for the couple (*Beyond the Glass*, p. 161): Clara believes that the world possesses 'highly personalised messages' for her, a symptom known as 'ideas of reference'.[74] Richard, however, expresses worry about moments when '"it's almost as if you suddenly weren't there. Usually it's only for a split second [. . .] and then you're back again and everything's real"' (*Beyond the Glass*, p. 154). These moments – 'bipolar blackouts' that resemble amnesia, whereby the person interacts with others but cannot remember what transpired – gradually increase in length. Kraepelin describes how a 'dreamy and profound clouding of consciousness may occur' as the patient succumbs to delirious mania,[75] and Clara indeed feels a 'strange drowsy feeling' overcome her, in which entire periods of time escape her memory. Her moods veer wildly, from joy to tears, from ecstasy to violence, the dysphoric and labile moods typical of delirious mania. A glimpse of herself in the mirror at the end of the evening recalls her distraught mirror image after her separation from Archie, when she imagined a strange, sinister double who could compel her to act. Whereas earlier she had been able to resist the compulsion of that sinister double, now a 'wild, helpless feeling' suddenly 'invades' her body, and in an act motivated by a 'blind, panic-stricken rage' she attacks Richard 'fiercely' (*Beyond the Glass*, p. 168). Although she tries to laugh it off, he does not, telling her, '"these days, I can't follow all your moods"' (*Beyond the Glass*, p. 169).

The three days that follow fluctuate between intervals of relative lucidity and intervals punctuated by delusions and hallucinations. Clara counsels herself to 'tiptoe through the day, holding herself carefully, until the turbulence of last night had subsided'; 'things had slipped out of focus' and she wants to 'recover the bright, sharp image' again (*Beyond the Glass*, p. 175). She is well aware that there had been moments the preceding day 'when the crystal sphere of security in which she was enclosed had nearly cracked and she had been giddily aware of a whirling darkness outside' (*Beyond the Glass*, p. 175). At the same time, she experiences the grandiose delusions typical of acute mania: she imagines that 'Soon money would begin to flow to her in larger and larger quantities', delusions she now shares openly with her father, much to his distress (*Beyond the Glass*, pp. 175, 173, 186–7). Her behaviour grows increasingly erratic. A Friday evening dinner with Richard and his sister ends with Clara slipping away and wading into the Thames, despite not being able to swim: she feels compelled by a voice that whispers in her head, 'This is the perfect moment. Go *now*' (*Beyond the Glass*, p. 181). After Richard rescues her, she cannot explain what seems to be a suicide attempt; again she shakes off his concern and his sense that '"sometimes you seem to go off where I can't follow you"' (*Beyond the Glass*, p. 183). She feels her 'gay confidence' return the following morning, but as her confidence increases so do her delusions (*Beyond the Glass*, p. 185). Messages reach her from external sources. Thus Clara believes she has 'been intended to come' to a Requiem sung for dead soldiers in honour of Armistice Day: chastising herself for not caring enough for the dead soldiers and holding herself unworthy of being a soldier's wife, Clara suddenly hallucinates a 'crowd of young men in torn and blood-stained uniforms' with faces 'turned reproachfully on her' (*Beyond the Glass*, p. 187). Clara asks for a test from God to prove her worthiness and the soldiers return, now smiling at her: Clara believes that they have a 'special claim' on her, something they want her to do (*Beyond the Glass*, p. 188). Grandiose delusions of a religious cast are extremely common in acute mania: patients may feel they are prophets, 'elected by God for a magnificent, yet hidden purpose'.[76]

Delirious mania is characterised by 'clouding of consciousness, hallucinations, and delusions'.[77] As her mood escalates from acute to delirious mania, the 'film of drowsiness' over Clara's mind deepens into a 'cloud of fog' (*Beyond the Glass*, pp. 175, 189). Clara now feels 'extraordinarily sleepy', in a 'kind of passive stupor', as she loses all sense of time or even 'separate thoughts': 'Her whole mind and body seemed to be arrested in a cataleptic state in which the only thing she knew was that she was being mysteriously prepared for something and that it was imperative to make no attempt to disturb this strange experience' (*Beyond the Glass*, p. 189). Increasingly delusional, Clara grows paranoid, hostile and even violent: she believes her mother and the family boarder speak in code; the boarder wants to become her mother's lover in order to give her smallpox; 'terrible danger' threatens her father; and so on. At the same time, she feels herself 'slowly charged with a mysterious magnetic force' that becomes so powerful that, helplessly rocking back and forth in her chair and feeling the rhythm change to 'a rapid, violent one', she falls over and strikes her head. Significantly, Clara imagines, just before she tumbles over, that 'Something is possessing you, like a medium. Just let it *happen*' (*Beyond the Glass*, p. 191): she does not perceive that she herself is the source of the energy. She reacts with violence when first the student and then the doctor try to restrain her, gripped by delusions of persecution and treachery. Still, left alone for a moment, she displays the astonishing lucidity the manic patient is often capable of: her senses 'preternaturally acute' and her mind making 'lightening decisions',

Clara slips out of the house, leaving a note for her father to warn him that '[t]he house is full of evil' (*Beyond the Glass*, pp. 193, 196).

In the final hours before Clara is committed to Nazareth Asylum, she succumbs to delirious mania. Convinced that evil spirits beset her – including a monk who looks like her father but is really a devil in disguise – she fights violently to free herself and defends herself by repeatedly singing hymns. She fights like a 'wild-cat', but then acts like a docile child; she sings and raves, but then has tiny moments of relative lucidity (*Beyond the Glass*, pp. 198–9). Persecutory delusions predominate in this manic stage, and in particular Clara believes that she is undergoing a 'terrible ordeal' to prepare her to be a soldier's bride. This ordeal entails living through deaths that have haunted her and for which she feels guilt, including those of Charles Cressett and a schoolmate from convent days. It finally entails living through the dying agony of young soldiers:

> Women wearing nurses' veils and aprons tiptoed in and sat beside her bed. She knew quite well that they were not nurses; they were women whose sons had been killed in the war. Each time a woman came in, Clara went through a new agony. She became the dead boy. She spoke with his voice. She felt the pain of amputated limbs, of blinded eyes. She coughed up blood from lungs torn to rags by shrapnel. Over and over again, in trenches, in field hospitals, in German camps, she died a lingering death. Between the bouts of torture, the mothers, in their nurses' veils, would kiss her hands and sob out their gratitude.
>
> 'She must never speak of the House of Mirrors', one said to another.
>
> And the other answered: 'She will forget when she wakes up. She is going to marry a soldier.' (*Beyond the Glass*, p. 207)

Here, Clara manifests the acutely psychotic delusions and hallucinations known as Schneiderian first-rank symptoms. She has delusions of control or somatic passivity, in which she believes others have taken possession of her body (Charles Cressett; her schoolmate; the dying soldiers); she has third-person hallucinations, in which she hears voices talking about her in the third person; she has audible hallucinations, in which her own thoughts become hallucinated voices; she has delusions, whereby she attributes false meanings to real perceptions (her father becomes a monk/devil; the nurses become the mothers of dead soldiers). Schneiderian first-rank symptoms, typically indicative of a diagnosis of schizophrenia, appear in 22–29 per cent of those suffering manic psychosis.[78] Before Clara finally succumbs completely to psychosis, she makes a last-ditch effort to regain control and re-establish contact with others, but she feels she has gone deaf and dumb, unable even to open her eyes, which are 'clamped down with leaden weights' (*Beyond the Glass*, p. 208). Instead, 'the darkness closed down', and her last (unspoken) words to Richard – 'I do, I do' she wants to cry – reference marriage vows even as her madness cuts her off from him for ever (*Beyond the Glass*, p. 208).

The psychosis chapter, which records the wholesale dissolution of Clara's identity, is a brilliant reworking of White's 1930 story 'The House of Clouds'. White establishes continuity with the previous three instalments by embedding many fragmented images of incidents and people from Clara's past in a delusional and hallucinatory swirl in which Clara loses all sense of time, place and even identity as she forgets her name and even her humanity. Psychosis thus assumes textual meanings consistent with White's manifest plot of psychic conflict as the genesis of psychosis. As Evelyne Keitel notes, whereas the psychotic 'going through a severe personality fragmentation is trapped in an autistically self-contained world of illusion', literary representation of psychosis becomes a device contributing to a 'network of interconnecting literary strategies. The function of a psychotic within such a literary frame of reference consists principally, in interplay with the other textual strategies, of controlling the reader's reaction to the text'.[79] Through her delirium come glimpses of the asylum, of doctors and nurses, padded cells, water treatments, restraints and force-feeding, all rendered as forms of torture and fright. There are glimpses, too, of the hyperactivity and superhuman strength and agility of delirious mania, for Clara is able to leap from the bed to the sill of a window high in the wall, where she crouches like a cat.

Clara's recovery from delirious mania is gradual. White's representation again is clinically accurate, for Clara's recovery retraces the path of her ascent, in keeping with the clinical literature that notes:

> Whether the peak of severity of the individual patient's episode is found in hypomania, in acute mania, or in delirious mania, once that peak has been reached, a more or less gradual and orderly subsidence of symptoms occurs, which to a greater or lesser extent retraces the same symptoms seen in the earlier escalation.[80]

Clara's descent from the peak of delirious mania begins with her 'remarkable' sense that, 'whenever she was fully awake, she was always the same person. This person was called Clara. She was almost sure that, in the other life, her name had also been Clara' (*Beyond the Glass*, p. 229). Gradually, the hospital and the nurses assume distinct outlines: 'A small space about her became solid and recognisable. In that space objects and people were always the same' (*Beyond the Glass*, p. 230). Blank spaces punctuate her account and she often 'finds' herself in a room or situation without actually knowing how she got there:

> [It was] extraordinarily difficult to remember things. Words like 'before' and 'after' no longer had any meaning. There was only 'now'. Very occasionally there was a tiny thread of continuity [. . .] But it always snapped off short and she would find herself in the middle of doing something without any idea of how she had come to be doing it. (*Beyond the Glass*, p. 231)

She gradually grows aware of these lapses in space and time, observing:

> Though she could now recognise certain sections of the place she was in, there was no way of connecting them together. They were like islands with a blank, featureless sea between them. How did one get from one to the other? It was the same with people; [they] materialised and dematerialised. What happened to them in between? (*Beyond the Glass*, p. 232)

She similarly observes the impossibility of establishing any sequence in time: 'Sometimes it went at a tremendous pace, as when she saw the leaves of the creeper unfurl before her eyes like a slow motion film, or the nurses, instead of walking, sped by as fast as cars', whereas at other times the simple motion of bringing a spoon from her plate to her mouth takes several hours (*Beyond the Glass*, p. 232).

In the second stage of her recovery, Clara works 'desperately to piece things together, to find some connection between Clara *here* and Clara *there*', now aware that the world of the hospital 'existed somewhere in the world she had once inhabited' (*Beyond the Glass*, p. 233). At this point she begins to draw distinctions between the other inmates and the doctors and nurses, and suddenly a 'bright idea' strikes her that she is in Looking-Glass Land (*Beyond the Glass*, p. 233). This ability to draw upon a literary analogy to make sense of her experience marks an important facet of Clara's recovery, for her return to sanity follows a trajectory in which her increasing capacity to communicate with those on the 'sane' side of the glass unfolds in tandem with her gradual remastering of the skills of reading and writing.[81] The publication date on an old magazine alerts her to the passage of time, while the words on the hospital plates, Nazareth Royal Hospital, alert her to her location (*Beyond the Glass*, pp. 234, 232). A bizarre game of croquet with the other inmates, which she again analogises to *Alice in Wonderland*, not only alerts her to the fact that she is 'imprisoned in a place full of mad people' but also brings back her memory of playing croquet with her father at the family's country home (*Beyond the Glass*, p. 243). In a passion of desire to communicate with her father, she struggles against the reversed writing required of those living in Looking-Glass Land, and, taking as a model the way letters appear in a Dornford Yates novel provided by a kindly doctor, manages to write a short note of appeal to her father, a note which eventually wins her release when her father immediately turns up at the hospital and lobbies for Clara's return to the family home.

Throughout this stage of recovery, Clara must deliberately work at maintaining her 'new awareness' and, in fact, her hope of hearing back from her father motivates her to fight against lapsing into the 'blank spells' by 'forcing herself to attend vigilantly to every detail', thereby managing 'to piece together the run of a whole day without once finding herself unable to account for how she came to be in a particular place or doing a particular thing' (*Beyond the Glass*, p. 252). In a sharp insight into how mental hospitals instil the very patterns of behaviour they are meant to ameliorate, Clara begins to study the other inmates' language and gestures, finding that trying them out 'was rather soothing; it dulled the new sharp edge of her mind [. . .] why not gently relapse to a state where no more effort was needed?' (*Beyond the Glass*, p. 252). She soon understands that it would be 'much easier [. . .] to slip into their ways than to keep up this tremendous effort of piecing things together in logical sequence' (*Beyond the Glass*, p. 252). Indeed, it is when Clara explains this temptation to the doctor that she wins her case for release (*Beyond the Glass*, p. 259). But once outside the hospital, Clara faces other obstacles. Her memory of the events leading up to her hospitalisation are hazy and uncertain, and her family, in a common but unproductive response, believe that Clara should just forget her illness ever happened: they worry that memories of her now-lost fiancé may trigger a recurrence and discourage her from talking about it. Thus, conversations with her family 'always edged away from the only two things that really interested her: Richard and her memories of Nazareth' (*Beyond the Glass*, p. 271). Clara, however, is determined to 'piece it all together' (*Beyond the Glass*, p. 275), despite the fact that the day she began to slip into delirious mania contains

> gaps [. . .] that, try as she might, she could not fill. She could remember more and more of what she had been through in the asylum but those last days with Richard remained a curious dazzle of brilliant light and utter darkness. (*Beyond the Glass*, p. 272)

As she explains to Richard's sister, '"what I can't stand is not knowing [. . .] I don't want to forget it, as Daddy thinks I should. You see, it was real, in its way. And it's desperately important for me now to know what's real and what isn't"' (*Beyond the Glass*, p. 282).

Clara's determination to piece together her experience of manic psychosis and integrate it as an important element of her identity narrative develops out of her appreciation of the intensity and power of manic perception:

> Beyond the glass, however agonising the nightmare experiences, they had had a peculiar intensity. If some had been terrifying, others had been exquisite. When those experiences had ceased, she had been as passive as a child until the tremendous, absorbing experience of willing herself back to consciousness. (*Beyond the Glass*, p. 271)

Like many manic-depressives, Clara finds euthymic or 'normal' life tortuous in its 'boredom and suspense': 'for all the kindness and love about her, she felt frustrated and only half alive. Her days were regulated to a routine of meals and walks and games of croquet' (*Beyond the Glass*, p. 271). This routine echoes that of the hospital and implicitly underscores the powerful attraction the spontaneity and intensity the manic 'high' has for many manic-depressives. To forego access to this realm of experience is difficult; to act as if it never happened is impossible. Thus, despite Clara's own embarrassment and reticence over her 'strange' behaviour and 'rows' with the Indian student and Richard's sister (*Beyond the Glass*, pp. 264, 280), she courageously undertakes the process of remembering all she can by revisiting her old ward and saying goodbye to a kind nurse; by interrogating the doctor about what happened to her leather coat (she had shredded it with her bare hands); and by demanding answers from Richard's sister about his marriage to another woman. The novel ends with Clara alone, tempted once again to wade into the Thames but, clutching the rosary that is her parting gift from her lost fiancé and feeling its weight like a 'detaining hand', vowing to 'hold on' (*Beyond the Glass*, p. 285).

The Sugar House and Beyond the Glass: the manifest plot

White's representation of manic depression is stunning in its uncanny reflection of medical accounts of the disorder, an uncanniness that develops out of its positioning 'beyond the glass' and from the sufferer's perspective. The psychosis sections of *Beyond the Glass*, in particular, evidence White's brilliant manipulation of narrative to capture exactly how it feels to escalate into psychosis. Clara's inability to fill in the gaps that open up, for example, accurately speaks to the fact that 'memory is often spotty for the events of delirious mania'; thus White deliberately embeds the gaps as textual jumpcuts that remain unexplained. Brief chapters of exposition, typically focalised through Claude or through conversations between Claude and Isabel, provide context and a timeline for Clara's hospitalisation and the stages of her illness.

Yet if manic depression is the latent plotline of *The Sugar House* and *Beyond the Glass*, the manifest plotline explains Clara's illness as the result of enduring psychological conflicts about her father and Catholicism, in which her inability to embrace a fully sexual adult femininity is entwined with her inability to fulfil her vocation as artist and writer. As Kylie Valentine observes of *Beyond the Glass*:

> The novel's appropriation of the discourses of psychoanalysis, nationalism, and spiritualism render the fact of Clara's madness explicable

and the content of it meaningful. The authority of these discourses situates the cause of an individual madness within a political and social network rather than locating this cause narrowly in the mind or body of that individual.[82]

Yet 'this appropriation of patriarchal discourses dovetails finally into a resituating of madness and recovery within these discourses'.[83]

From the outset of *The Sugar House*, White emphasises Clara's troubling inability to define herself: she has taken up acting 'just as she had gone, at seventeen, to be governess to the Cressetts simply because someone else had suggested it and she had been anxious for a change' (*The Sugar House*, p. 15). White thus builds upon the themes introduced in the two earlier novels, that Nanda's will was shattered by her father's repudiation of her as his daughter and that the structure and discipline of the convent has made it impossible for Clara to regulate herself: 'She was so used to obeying other people that it was impossible to obey herself' (*The Lost Traveller*, p. 178). When Clara is jilted by a man she hopes to marry, her father and Charles's mother between them propel her back to Archie, and part two of *The Sugar House* opens with her wedding. Just as these two represent patriarchal and Catholic authority in motivating Clara's engagement in *The Lost Traveller*, so, too, do they here: once again, Clara perceives the Cressett home, the aristocratic Maryhall, 'as the symbol of order and tradition; of a life oriented beyond time'. Maryhall serves as a kind of secular convent and marriage functions as a vocation undertaken for the promise of the future family (*The Sugar House*, p. 112). The stable structures of the convent and Maryhall remain deeply appealing to Clara, who continues to feel as if she doesn't belong anywhere. At the same time, Clara has longed to become fully adult since her passionate encounter with the man who jilted her.

Her marriage to Archie, however, does not separate her from her father but instead underscores her indissoluble bond to him. As Flood points out, 'Archie's impotence makes him most suitable as Clara's husband, for the object of her marriage is to preserve her oedipal tie to her father.'[84] White emphasises the oedipal aspects of the marriage: the night after the wedding, Clara imagines her father knocking at the door and, realising 'with horror that she was in bed with Archie', Clara is overcome with 'shame and guilt' (*The Sugar*

House, p. 127). The entrance of a maid with a congratulatory letter from her father seems to

> link her once more to her old self. However disjointed her life might be, however much she was haunted by the sense that everything she undertook was doomed to failure, she remained Claude Batchelor's daughter. In marrying Archie she had perhaps made up to him for all the times she had disappointed him in the past. (*The Sugar House*, p. 128)

She goes on to imagine how her marriage 'had restored her to her father; henceforth the three of them were bound in a new tie from which her mother was excluded. She thought how passionately Claude had wanted a son; how passionately she herself had wanted a brother' (*The Sugar House*, p. 129). Thus the bohemian Chelsea house, which should have provided an escape from her father –'a symbol of her new-found freedom', 'a place where she could do as she chose' and where 'her father had no right to come here unless she invited him' (*The Sugar House*, p. 140) – simultaneously functions as 'a room in a horrible story she had once heard where each day the walls of a prisoner's cell drew imperceptibly nearer together' (*The Sugar House*, p. 142). The looming presence of a Catholic church outside reinforces this sense of claustrophobic entrapment.

Clara's reference to Archie as her brother, not husband, is telling, for in marrying the impotent man – whose gift to Clara of an empty gun makes his condition sadly apparent – Clara not only confirms the centrality of her father in her psychic life but confirms her own sense of femininity as castrated and inferior. For Archie reflects Clara's own sense of psychic incompletion and impotence, a doubling White develops through a muted allusion to the conceptualisation of the female castration complex that had informed her own analysis with Carroll during the 1930s. In a passage in which Archie scalds his hand, Clara urges him to treat the burn lest the hand get infected; she implies, but doesn't state, the thought that Archie finishes: 'Even have to have it cut off; is that it?' (*The Sugar House*, p. 188).[85] Underpinning this passage is Abraham's discussion of the attraction the 'mutilated man' has for the woman who herself feels mutilated: 'such women feel an affinity to the mutilated man; they consider him a companion in distress and do not need to reject him with hate like the sound man'.[86] Indeed, Clara's and

Archie's kinship develops out of their mutual sense that they are 'two of a kind', misfits who do not fulfil the conventional norms of femininity and masculinity (*The Sugar House*, pp. 172–3). Their marriage, moreover, comes about because Archie was present at the scene of Charles Cressett's death and championed Clara's innocence afterwards; in fact, Clara wonders, 'if Charles had not been killed, would there have been any question of her marrying Archie?' (*The Sugar House*, p. 173). Flood notes that a later scene, in which Clara has 'a kind of instantaneous dream in which she was a railway engine driven by Charles Cressett and Archie' (*The Sugar House*, p. 142), fuses dead boy and impotent man, functioning as an image of Clara's psychic state and as an image of her as 'an undesirable but irreducible female who has incorporated the male'.[87] It also suggests that Clara is a castrated (fe)male, without 'male' agency and drive but unable to become wholly 'feminine'. The fusion of dead boy/half-woman and impotent man thus captures the tragic aspect of Clara's and Archie's marriage: they play like children in the Sugar House, for their journey to psychological and sexual maturity has hopelessly veered off course.

Clara's 'instantaneous dream', significantly, occurs during their honeymoon, at a moment after Archie has dammed up a stream with her assistance: 'she had had to use all her self-control not to pull away some of the stones and release the imprisoned water. The impulse was so violent that for a second she had almost lost consciousness' (*The Sugar House*, p. 142). This passage references Clara's increasing sexual frustration, for after Archie fails to consummate their relationship Clara admits to herself that she had desired as well as dreaded 'that unknown, violent contact with another person' that would 'break down some barrier in herself' – a barrier that encompasses not only the physical barrier of the hymen but a psychological barrier as well (*The Sugar House*, p. 129). Increasingly aware that, since their wedding, 'she had grown older and Archie younger' (*The Sugar House*, p. 141), Clara longs to move fully into adulthood: the games the two had played with Charles at Maryhall now bore her and she wonders 'how long she was going to have to keep up the part of Wendy to Archie's Peter Pan' (*The Sugar House*, p. 141).

White's use of train imagery, both here and in the Maryhall sections of *The Lost Traveller*, draws upon two related but distinct phenomena familiar in late nineteenth- and early twentieth-century medical and psychological discourse: the railway collision that results in 'railway brain' and 'traumatic neurosis', on the one hand, and the ongoing successive jolts of railway travel that were experienced as 'a condition of continuous vibration'[88] on the other. Whereas the first came to be recognised as a form of psychic trauma or shock – anticipating the development and recognition of war neurosis and shell shock during the First World War – the latter, a more nebulous but still insidious form of shock, developed out of the enforced passivity and simultaneously overstimulated condition of the railway passenger. Freud describes railway travel as one form of 'the production of sexual excitation by rhythmic mechanical agitation of the body', and he goes on to associate trains with masculine development and puberty:

> [Every boy] has at one time or other in his life wanted to be an engine driver or coachman [. . .] A compulsive link of this kind between railway travel and sexuality is clearly derived from the pleasurable character of the sensations of the movement.[89]

The train became a dominant image for the Surrealists: notably, in *Nadja* André Breton 'underscores the connections between violent movement, psychological shifts, and romantic emotion', writes Marylaura Papalas.[90] In particular, the juxtaposition of violence and sexuality 'is a way of expressing the repressed sexuality that the Surrealists felt governed social behaviours of the modern era'.[91]

White's use of train imagery speaks to both trauma and sexual excitation. In *The Lost Traveller* Clara plays with trains as eagerly as Charles Cressett, entering into his world 'as if she had been ten years old herself' and resembling the prepubescent boy of Freud's description (*The Lost Traveller*, p. 228); at her first meeting with Archie, his skill with trains and ability to 'command' Clara transforms him from 'an overgrown schoolboy' into a man in her eyes (*The Lost Traveller*, p. 237). The accident he stages evokes the model of psychological trauma associated with 'railway brain': 'The railway had become so real to Clara that when the locomotives crashed into each other and a tiny coach came uncoupled and toppled over a precipice eighteen inches deep, she felt a shock of horror' (*The Lost Traveller*, pp. 237–8). In hindsight, as their marriage collapses, Clara will recall this accident as a premonition of both their disastrous marriage and

Charles's death, for she first agrees to marry Archie to assuage his misery after the accident (*The Sugar House*, p. 217). The 'shock' of the tiny coach's derailment anticipates Charles's fall to his death, which in turn inaugurates Clara's sense of unreality and incompletion, 'as if some part of [her] died when Charles did' (*The Sugar House*, p. 76).[92] In imagining herself as an engine driven by Charles and Archie, then, Clara imagines herself as driven by fate (Charles's death) into a farcical and childish caricature of marriage, one steered by a man in a permanent state of arrested development.

This second use of the train thus speaks to Clara's sexual frustration in the face of her unconsummated marriage, for Clara clearly perceives sexual initiation as an initiation into adulthood: the 'continuous vibration' of the moving engine on a track to nowhere captures her state of futility, frustration and entrapment. These feelings contribute to her deteriorating mental state, as she lapses into lethargy, inertia and finally depression, a depression in which she explicitly connects her inability to write to her sterility as woman. Feeling as if everything is 'jammed up inside and out' and likening herself to the parched courtyard of 'sour soil where nothing will grow' (*The Lost Traveller*, pp. 172, 210), Clara recalls some lines of poetry: 'Abstinence sows sand all over the ruddy limbs and flaming hair' (*The Lost Traveller*, pp. 208–9). These unattributed lines from Blake's 'Epigram 465' continue with an explicit image of sexual fulfilment and fecundity: 'But Desire Gratified/ Plants fruit of life & beauty there'.[93] Clara feels barred from sexual and artistic fruition, and she despairingly wonders whether her 'numbed body' could produce a 'living creation any more than her numbed mind could produce even a fragment of living work' (*The Sugar House*, p. 210). Her desperation eventually drives her into the arms of Marcus Gundry, a successful painter whose artistic creativity and sexual appetite represent an ideal to her. But Clara cannot, finally, acquiesce to desire. Instead, she finds Gundry's sexual advances overwhelming, producing 'a blank darkness in her mind and a sense of suffocation' (*The Sugar House*, p. 233). Her inhibitions thwart her attempts to move into autonomy: tellingly, she imagines her father, not her husband, accusing her after a flirtatious conversation with Gundry (*The Sugar House*, p. 213). Characteristically, Clara twins her father's censorious authority with that of the Catholic church which looms outside the Sugar House, initially in the guise of a 'firm Nannie' intruding into the nursery and, later, more ominously, as the witch who entrapped Hansel and Gretel (*The Sugar House*, pp. 142, 212).

The Sugar House thus connects artistic and sexual frustration explicitly to Clara's unresolved and conflicted relationship with her father in general and with the repudiated convent novel in particular. As depression sets in and Clara finds herself unable to write, she buys herself a black notebook like her father's and begins to 'keep a kind of diary. Writing in it gave her the illusion that she was at least producing something' (*The Sugar House*, p. 154). On her twenty-second birthday, the eighth anniversary of the discovery of her 'depraved' novel, Clara hopes that her father will finally give her the opportunity to explain her plans for the novel's conclusion and receive his forgiveness for 'what had outraged him in what she had written, in all innocence, at fourteen':

> Might that relieve the appalling guilt and self-mistrust which overcame her every time she tried to write anything which was not merely confected? In the last two months, this guilt and impotence had spread to anything she wrote at all [. . .] to anything, in fact, designed to be read by others. Only the black notebook, though it contained much that might reasonably make her feel guilty, was exempt from the blight, simply because it was secret. (*The Sugar House*, p. 163)

The Sugar House thus enshrines in fiction the explanation White had developed in her identity narrative to explain her writer's block and her illness. *Beyond the Glass* follows up by providing a plausible explanation for Clara's swing into mania. Here, White develops the psychoanalytic understanding of schizophrenia as developing from 'the splitting of the psyche in accordance with the emotionally charged complexes'. The unacknowledged rage at the father's failure to equip the daughter with access to expressive power (writing/sexuality) eventually results in her disintegration as the 'emotionally charged complexes' begin to break through. Other conceptualisations of both schizophrenia and the unconscious also shape White's vision. Jung, whose formulations influenced White's second analysis, attributed schizophrenia to the splintering of the psyche into fragments when uninhibited and primitive unconscious content intrudes upon the conscious ego, a process he imaged as the splintering of a mirror.[94] Hence it is significant that both *The Sugar House* and *Beyond the*

Glass describe Clara's intensifying fragmentation and depersonalisation through the imagery of a complex interplay of windows, mirrors and glass.[95] At the same time, White's use of mirrors speaks to her understanding of schizophrenia as split personality, the Jekyll and Hyde of popular (mis)conception. Clara's disturbing vision of a menacing, mocking stranger in the mirror who wants to pull her over to the other side, for example, suggests the takeover of Jekyll by Hyde in Stevenson's novel: as in Stevenson, this menacing alter ego unleashes primitive emotions and actions (*Beyond the Glass*, p. 168).[96]

Beyond the Glass locates psychic fragmentation and madness within several other important contexts. The title alludes, of course, to Lewis Carroll's *Through the Looking Glass, and what Alice Found There*. Although Elaine Showalter has described women writers' pervasive imaging of mental asylums in terms of Carroll's book as 'an allusion from the nursery world which the infantilization of the institution brings to mind'[97], White's use of Carroll may have been influenced by the Surrealists' promotion of Alice as a figure of the *femme-enfant* and the world through the looking glass as a figure of the unconscious; indeed, William Empson dubbed Alice 'the patron saint of surrealism' in 1935[98] and, in the same year, David Gascoyne, who introduced White to surrealism, claimed Carroll as an important British forerunner to surrealism in his survey of the subject.[99] Catriona McAra has shown how the Surrealists 'co-opted the curiosity of his heroine Alice as an investigatory trope': Alice becomes an 'agent of critique and disruption' who, while appearing 'sweet and wholesome [. . .] transgresses the confines of her bourgeois nursery, through escape into imaginative, fantastical domains'.[100] McAra points out, moreover, that those domains could be 'dark, frightening places full of violence, monsters and latent meaning where the Alice-child must trump her obstacles'.[101] Alice's forays through the looking glass resonate with the use of mirrors in women's surrealist art in general. Whitney Chadwick writes that 'the mirror image, rather than confirming our assumptions about the nature of the real (and its replicability), defamiliarizes the real and opens it up to the forces of the dream, the irrational, and the unconscious'.[102] For women Surrealists in particular, 'the problem of self-representation is epitomized as the problem of the mirror':

> Women Surrealists were tied to and grounded in the idea of the mirror image giving something back, but the giving back was only the beginning. It was not to be taken as the end of the process, or as

the embodiment of self, but rather as simply the starting point from which the self might be doubled, fragmented, fractured or erased. The issue of misrecognition in the mirror is very important here.[103]

Chadwick's remarks concern visual artists, but they seem widely applicable to White's work. The sitting room of the Sugar House, hung with mirrors to give the illusion of space, instead surrounds Clara with a claustrophobic impression of herself fractured and refracted from multiple angles:

> She jumped up from the chair. Immediately she was conscious of the number of mirrors in the tiny space. Three different angles of her head and shoulders and one full-length figure sprang towards her. The little room [. . .] seemed to close in on her. (*The Sugar House*, p. 142)

At a later point in the novel, fearing that she doesn't exist at all, Clara rushes into the sitting room full of mirrors 'almost expecting to find nothing reflected in them. But her face stared back at her anxiously from various angles and she was horrified to see how much she had changed' (*The Sugar House*, p. 154). In *Beyond the Glass*, the mirror becomes a site of eerie doubling, in which Clara's split-off dark double pulls her into the Looking-glass Land of the unconscious.[104] Notably, when Clara succumbs to psychosis, she looks into a mirror at the nurses' urging and 'saw a face in the glass, the face of a fairy horse, or stag, sometimes with antlers, sometimes with a wild golden mane, but always with the same dark stony eyes and nostrils red as blood' (*Beyond the Glass*, p. 212). Such passages function as verbal equivalents to the kinds of visual images produced by women Surrealists: Claude Cahun's photographic self-portraits distort and refract her image through the use of multiple mirrors, for example, while Leonora Carrington often uses animals, particularly horses, as emblems of self-transformation and 'symbolic intermediaries between the unconscious and the natural world'.[105]

As in *The Lost Traveller*, White also positions the unconscious within a Catholic context. Julie Vandivere has shown how the title alludes not only to Carroll but also to a well-known Biblical passage: 'For now we see through a glass, darkly; but then face to face: now I know in part; but then shall I know even as also I am known' (1 Corinthians: 13).[106] The conventional interpretation of the passage – that in life we see only with imperfect and obscure vision but in the afterlife in the presence of God we will see clearly – reads it as referencing clouded glass. But as a number of Biblical commentaries posit, the 'glass' in the passage derives from the King James translation, when 'glass' meant 'mirror': mirrors in ancient times were made of polished brass, in which reflections were dark, dim and distorted.[107] This conceptualisation of the glass or mirror posits that we cannot see ourselves clearly in this life, but can do so in the perfect glass of the afterlife, when we come into the presence of God 'face to face'.[108] Other commentaries suggest that the passage gestures to the difficulty of seeing through such a mirror: our attempts to gain understanding will always be circumscribed by our inability to see beyond our own egotism.[109] Hence the Biblical passage gestures to the double meaning of glass in the final instalment: on the one hand, glass permits some vision of what lies on the other side (the unconscious); on the other hand, vision is always imperfect, a reflection of one's own (fallen) nature. In life, one can only see 'darkly', that is, imperfectly and through the lens of one's inevitable distortions. A diary entry White recorded about her reconversion in 1941 explicitly positions the limitations of human vision within a framework of faith:

> About a week ago, after months of hesitation and doubt, I felt I reached firm ground. I do not pretend to explain it: in fact I can't explain it anyhow except by 'grace'. It is not as if I had had any miraculous revelation or had arrived at a satisfactory reconciliation of all the problems. All that I know is that an eye seemed to open somewhere inside me, an eye very filmed and feeble, seeing nothing definite but yet knowing that there *was* something to see. This is the nearest to 'faith' I have ever come in my life . . . (*Diary* 1, p. 177)

In a revised version of this passage for publication, White foregrounded the allusion to 1 Corinthians: 13 by explaining that the 'filmed and feeble' eye could just 'make out a dim outline':

> as if, with the eyes of the mind wide open, seeing all the loose ends, all the contradictions, all the gaps to be bridged, this inner eye perceived that the surface was not quite opaque and that an infinite perspective opened out beyond it. (*The Hound and the Falcon*, pp. 163–4)

This Catholic shading of the unconscious plays an important role in understanding the novel's conclusion, as I show below.

Glass also plays an important role in White's imaging of two related but distinct psychological manifestations of Clara's psychic disintegration, derealisation and depersonalisation. The first of these, derealisation, is the sense of being cut off or estranged from the world: common images to describe the experience include entrapment in a bell jar; entrapment in a goldfish bowl; and the sense of being separated from the world by a pane of glass.[110] Clara experiences all three: she feels suffocated under a bell jar; she identifies Archie through a glass door, 'glaring at him speechlessly like a fish in an aquarium' (*Beyond the Glass*, p. 77); she feels cut off from others as if 'forever outside, forever looking in through glass at the bright human world which had no place for her and where the mere sight of her produced terror' (*Beyond the Glass*, p. 65). Depersonalisation, by contrast, is the sense of disconnection between body and consciousness: here the mind stands apart from the body, an onlooker to its experiences, which seem to be happening to somebody else.[111] Clara experiences this sense of disconnection when she packs up her belongings in the Sugar House: 'she had the odd impression that it was not she [. . .] but some callous, efficient stranger. She herself was lying on the unmade bed, staring blankly at the cracks in the sugar-pink ceiling' (*Beyond the Glass*, p. 39). Similarly, during the gynaecological examination 'she managed to detach herself so completely from what was going on that her body seemed to have no connection with her' (*Beyond the Glass*, p. 80). An extreme form of depersonalisation occurs when Clara gazes into a mirror, only to see a stranger staring back. Derealisation and depersonalisation tend to occur in tandem with each other and are considered co-symptoms of dissociative disorder[112]; they are sometimes considered early signs of schizophrenia. That they were so considered at the time that White was composing her novels during the early 1950s is suggested by an anecdote reported by Janet Frame in her autobiography. Newly released from the mental hospital where she had been incarcerated for almost eight years, Frame applied in 1954 for a sickness benefit to help her resettle after years of institutionalisation. When the supervisor of the hospital refused to support the application, admonishing her to find work, she wrote a poem to him in which she deliberately 'chose imagery known to be "schizophrenic" – glass, mirrors, reflections, the sense of being separated from the world by panels of glass'.[113]

This 'schizophrenic' imagery, which incorporates meanings drawn from psychoanalysis, surrealism and Catholicism, encodes the father–daughter complex White had addressed explicitly in the plotlines of her earlier three instalments. Hence *Beyond the Glass* displaces Clara's psychological conflicts from plot on to symptom. Of all the instalments in the series, this novel shows the least overt conflict between Claude and Clara. Instead, White suggests that the damage has been done: the split that opened up in *Frost in May* between compliance with the authority of the father and the Church on the one hand and self-assertion on the other has widened as Clara has grown to maturity and as her sexual and artistic desires have intensified and gone unfulfilled. In this respect, Clara's will – shattered by the father's repudiation of the convent novel and by habits of obedience and compliance to convent and paternal discipline – plays a key role in predisposing her to breakdown: in the Jungian conceptualisation of schizophrenia, the complexes break through as a result of a *faiblesse de la volonté*, a weakening of willpower.[114] Clara's inability to channel complexes into artistic productions may here play a crucial role. As Juan Terblanche explains:

> Where, in a normal situation the ego would allow (through active imagination) the unconscious material to rise to consciousness in order to 'make sense' of the vast plethora of material housed in the unconscious (either through writing, painting, drawing), the ego in the schizophrenic is bombarded without warning with archetypal images from the collective unconscious, thus, the psyche is in disarray.[115]

The very suddenness with which Clara falls in love with Richard precipitates this bombardment, for her mind shatters when the conflicts associated with sexuality and artistry abruptly surface.[116] As Penny Brown observes:

> In her new conviction that she will one day be able to write a wonderful book imbued with 'this dazzling new intensity of vision' (her literary ability as a means of self-expression thus clearly associated with emotional and sexual fulfilment) and her longing to bear Richard's children, her insatiable urge to create and the mental acceptance of, even longing for pain, indicate the too rapid unblocking of her inhibitions.[117]

In fact, the novel supplies this explanation: Claude worries about the 'extraordinary change' in Clara and questions the intensity and impetuosity of the romance, while Isabel, wanting to imagine that the romance will be a happy version of *Romeo and Juliet*, finds lines from the play rising to her lips unbidden: '"It is too rash, too unadvised, too sudden/ Too like the lightening which doth cease to be/ Ere one can say: It lightens"' (*Beyond the Glass*, p. 174).

Clara's image of herself as balanced within a 'crystal sphere of security' that spins in the sunlight points to this psychological fragility: her violent moods threaten to 'shatter' and 'crack' it, and she is 'giddily aware of a whirling darkness outside' (*Beyond the Glass*, pp. 169, 175). White almost certainly drew this image from Freud, for he explicitly compares the psyche to a crystal that can fracture from a sudden shock or trauma:

> If we throw a crystal to the floor, it breaks; but not into haphazard pieces. It comes apart along the lines of its cleavage into fragments whose boundaries, though they were invisible, were predetermined by the crystal's structure. Mental patients are split and broken structures of this same kind.[118]

Clara's mind indeed fractures along the faultlines established by the previous instalments. Kylie Valentine has shown how White adapts the psychoanalytic conceptualisation of over-determination to image Clara's initial delusions about soldiers, whereby 'multiple causes of a symptom (in Clara's case, the multiple meanings obtained through the figuring of soldiers)' find expression in 'that symptom (Clara's delirium)'.[119] The multiple meanings that soldiers accrue throughout the series become, in *Beyond the Glass*, 'a site of convergence of otherwise unconnected events: the death of Charles Cressett; parental disapproval and disappointment; failure to share her father's grief and loss; unworthiness because of all of these to be a soldier's wife'.[120] Thus the 'pressures brought to bear by her sense of unworthiness, her father's disappointment, and the death of a child for which she feels responsible' are all 'linked back to the figure of the soldier, a link that compounds the original effect of each event into a torment easily recognised as unbearable'.[121] Clara's delusional belief that she must suffer through the agonies of multiple dying soldiers functions as a form of absolution as well as 'an act of resurrection and redemption for the soldiers' mothers'.[122]

Delusions about her unworthiness to become a soldier's bride mark only the onset of Clara's psychosis, however. As her psychic fragmentation increases, the images her mind throws up become far more surrealistic and less explicable. Hal Foster argues that 'the surrealist image is patterned upon the symptom as an enigmatic signifier of a psychosexual trauma'.[123] Focusing on the darker psychic undercurrents of surrealism rather than on its avowed alliance with pleasure, love and liberation, Foster connects the surrealist image to the uncanny, the death drive and the compulsion to repeat: the traumatised subject, caught between Eros and Thanatos, contemplates objects from the past which now appear familiar and yet unfamiliar in their relocation to a world where they acquire now-fantastic meanings that amplify or contradict their earlier ones. This conceptualisation of the surrealist image illuminates the imagery that swirls through Clara's psychosis, in which familiar scenes and people from the past are displaced into an hallucinatory present: the Cossack cap she wears in a childhood photograph now appears on Richard's head; stories heard in the convent – a saint martyred by being crushed to death; a bride lost in a dungeon on her wedding day and discovered years later as a skeleton – unwind in the present, with Clara living the stories out. Images of birth and death, creation and destruction, intermingle and succeed one another. Notably, while a number of Clara's hallucinations embody impediments to her union with or marriage to Richard, others suggest sexual inhibition and anxiety. Hence at one point Clara becomes a girl aged twelve, dressed in a blue pinafore (reminiscent of Alice), while Richard is her brother; they share a love 'far deeper and more subtle than any love between husband and wife' (*Beyond the Glass*, p. 215). At another point, Clara is both herself and Richard simultaneously: 'she was Richard, endlessly climbing up the steps of a dark tower by the sea, knowing that she herself was imprisoned at the top' (*Beyond the Glass*, p. 213). This tower, suggestive of fairy tales such as *Rapunzel*, also recalls the tower in which Claude had fantasised his ideal union with his daughter. Above all, Clara's transformations into animals, fish and plants blur the boundaries between the human and natural world. Sometimes these transformations eradicate sexual difference; others empower femininity. In her guise as a magic horse, for example, Clara evokes the Queen of Horses, the British goddess Epona or Celtic goddess Rhiannon (source of the 'night mare'), whose travel across the sky emblematises her ability to access the Other World and bridge the worlds of life and death.

Clara's return to 'sanity' and the world on the 'sane' side of the looking glass is a return to the strictures and structures of patriarchy, as most commentators have pointed out.[124] As in the world of the convent, where nuns enforced the rule of God the Father, nurses teach Clara how to be a 'good' girl under the direction of male doctors (*Beyond the Glass*, p. 242). White draws explicit parallels between the convent discipline and that of the hospital; even the name of the hospital, Nazareth Royal Hospital – a hospital for girls who, like Alice, 'ask too many questions' (*Beyond the Glass*, p. 219) – reproduces that of the Nazareth dormitory in *Frost in May* (p. 33).[125] Clara's written appeal to her father for release from the hospital, which entails reversing the mirror writing of Looking-glass Land and painfully copying the writing of a male-authored novel, affirms her identity as the 'loving daughter' of 'Dearest Daddy' (*Beyond the Glass*, p. 245); her father responds to this affirmation by immediately visiting the hospital to secure her release, and they leave together 'like reunited lovers' (*Beyond the Glass*, p. 263).[126] During Clara's incarceration, moreover, Claude has engineered a break between Clara and Richard by informing the latter of Clara's prognosis of chronic insanity: Richard has in the meantime married an Irish girl, also a Catholic, whose pilgrimage to Lourdes to pray for Clara's recovery has telepathically reached Clara in her psychotic delirium. Thus the novel ends, as Flood remarks, by leaving Clara 'firmly but guiltlessly united to her father in the incestuous bond'.[127]

And yet not quite. Clara's refusal to renounce her memories of Nazareth has left her in an uneasy relationship to the 'world beyond the glass': knowing she no longer belongs there, 'There were moments when she almost wished she did' (*Beyond the Glass*, p. 271). Richard's conversion to Catholicism, which resonates with the conversion of a schoolmate at the close of *Frost in May*, similarly opens up the novel's conclusion to a broader context. As Philip O'Mara points out, throughout the series White emphasises the mysterious working of grace and faith, whereby the limited vision of human beings can never see beyond the imperfect glass of mortality: 'The action of grace is always mediated through imperfect human motives and is often perilously close to tragedy', he remarks.[128] Hence her schoolmate's conversion, which Nanda imagines she is prepared to sacrifice anything to achieve, occurs in tandem with her expulsion, suggesting that her 'implicit sacrificial offering has been accepted, her prayer answered'.[129] O'Mara suggests that Clara's loss of Richard functions as a similar sacrificial offering, answering Clara's prayer that she be allowed to share in the suffering of the soldiers and become worthy to be a 'soldier's bride': 'She is about to find herself called on, as they were, to lose her own hope of earthly happiness and accomplishment [. . .] she, like the soldiers, will suffer involuntarily, and for no reason that she can understand'.[130] Thus Richard's conversion means that 'Clara's agony has borne fruit in the life of another without ending in any consolation for her, and the pattern is complete'.[131] The emphasis on Mary as the intermediary suggests further that Clara turns, not to her father, but to the Divine Mother as her support. Not only does the woman who becomes Richard's wife communicate with Clara during her psychosis by reciting the Litany of Our Lady, Richard's gift of a rosary – the prayer beads that promote access to Jesus through Mary's intercession – functions as a 'detaining hand', preventing Clara from succumbing to despair and suicide. In this sense, Clara fulfils the Catholic ideal first laid out for her in the convent long ago, when Mother Radcliffe explained that the Catholic mission was to turn out neither 'accomplished women nor agreeable wives, but soldiers of Christ, accustomed to hardship and ridicule and ingratitude' (*Frost in May*, p. 118). Clara's final affirmation is not to her father, nor to Richard, but to faith.

Epilogue: Composing a Self

White's writing out of Clara's life stalled at the point when Clara had left the asylum and returned to her father's home. The next instalment was to tell the story of the loss of White's virginity, the resulting pregnancy with the only son she ever conceived, and the termination of that pregnancy by an illegal abortion arranged with her father's help. Entries about this unwritten novel recur throughout the 1950s, as White tries to reconstruct the chronology, a reconstruction she finds difficult because 'That is one of the most tangled parts of my life to look back on' (*Diary* 1, p. 274). 'The beginning is terribly important,' White writes (*Diary* 1, p. 292): 'we know her father's state of mind. Relief that she is decertified [. . .] Unconscious delight that she is "his" again' (*Diary* 1, p. 292). While Clara's father wants her to have the child abroad, 'He does not *seriously* attempt to dissuade her from the abortion: merely puts the responsibility on her'; afterwards, 'Paris [with her father] is definitely a sort of honeymoon. Yet in a way he wants to see her married. Why did he encourage D[ougal]? For he *did*' (*Diary* 1, p. 293). White slips from the fictional scene to the actual event in this passage: she stops herself at the point where she confronts her sense that her father was somehow complicit in Dougal's behaviour. In another entry, White again imagines the father as complicit: 'It is the father who asks him to stay the night. Clara does not even know he is in the house because of her having to go to bed at ten. So when he comes into her room, it is almost like a dream. He is wearing a dressing-gown of her father's' (*Diary* 1, p. 290). A third entry connects Dougal to both her father and her former analyst Carroll (*Diary* 1, p. 243); here White calls Dougal 'The liar: the man who got me on false pretences' (*Diary* 1, p. 243). Finally White concludes, 'The impossible thing to explain to myself is the Dougal thing' (*Diary* 1, p. 293).

White's entries suggest that the impossible thing to explain to herself is that, in imagining Clara's acquiescence to the intruder in her bedroom, White at some level imagines that she herself allowed Dougal to have sex with her because she thought he was her father. In an unpublished portion of the diary, White admitted that she 'certainly "provoked" this intercourse'.[1] Not only did White compose the Ritual Rape Dream during this period, but she records another dream in which her father returns to her from death: she writes that she 'was so happy, so relieved. I would not be lonely anymore' (*Diary* 1, p. 252). From this dream, too, White awakes 'aware of a very faint sexual tremor', and she goes on to interpret the dream as giving her 'a sense of peace, a sense that *something* [. . .] had changed [. . .] I suppose it means I have truly "forgiven" my father' (*Diary* 1, p. 252). In an entry recorded some days later, White returns to the dream again, speculating that it also suggests that her father has forgiven her; but she adds 'Fear . . . about my novels. Slightly wrong love . . . the sexual element. A touch obviously of wanting the father as a *husband*' (*Diary* 1, p. 253). What White comes up against in her planning of the next instalment of Clara's story is the exposure not just of the father's desire for the daughter, but the daughter's answering desire for the father, a desire inculcated by the master narratives of family, religion and psychology. Although she repeatedly tried to change the chronology of her alter ego's life so that she could eliminate the 'Dougal episode', White remained uncertain about whether Clara's life made sense without it. She wavered for years:

> I have decided to do the abortion book after all. This doesn't solve *my* problems for it will be *very* difficult. But I am sure it is right for the sequence. It is the only logical lead-up to Clara's marriage to Clive. (*Diary* 2, p. 23)[2]

White's fear of her 'depraved' imagination clearly played some role in making it impossible for her to continue with Clara's story. That fear was justified: her second analyst, for whom White composed her dream diaries (including the two 'reconciliation' dreams about her father), broke with White during this period; White records in her diary that her analyst 'cast me out very crudely and definitely. Something all wrong with me . . . I am "depraved" and she must "withdraw from me and my situation"' (*Diary* 1, p. 217). One of her father's former students, a woman who had been instrumental in his conversion to Catholicism, repeatedly urged White to burn her work instead of publishing it (*Diary* 2, p. 210); she specifically disapproved of the way White wrote about her father and accused her of injuring his reputation (*Diary* 2, pp. 177, 143). White herself worried that she was transgressing in some way:

> I find I *am* still worrying about 'exposing' my father in this [book]. 'Thou shalt not uncover thy father's nakedness.' In church this morning I remembered that strange temptation when I looked at my father's dead body to which mercifully I did not yield. I don't really think it was a wish to do anything wrong. I cannot analyse it. Perhaps I wanted to see for myself that my father was a man like other men. (*Diary* 2, p. 38)

Toppling her father from the pedestal she had erected for him was something White was never able to do: in her seventies she dreamt that 'my father appeared to me naked. A great colossal naked figure. *Most* extraordinary. No sense of embarrassment on my part and certainly no sexual association. He was massive, more than life size, like a primitive statue' (*Diary* 2, p. 217). That she could not finish Clara's story – or even write the next instalment of it – speaks to the ways in which this colossus dominated White's imagination as well as her emotional and sexual life. What she did not write as fiction, however, is inscribed in the identity narratives she repeatedly constructed, in which the father's centrality in social and cultural narratives colonises the daughter's imagination and requires her seduction by paternal authority.

Yet, as much and as often as White attributed her writer's block to her father's disapproval, that attribution had its source in a misreading and misunderstanding of her illness. White did not understand the ways in which her chaotic moods generated feelings, particularly the soul-destroying feelings of self-hatred, guilt and worthlessness. Her moods were as inexplicable to her family and friends as they were to her, and White experienced tremendous difficulties with interpersonal relationships, evidenced not only by her failed marriages and affairs but also by her estrangement from her daughters. She spent most of the last thirty years of her life alone, sharing her flat with a succession of boarders. Often struggling with depression and harassed by financial worries and an inability to control her spending, White supported herself through translating French texts, literary grants and subsidies, and handouts from friends. Unlike Virginia Woolf, whose experiences of illness in many ways are congruent with those of White, White had no secure network of emotional and financial support to help her in managing her debilitating moods and resultant sense of incoherence. In fact, by her later years an entry in her diary reads 'association of writing with loss of love and feeling something bad comes out of my writing wh. will alienate those I love'; White includes her third husband and oldest daughter among those lost to her (*Diary* 2, p. 186). Her difficult personal relations seemed to confirm her in her own mind as worthless, corrupt or even non-existent. When her analyst calls her depraved, White has a 'classic bad turn [. . . her] mention of "depravity" obviously touched a very raw place: the sense I always have during a "bad" turn of being a kind of leper' (*Diary* 1, p. 215). Estranged from her daughter, White writes that 'It is as if when people remain deliberately unaware of me, I cease to exist, can make no decisions, do no work' (*Diary* 1, p. 253). '[S]o often I don't feel as if *I* existed unless I'm the object of someone's concern', reads another entry (*Diary* 1, p. 143). She identifies herself with the little boy in the Andersen fairy tale 'The Snow Queen':

> with the fatal splinter of glass in his eye who sees everything distorted – the boy scorning love and trying to build up everything by reason [. . .] he is only saved from being frozen to death by the child who loves him and by regaining his own childhood. (*The Hound and the Falcon*, p. 118)

That sense of unconditional acceptance never came.

White's isolation, which intensified her feelings of disintegration and nonexistence, played an enormous role in her writer's block. One of the major benefits she attributes to analysis was that her analysts listened to her. In an entry recorded when she was in her sixties, White describes her reaction when her doctor identified symptoms of a major episode of illness: 'The mere fact of someone asking me – listening – showing interest – was such an amazing relief – I was so grateful – I thanked him and even cried a little with gratitude' (*Diary* 2, p. 130). When her second analyst cast her off, White writes, 'Certainly I needed a friend: who doesn't? I was too weak to put up with human loneliness. Oh, the analyst, the analyst, the person who gives us their exclusive undivided attention' (*Diary* 1, p. 215). Analysis provided a much-needed space where White could explain what she felt to someone who could help her figure out who she was. That kind of analytic 'holding environment' never materialised for White elsewhere, and without it she felt insecure, incoherent and anchorless. Indeed, she came to imagine that her desire to have others recognise her work revealed shameful exhibitionist tendencies, a desire to be remarkable and to display herself to others. White's fear that her writing would expose her to punishment and contempt, moreover, had a basis in fact. In an entry where she identifies her 'need for an audience', White writes, 'I would never have been expelled . . . if I hadn't yielded to the temptation of letting someone read my book . . . *Frost in May* written entirely because Tom listened [. . .] It seems odd neither of the analysts got on to this" (*Diary* 1, 215). Her unconscious can only accept a 'not guilty' verdict, she writes, through the agency of 'another human being whom one loves and trusts and who loves and trusts oneself. I need a friend far more than an analyst' (*Diary* 1, 216). Alone and trying to imagine an 'ideal reader' who can instil confidence, White goes through a long list of friends and family members, none of whom suffice, because they are too busy or too uninterested (*Diary* 1, p. 234). Yet 'if someone can give me confidence I can do better than I thought possible' (*Diary* 1, p. 227).

White repeatedly complained that she could only write fiction based on her own life, that she was incapable of invention and imagination. Some of that may indeed have stemmed from her overly controlling and intrusive father, who demanded her compliance and curbed her spontaneity. But it also came from her sense that she was psychically adrift in a world where she could not be sure of herself: her imagination spoke most clearly in her diaries and her dreams – and her insanity. It is significant that her second analyst was able to help White break through her block long enough to write three of the four novels in the quartet by helping White recognise her maternal inheritance: her mother, the more playful and tolerant parent, was, White recognised belatedly, the more imaginative one as well. But White feared this inheritance as well, seeing in her 'cuckoo' (*Diary* 2, p. 159) mother someone who had lost touch with reality and lived in a fantasy world White considered grotesque: 'My mother's mind is like a fruit rotten before it ripened [. . .] I am so frightened of becoming like her that I must have some grounds for fear' (*Diary* 1, p. 125). Deeply depressed and suicidal, White conjures her ideal companion, a maternal presence that tethers her in complete security and thereby enables the buoyant flight of the imagination:

> It is as if, sitting here at my desk . . . I were venturing out into an unknown terrifying world from which I might not find my way back. Yet all is safe, friendly, benevolent in the room. Though I sit with my back to it, nothing looks over my shoulder. No mirror is behind me . . . I wish someone were sitting in the chair behind, absorbed in reading or knitting, yet holding on to me as a child twists the string of a balloon round its wrist, ignores it, yet keeps it safely tethered . . . Never in writing, except perhaps occasionally in the notebooks have I felt out of my depth . . . In writing, when I can write at all, I hug the shore all the time. (*Diary* 1, p. 57)

White's identification of her father as the agent of her imaginative blight emblematises the genesis of her fractured self-structure: for the rest of her life she would yearn for a prelapsarian time and space where the child could scribble freely in her nursery, secure in the safety of a protective parent's love. But it was not, finally, her father who blasted her sense of self: the frost that blighted White's life and shrivelled her confidence was the illness that threatened to leave her stranded, alone and insane, in an unknown, terrifying world. She had made it back once. She could never be sure she would come back again.

Notes

Introduction

1. Suzette Henke has coined the term 'scriptotherapy' to characterise the use of writing as a form of self-clarification and healing. See her *Shattered Subjects: Trauma and Testimony in Women's Life-Writing* (Palgrave Macmillan, 2000).
2. I discuss the history of White criticism in the second half of this introduction.
3. Jane Dunn, *Antonia White: A Life* (London: Jonathan Cape, 1998), p. 309.
4. Patrick Allitt, *Catholic Converts: British and American Intellectuals' Turn to Rome* (Ithaca: Cornell University Press, 1997), p. 10.
5. See Marcia Anne Newton's unpublished dissertation, 'Sexual Trauma, Psychosis, and Betrayal in Antonia White's Autobiographical Fiction: A Critical Examination of the Freudian Perspective' (University of Sheffield, 2014) and Sherah Wells' 'Strand by Strand: Untying the Knots of Mental and Physical Illness in the Correspondence and Diaries of Antonia White and Emily Holmes Coleman', in Vera Kalitzkus and Peter L. Twohig (eds), *The Tapestry of Health, Illness, and Disease* (Amsterdam and New York: Rodopi, 2009), pp. 43–55. Both discuss the interweaving of psychoanalysis and Catholicism, although they do not read them as providing identity structures. Elizabeth Podnieks also discusses psychoanalysis and Catholicism in *Daily Modernism: The Literary Diaries of Virginia Woolf, Antonia White, Elizabeth Smart, and Anaïs Nin* (Montreal, Kingston, London and Ithaca: McGill-Queen's University Press, 2000), pp. 165–224. Almost all scholars of White touch on these subjects, which were central to White's writing and life. I discuss this body of work in more detail in the second part of this introduction.

6. Hilary Clark, 'Introduction: Depression and Narrative', in Hilary Clark (ed.), *Depression and Narrative: Telling the Dark* (Albany: State University of New York Press, 2008), p. 4.
7. I discuss these interpretations in the second part of this introduction.
8. Kay Redfield Jamison, *An Unquiet Mind: A Memoir of Moods and Madness* (1995: Great Britain: Picador Press, 1996), p. 6.
9. Edward Shorter, 'The History of Lithium Therapy', *Bipolar Disorder* 11, 2 (June 2009), pp. 4–9. As Shorter makes clear, Cade's discovery was to some extent a rediscovery, as forms of lithium had been in medical use much earlier.
10. Edward Shorter, *A History of Psychiatry: From the Era of the Asylum to the Age of Prozac* (New York: John Wiley and Sons, 1997), p. 245.
11. Ibid. pp. 145–89.
12. Ibid. p. 145.
13. Thomas C. Caramagno, *The Flight of the Mind: Virginia Woolf's Art and Manic-Depressive Illness* (Berkeley, Los Angeles and London: University of California Press, 1992), p. 27.
14. Susan Sontag, 'Against Interpretation', in *Against Interpretation and Other Essays* (1966. New York: MacMillan, 2001), p. 7.
15. Ibid. p. 6.
16. Arnold M. Cooper, 'Will Neurobiology Influence Psychoanalysis?', in Arnold M. Cooper, Otto Kernberg and Ethel Spector Person (eds), *Psychoanalysis: Towards the Second Century* (New Haven: Yale University Press, 1989), pp. 211–12.
17. The five specific therapies designed for those with bipolar illness include Prodrome Recognition; PsychoEducation; Cognitive Behavioural Therapy; Interpersonal and Social Rhythm Therapy; and Family-Focused Therapy. For discussion of the research that informs these approaches and the differences between them, see the detailed descriptions on Dr James R. Phelps' website, psycheducation.org/treatment/psychotherapy-for-bipolar-disorder.
18. Caramagno, *The Flight of the Mind*, p. 32.
19. Mark S. Bauer, 'Psychosocial Interventions for Bipolar Disorder: A Review', in Mario Maj, Hagop S. Akiskal, Juan José Lopez-Ibor and Norman Sartorius (eds), *Bipolar Disorder* (John Wiley and Sons, 2002), p. 282.
20. Ibid. p.282.
21. Frederick K. Goodwin and Kay Redfield Jamison, *Manic-Depressive Illness: Bipolar Disorders and Recurrent Depression,* 2nd edn (Oxford and New York: Oxford University Press, 2007), p. 249.
22. Ibid. p. 249.

23. David J. Miklowitz, *Bipolar Disorder: A Family-Focused Treatment Approach*, 2nd edn (New York and London: Guilford Press, 2008), p. 23.
24. Goodwin and Jamison, *Manic-Depressive Illness*, p. 134.
25. Ibid. p. 134.
26. Ibid. p. 135.
27. Ibid. p. 138.
28. Ibid. pp. 128–31.
29. Miklowitz, *Bipolar Disorder*, p. 23.
30. Dunn, *Antonia White*, p. 137.
31. Personal communication.
32. Elaine Showalter, *The Female Malady: Women, Madness, and English Culture, 1830–1980* (New York: Pantheon, 1985), p. 203.
33. Goodwin and Jamison, *Manic-Depressive Illness*, p. 36.
34. Ibid. p. 35.
35. Qtd. in Goodwin and Jamison, *Manic-Depressive Illness*, p. 36.
36. In addition to *Beyond the Glass* and White's own descriptions in her diaries and *The Hound and the Falcon*, see Dunn, *Antonia White*, pp. 79–86. Dunn had access to White's medical records and quotes extensively from them.
37. See Sergio Della Sala, Clara Calia, Maria Fara De Caro and Robert D. McIntosh, 'Transient involuntary mirror writing triggered by anxiety', *Neurocase: The Neural Basis of Cognition* (17 October 2014), pp. 1–9. http://dx.doi.org/10.1080/13554794.2014.969278. This article discusses the first documented case of mirror writing triggered by angst and anxiety, although anecdotal cases had been reported in prior studies. See also G. D. Schott, 'Mirror writing: neurological reflections on an unusual phenomenon', *Journal of Neurology, Neurosurgery and Psychiatry* 78, 1 (January 2007), pp. 5–13.
38. Stephen P. Hinshaw, 'Growing Up in a Family with Bipolar Disorder: Personal Experience, Developmental Lessons, and Overcoming Stigma', in Maj, Akiskal, López-Ibor and Sartorius (eds), *Bipolar Disorder* (John Wiley and Sons, 2002), p. 543. See also Hinshaw's memoir about his father, *The Years of Silence are Past: My Father's Life with Bipolar Disorder* (Cambridge: Cambridge University Press, 2002), particularly Chapter 7, 'Diagnosis and Misdiagnosis' (pp. 81–103). Hinshaw describes in that chapter the impact of Eugen Bleuler's contention that psychotic symptoms are 'actually secondary features of schizophrenia's basic pathologic process' (p. 90). 'The upshot, from this perspective', Hinshaw remarks, 'is that the presence of psychosis warrants a diagnosis of schizophrenia' (p. 90). The misdiagnosis of manic depression as schizophrenia was particularly prevalent in the

United States; it is significant that White's analyst and not her doctors at Bethlem provided the diagnosis of schizophrenia.

39. Karl Abraham, 'Notes on Manic-Depressive Insanity', in Ernest Jones (ed.) and Douglas Bryan and Alix Strachey (trans.), *Selected Papers of Karl Abraham* (London: Hogarth Press, 1927), p. 150.

40. Ibid. p. 151.

41. Jamison, *An Unquiet Mind*, pp. 82–3.

42. Jamison, *An Unquiet Mind*, p. 182.

43. See Michel Foucault, *Madness and Civilization: A History of Insanity in the Age of Reason*, trans. Richard Howard (New York: Vintage, 1973); and Roy Porter, *A Social History of Madness: The World through the Eyes of the Insane* (New York: Weidenfeld and Nicolson, 1987).

44. David A. Karp, *Speaking of Sadness: Depression, Disconnection, and the Meanings of Illness* (Oxford and New York: Oxford University Press, 1996), p. 55.

45. See Phyllis Chesler, *Women and Madness* (Garden City, NY: Doubleday, 1972); Elaine Showalter, *The Female Malady* (New York: Pantheon, 1985); and Jane M. Ussher, *Women's Madness: Misogyny or Mental Illness?* (New York and London: Harvester Wheatsheaf, 1991).

46. Showalter, *The Female Malady*, pp. 203–14.

47. The anti-psychiatry movement of the 1960s and 1970s argued that mental illness did not exist but was a social and disciplinary construct. In addition to Thomas Scheff, who discussed the damaging effects of psychiatric labelling (*Being Mentally Ill* [Chicago: Aldine, 1966]), see Erving Goffmann, *Asylums: Essays on the Social Situation of Asylum Patients and Other Inmates* (New York: Doubleday, 1961). Psychiatrists such as R. D. Laing (*The Politics of Experience* [New York: Pantheon, 1967]) and Thomas Szasz (*Ideology and Insanity* [Garden City, NY: Anchor Books, 1970]) were also influential spokespeople for this position.

48. Karp, *Speaking of Sadness*, p. 65.

49. Ibid. p. 55.

50. For some representative studies, see Phil Barker, Peter Campbell and Ben Davidson (eds), *From the Ashes of Experience: Reflections on Madness, Survival and Growth* (London: Wiley-Blackwell, 1999); Judi Chamberlin, *On Our Own: Patient-Controlled Alternatives to the Mental Health System* (New York: McGraw-Hill, 1978); Jim Read and Jill Reynolds (eds) *Speaking Our Minds: An Anthology* (New York: Palgrave Macmillan, 1996); and Peter Stastny and Peter Lehmann (eds) *Alternatives Beyond Psychiatry* (Berlin: Peter Lehmann, 2007).

51. Gail A. Hornstein, *Agnes's Jacket: A Psychologist's Search for the Meanings of Madness* (New York: Rodale Press, 2009), p. xxii.

52. Clark, 'Introduction', p. 2.

53. See Anna Bentinck van Schoonhetan, *Karl Abraham: Life and Work, A Biography* (London: Karnac Books, 2015) for a discussion of Abraham's centrality to early psychoanalysis.

54. Christine C. Kieffer, 'Selfobjects, Oedipal Objects and Mutual Recognition: A Self-Psychological Reappraisal of the Female "Oedipal Victor"', *The Annual of Psychoanalysis* 32 (2004), pp. 69–80.

55. Chitty, 'Introduction', *Diary* 1, p. 7.

56. Connections between White and Joyce are touched on by Elizabeth Bowen, 'Introduction', *Frost in May*, p. vii; Bowen also discusses *Frost in May* as a 'school novel' (pp. v–x). Podnieks develops a comparison between Joyce and White in *Daily Modernism*, pp. 206–9. Paulina Palmer reads *Frost in May* as a school novel encoding lesbianism in 'Antonia White's *Frost in May*: A Lesbian-Feminist Reading', in Susan Sellers (ed.), *Feminist Criticism: Theory and Practice* (New York: Harvester Wheatsheaf, 1991), pp. 89–108. Ellen Cronan Rose reads White's work as a counterpoint to Joyce as well as discussing her conflicts as a woman writer more generally in 'Antonia White: Portrait of the Artist as a Dutiful Daughter', in *Literature, Interpretation, Theory* 2, 3 (1991), pp. 239–48. Penny Brown discusses the novel sequence as a failed *Künstlerroman* in *The Poison at the Source: The Female Novel of Self-Development in the Early Twentieth Century* (Basingstoke and London: Macmillan, 1992), pp. 121–50. Jeanne A. Flood's study of the novel sequence appeared soon after its republication; see 'The Autobiographical Novels of Antonia White', in *Critique* (Spring 1983), pp. 131–49.

57. An excellent analysis of the impact of Catholicism on the novel sequence appears in Philip F. O'Mara, 'Trust Amid Sore Affliction: Antonia White's Novels', in *Cithara: Essays in the Judaeo-Christian Tradition* 28, 1 (November 1988), pp. 33–43. For a discussion of Catholic conflicts in White's writing more generally, see Julietta Benson, '"Varieties of Disbelief": Antonia White and the Discourses of Faith and Scepticism', *Literature and Theology: An Interdisciplinary Journal of Theory and Criticism* 7, 3 (September 1993), pp. 284–301.

58. Mary Lynn Broe, 'My Art Belongs to Daddy: Incest as Exile, The Textual Economies of Hayford Hall', in Mary Lynn Broe and Angela Ingram (eds), *Women's Writing in Exile* (Chapel Hill and London: University of North Carolina Press, 1989), pp. 41–86.

59. Podnieks, *Daily Modernism*, pp. 164–224.

60. Elizabeth Podnieks and Sandra Chait (eds), *Hayford Hall: Hangovers, Erotics, and Modernist Aesthetics* (Carbondale: Illinois University Press, 2005).

61. See Sandra Chait, 'Site also of Angst and Spiritual Search', and Sandra Jeffery, 'Antonia White and the Subversion of Literary Impotence at Hayford Hall', both in Podnieks and Chait (eds) *Hayford Hall*, pp. 150–69 and pp. 70–88 respectively.

62. Julie Vandivere, 'Framed Liminalities: Antonia White's *Beyond the Glass* and Emily Coleman's *The Shutter of Snow*', in Podnieks and Chait (eds), *Hayford Hall*, pp. 46–69.

63. Kylie Valentine, 'Mad and Modern: A Reading of Emily Holmes Coleman and Antonia White', *Tulsa Studies in Women's Literature* 22, 1 (Spring 2003), pp. 121–47; and *Psychoanalysis, Psychiatry and Modernist Literature* (Basingstoke and New York: Palgrave Macmillan, 2003).

64. O'Mara, 'Trust Amid Sore Affliction', p. 43.

65. Podnieks, *Daily Modernism*, p. 193.

66. Chait, 'Site', p. 156.

67. Jeffery, 'Antonia White', p. 81.

68. Ibid. p. 80.

69. See, for example, Newton, 'Sexual Trauma, Psychosis, and Betrayal in Antonia White's Autobiographical Fiction'; and Wells, 'Strand by Strand', p. 44.

70. Podnieks, *Daily Modernism*, p. 190.

71. Mary Therese Strauss-Noll, 'A Passionate and Troubled History: Antonia White and Her Father', *Pennsylvania English* 22, 1–2 (2000), pp. 141–5.

72. Hopkinson, *Nothing to Forgive*, p. 178.

73. Chitty, *Now to My Mother*, p. 155. The extract Chitty includes forms part of a much longer narrative in White's unpublished dream diaries.

74. Hopkinson, *Nothing to Forgive*, p. 354.

75. Judith Lewis Herman, *Father–Daughter Incest* (Cambridge, MA and London: Harvard University Press, 1981), p. 109.

76. Chitty, *Now to My Mother*, p. 3.

77. Podnieks, *Daily Modernism*, p. 191.

78. Unpublished diaries, 27 August 1951.

79. Unpublished diaries, 3 October 1960.

80. 'Two Instances of Pathogenic Phantasies Revealed by the Patients Themselves', in James Strachey (ed.), *The Standard Edition of the Complete Psychological Works of Sigmund Freud*, Volume XI (London: The Hogarth Press and the Institute of Psychoanalysis), pp. 236–7. The first anecdote related here attributes the return of a man's psychosis to his incestuous fantasies about his mother.

81. White's unpublished diaries reveal that Carroll provided analysis at a cheaper rate than was the norm, another indication that he was still in

training (unpublished analysis diary, 13 March 1935). I discuss Carroll's status more fully in Chapter 3.

82. Unpublished analysis diary, 13 March 1935.
83. Unpublished diaries, 1 June 1937.
84. Chitty, *Now to My Mother*, p. 20.
85. Ibid. p. 21.
86. Unpublished diaries, 25 June 1938.
87. Strauss-Noll, 'A Passionate and Troubled History', p. 136.
88. Unpublished diaries, 28 June 1938.
89. Ibid. 28 June 1938.
90. Ibid. 27 June 1937.
91. The research in this field is extremely rich. Works consulted include Martin A. Conway (ed.), *Recovered Memories and False Memories* (Oxford: Oxford University Press, 1997); Janice Haaken, *Pillar of Salt: Gender, Memory, and the Perils of Looking Back* (New Brunswick, NJ and London: Rutgers University Press, 1998); Ian Hacking, *Rewriting the Soul: Multiple Personality Disorder and the Sciences of Memory* (Princeton: Princeton University Press, 1995); and Daniel L. Schacter, *Searching for Memory: The Brain, the Mind, and the Past* (New York: Basic Books, 1996).
92. Martin A. Conway, 'Introduction: what are memories?', in Martin A. Conway (ed.), *Recovered Memories and False Memories*, p. 1.
93. Dunn also interprets the explicitly incestuous dreams as expressions of reconciliation. See *Antonia White*, p. 219.
94. Unpublished dream diaries, 6 November 1947.
95. Dunn's caution – 'It would be a mistake to interpret such a dream literally and superficially' – is sound: her contention that the dream symbolised reconciliation and forgiveness is one with which I agree (*Antonia White*, p. 219).
96. Podnieks, *Daily Modernism*, p. 191.
97. Black masses feature in a number of well-known books from the eighteenth and nineteenth centuries, including the Marquis de Sade's *Juliette* (1791) and *Justine, or The Misfortunes of Virtue* (1791–1801); Joris-Karl Huysman's *Là-bas* (1891); and Leopold von Sacher-Masoch's *Venus in Furs* (1870). Dr Iwan Bloch, author of the 1899 *Marquis de Sade: His Life and Works*, describes the basic outlines of one such black mass: 'A Maiden, as the Holy Virgin, with arms raised to heaven, was bound in a niche in the church. Later she was laid naked on a great table, candles were lit, a crucifix decorated her buttocks, and they celebrated on her buttocks the most absurd mysteries of Christianity.' White's rewriting of this scene restores the sacred element to what was a pornographic parody of the Catholic Mass.

98. Sandra Chait analyses the complex way in which the sexual and the spiritual intertwine in White's writing. See her 'The Psychospiritual in the Literary Analysis of Modernist Texts', in Heather Walton and Andrew W. Hass (eds), *Self/Same/Other Revisioning the Subject in Literature and Theology* (Sheffield: Sheffield Academic Press, 2000), pp. 54–69.
99. Chitty, 'Introduction', in *Diaries* 1, p. 8.
100. Chitty, *Now to My Mother*, pp. 2–4.
101. Haaken, *Pillar of Salt*, p. 2.
102. Ibid. p. 3.
103. Ibid. p. 3.
104. Ibid. pp. 3, 174.
105. Ibid. p. 32.
106. Ibid. p. 80.
107. Ibid. p. 92.
108. Ibid. p. 91.
109. Ibid. pp. 178–9.
110. Ibid. pp. 183, 193.
111. Broe, 'My Art Belongs to Daddy', p. 44.
112. Ibid. p. 44. Broe does not cite Chitty's memoir as the source of this collage, but not only does she use the same sequence of passages, the wording used to introduce the passages is at points identical to that of Chitty. Additionally, White's remark that the fictional father's assault of Patsy explained 'things' in her own father is an anecdote reported by Chitty (*Now to My Mother*, pp. 2–3).
113. Ibid. p. 44. In the unreferenced source for this anecdote, the wording is actually as follows: 'She later admitted that the *passage* was pure invention, "to explain things in Daddy"' (Chitty, *Now to My Mother*, p. 3; my emphasis). Broe's substitution of the word 'friend' for 'passage' creates the impression that the fictional event was based on a biographical one.
114. Ibid. p. 44.
115. Ibid. p. 44.
116. Ibid. p. 73.
117. Podnieks, *Daily Modernism*, pp. 164–224.
118. Ibid. p. 189.
119. Ibid. pp. 188, 190.
120. Ibid. p. 178.
121. Ibid. p. 197.
122. Ibid. p. 193.
123. Ibid. pp. 192, 193.
124. Ibid. p. 189.
125. Ibid. p. 195.

126. Ibid. p. 193.
127. Ibid. p. 192.
128. Ibid. pp. 197–8.
129. My own reaction to seeing this passage in the manuscript diaries was one of disappointment: Chitty, Hopkinson, Dunn and, of course, Podnieks had all described this passage as so extraordinary that I believed that I, too, would have some kind of revelation. White just seemed angry to me.
130. Podnieks, *Daily Modernism*, p. 198.
131. Broe, 'My Art Belongs to Daddy', p. 73.
132. Ibid. pp. 74–5.
133. Strauss-Noll, 'A Passionate and Troubled History', p. 135.
134. Haaken, *Pillar of Salt*, p. 254.
135. Ibid. p. 97.
136. Ibid. p. 255.
137. Ibid. p. 190.
138. White expands considerably on her internal sense of corruption in the full version of this entry in the unpublished diaries, 4 August 1949.
139. See Richard T. Liu, 'Early life stressors and genetic influences on the development of bipolar disorder: The roles of childhood abuse and brain-derived neurotrophic factors', *Child Abuse and Neglect* 34, 7 (July 2010), pp. 516–22; Alex Fowke, Susan Ross and Katie Ashcroft, 'Childhood Maltreatment and Internalized Shame in Adults with a Diagnosis of Bipolar Disorder', *Clinical Psychology and Psychotherapy* 19 (2012), pp. 450–7; Robert M. Post et al., 'Verbal abuse, like physical and sexual abuse, in childhood is associated with an earlier onset and more difficult course of bipolar disorder', *Bipolar Disorders* 17, 3 (May 2015), pp. 323–30; and Stuart Watson et al., 'Childhood Trauma in Bipolar Disorder', *Australian and New Zealand Journal of Psychiatry* 48, 6 (2014), pp. 564–70.
140. Liu, 'Early life stressors', p. 516.
141. Fowke, Ross and Ashcroft, 'Childhood Maltreatment', p. 450.
142. Ibid. p. 450.
143. Jamison, *Touched with Fire*, pp. 58–9.
144. Ibid. p. 59.

Chapter 1

1. My summary of White's symptoms draws primarily upon White's *Diaries* and *The Hound and the Falcon* as well as the unpublished diaries. Other sources include the two memoirs by her daughter and Dunn's biography, which fill out White's own accounts.

2. Dunn, *Antonia White*, pp. 82–3.
3. Ibid. p. 172.
4. Dunn had access to White's medical records and she provides a thorough account of her hospitalisation (*Antonia White*, pp. 79–85).
5. In a letter, White wrote, 'Ever since I grew up, and even to this day (I am 41 now), I am usually taken for considerably more or considerably less than my age owing to this peculiar variability which affects not only features and shape of face but actual colouring of skin and hair. Someone who knew me very well once said to me: "I have seen you vary in the course of a day from a daughter of the morning to a debauched Roman Emperor and back again"' (*The Hound and the Falcon*, p. 10). The 'someone' was White's third husband Tom Hopkinson.
6. In *A Mood Apart: Depression, Mania, and Other Afflictions of the Self* (New York: Basic Books, 1997), Peter C. Whybrow remarks that 'grief can precipitate mania just as it will trigger melancholia. Mania is sometimes a pathological reaction to death or disappointment. Many studies have shown that acute or chronic stress may both precede the onset of mania and help precipitate repeated episodes' (p. 64). White's 'compulsive' response to Tom Hopkinson may indicate symptoms of mania or hypomania.
7. Unpublished diaries, 19 March 1934.
8. Ibid. 19 March 1934.
9. Ibid. 19 March 1934.
10. Chitty, *Now to My Mother*, p. 30; Tom Hopkinson, *Of This Our Time: A Journalist's Story 1905–50* (London: Hutchinson, 1982), pp. 128–9.
11. Qtd. in Chitty, *Now to My Mother*, pp. 30, 35.
12. Hopkinson, *Of This Our Time*, p. 125.
13. Unpublished diaries, 27 September 1934.
14. Unpublished diaries, 11 January 1935.
15. Unpublished diaries, 16 March 1935.
16. Chitty, *Now to My Mother*, p. 65.
17. Qtd. in Dunn, *Antonia White*, p. 152.
18. Ibid. Dunn cites an interview with Maggie Pringle in which White stated, '[*Frost in May*] wrecked our marriage [. . .] so I thought psychologically whenever I wrote anything I destroyed love' (p. 152).
19. Ibid. p. 161.
20. Frank, *Treating Bipolar Disorder*, pp. 18–20.
21. Dunn, *Antonia White*, p. 203.
22. Chitty, *Now to My Mother*, p. 79. See also White's description of her suicidal plans in *Hound*, p. 114.

23. Hopkinson, *Nothing to Forgive*, p. 174.
24. Chitty, *Now to My Mother*, pp. 85, 101.
25. Qtd. in Chitty, *Now to My Mother*, p. 92.
26. Dunn, *Antonia White*, pp. 235–6.
27. Hopkinson, *Nothing to Forgive*, p. 173.
28. Ibid. p. 110.
29. Chitty, *Now to My Mother*, pp. 110–16.
30. Qtd. in Dunn, *Antonia White*, p. 243.
31. Chitty, *Now to My Mother*, p. 118.
32. Chitty, 'Introduction', *Diary* 1, p. 6.
33. See Chitty, *Now to My Mother*, pp. 161–3.
34. Hopkinson, *Nothing to Forgive*, p. 244.
35. Ibid. p. 246.
36. Ibid. p. 246.
37. Chitty, 'Introduction', *Diary* 1, p. 6.
38. Chitty, 'Introduction', *As Once in May*, p. 7.
39. Ibid. p. 187.
40. Unpublished diaries, 23 July 1968.
41. Unpublished diaries, 27 November 1977.
42. See, for example, unpublished diaries, 13 December 1960.
43. Unpublished diaries, 28 July 1954.
44. Unpublished diaries, 13 February 1958.
45. See, for example, unpublished diaries, 27 June 1937. These entries cluster in the years 1937–9 and 1942–4, when White held various office jobs.
46. Unpublished diaries, 4 August 1949.
47. Unpublished diaries, 28 February 1965.
48. *The Diagnostic and Statistical Manual of Mental Disorders*, 5th edn (Washington, DC and London: American Psychiatric Publishing, 2013), p. 124.
49. Ibid. p. 124.
50. Ibid. p. 124.
51. Danai Dima and Gerome Breen, 'Polygenic risk scores in imaging genetics: Usefulness and applications', *Journal of Psychopharmacology* (2015), 1. DOI: 10.1177/0269881115584470
52. Ibid. p. 3.
53. Goodwin and Jamison, *Manic-Depressive Illness*, p. 464.
54. Ibid. p.464.
55. Ibid. p.464.
56. Ibid. p. 240.
57. Ibid. p. 128.

58. Jamison, *Night Falls Fast*, p. 210.
59. Goodwin and Jamison, *Manic-Depressive Illness*, p. 252.
60. Jamison, *Night Falls Fast*, p. 209. In *The Years of Silence*, Hinshaw identifies the seasonal onset of mania in late summer or early autumn (p. 89). Goodwin and Jamison observe that mixed mania peaks in the late summer, whereas 'pure' mania peaks in the spring (*Manic-Depressive Illness*, p. 80).
61. Goodwin and Jamison, *Manic-Depressive Illness*, p. 80.
62. Whybrow, *A Mood Apart*, p. 171.
63. Frank, *Treating Bipolar Disorder* p. 22; Whybrow, *A Mood Apart*, pp. 165–72.
64. Whybrow, *A Mood Apart*, p. 167.
65. Ibid. pp. 167, 324; Frank, *Treating Bipolar Disorder*, pp. 24–5. Interpersonal and social rhythm therapy, a therapy designed for the treatment of manic depression, has been designed around the connection between circadian rhythms and social and interpersonal factors. See Frank, *Treating Bipolar Disorder*, for a comprehensive explanation of this approach.
66. Whybrow, *A Mood Apart*, p. 324.
67. Unpublished diaries, 8 January 1937; *Diary* 2, p. 110.
68. Warren Mansell and Rebecca Pedley, 'The ascent into mania: A review of psychological processes associated with the development of manic symptoms', *Clinical Psychology Review* 28 (2004), p. 496.
69. Ibid. p. 496.
70. Goodwin and Jamison, *Manic-Depressive Illness*, p. 40.
71. Kraepelin, qtd. in Goodwin and Jamison, *Manic-Depressive Illness*, p. 32.
72. Mansell and Pedley, 'The ascent into mania', p. 496.
73. Ibid. p. 496.
74. David J. Miklowitz, *Bipolar Disorder: A Family-Focused Treatment Approach*, 2nd edn (New York and London: Guilford Press, 2008), pp. 28–30; Goodwin and Jamison, *Manic-Depressive Illness*, pp. 42–3.
75. Goodwin and Jamison, *Manic-Depressive Illness*, p. 133.
76. Ibid. p. 133
77. *ICD*-10, p. 97. Available at <apps.who/classifications/icd10/browse/2016/en>(last accessed August 2017)
78. Goodwin and Jamison, *Manic-Depressive Illness*, pp. 35–6.
79. See Caramagno, *The Flight of the Mind* (pp. 101–2), for a description of the onset and course of James Stephen's illness.
80. Irving Derby, 'Manic-Depression "Exhaustion" Deaths', *Psychiatric Quarterly* 7 (1933), pp. 436–9; cited in Caramagno, *The Flight of the Mind*, p. 102.

81. Stephan C. Mann, Stanley N. Caroff and Henry R. Bleier, 'Lethal Catatonia', *American Journal of Psychiatry* 143 (November 1986), pp. 1374–81.
82. Frank R. Farnham and Henry G. Kennedy, 'Acute excited states and sudden death', *British Medical Journal* 315, 7116 (1 November 1997), p. 1107.
83. Ibid. p. 1108.
84. Goodwin and Jamison, *Manic-Depressive Illness*, p. 33.
85. Ibid. p. 37.
86. *DSM-5*, p. 129; *ICD*-10, p. 95.
87. Jamison's *Touched with Fire* studies the relationship between creativity and manic-depressive illness; see in particular Chapter 3, pp. 49–99.
88. Frank, *Treating Bipolar Disorder*, pp. 32, 43. Jamison candidly explores her own history of non-adherence to a medication regime in *An Unquiet Mind*.
89. *DSM-5*, p. 128.
90. Ibid. p. 128.
91. Ibid. p. 129; Goodwin and Jamison, *Manic-Depressive Illness*, p. 39.
92. *DSM-5*, p. 129.
93. Goodwin and Jamison, *Manic-Depressive Illness*, p. 33.
94. Jamison, *An Unquiet Mind*, p. 67.
95. *ICD*-10, p. 96; *DSM-5*, p. 128.
96. *DSM-5*, p. 128.
97. Ibid. p. 38.
98. *ICD*-10, p. 96.
99. Miklowitz, *Bipolar Disorder*, p. 29.
100. Goodwin and Jamison, *Manic-Depressive Illness*, p. 58.
101. Jamison, *An Unquiet Mind*, p. 68.
102. Miklowitz, *Bipolar Disorder*, pp. 52–3.
103. Ibid. pp. 52–3.
104. *DSM-5*, p. 123.
105. Frank, *Treating Bipolar Disorder*, pp. 29–30; Miklowitz, *Bipolar Disorder*, p. 23.
106. Goodwin and Jamison, *Manic-Depressive Disorder*, p. 133; Miklowitz, p. 30.
107. Miklowitz, *Bipolar Disorder*, p. 30.
108. In *Speaking of Sadness*, Karp charts the stages through which people pass before acknowledging depression (p. 57).
109. Hans-Peter Kapfhammer, 'Somatic symptoms in depression', *Dialogues in Clinical Neuroscience* 8, 2 (2006), pp. 229–30.
110. *DSM-5*, pp. 160–3.
111. *DSM-5*, p. 163.

112. Goodwin and Jamison, *Manic-Depressive Illness*, p. 243.
113. Ibid. p. 240.
114. Ibid. p. 19.
115. Andrew Solomon, *The Noonday Demon: An Anatomy of Depression* (London: Vintage, 2002), pp. 18–19.
116. Goodwin and Jamison note that 'Interpersonal tension may be further intensified by the depressed individual's marked guilt and feelings of worthlessness and self-blame for real or perceived negative social encounters' (*Manic-Depressive Illness*, p. 339).
117. Ibid. p. 343.
118. Ibid. p. 339.
119. *DSM-5*, p. 164.
120. Solomon, *The Noonday Demon*, p. 19.
121. Styron, *Darkness Visible* (London: Vintage, 2001), p. 29.
122. Ibid. p. 31.
123. Ibid. p. 32.
124. Jamison, *Night Falls Fast*, p. 112.
125. M. Alvarez Ariza, R. Mateos Alvarez and G. E. Berrios, 'A review of the natural course of bipolar disorders (manic-depressive psychosis) in the pre-drug era: Review of studies prior to 1950', *Journal of Affective Disorders* 115 (2009), pp. 293–301.
126. Ibid. p. 296.
127. Ibid. p. 296.
128. Ibid. p. 296.
129. Qtd. in Goodwin and Jamison, *Manic-Depressive Illness*, p. 129.
130. Goodwin and Jamison, *Manic-Depressive Illness*, p. 138.
131. Woolf, in Nigel Nicolson and Joanne Trautmann (eds), *The Letters of Virginia Woolf*, vol. 4 (New York: Harcourt Brace Jovanovich), pp. 144–5.
132. Woolf, 'A Sketch of the Past', in Jeanne Schulkind (ed.), *Moments of Being*, 2nd edn (San Diego, New York and London: Harcourt Brace Jovanovich, 1985), p. 68.
133. Caramagno, *The Flight of the Mind*, pp. 307–11.
134. Ibid. pp. 307–11.
135. Ibid. pp. 307–11.
136. Goodwin and Jamison, *Manic-Depressive Illness*, pp. 205–6.
137. Jamison's *Touched with Fire* studies this connection.
138. Leonard Woolf, *Beginning Again: An Autobiography of the Years 1911 to 1918* (New York: Harcourt Brace Jovanovich, 1964), p. 161.
139. Caramagno, *The Flight of the Mind*, p. 20.
140. Leonard Woolf, *Beginning Again*, p. 76.

141. Leonard Woolf, *Downhill All the Way: An Autobiography of the Years 1919 to 1939* (New York: Harcourt Brace Jovanovich, 1967), p. 49.

142. Goodwin and Jamison, *Manic-Depressive Illness*, p. 815.

143. See Caramagno, *The Flight of the Mind* (pp. 109–10) for a discussion of Isabella Makepeace Thackeray.

144. Thomas Wehr et al., 'Sleep Production as a Final Common Pathway in the Genesis of Mania', *American Journal of Psychiatry* 144, 2 (1987), pp. 201–4.

145. Caramagno, *The Flight of the Mind*, pp. 20–1.

146. Thomas A. Wehr et al., 'Fostering sleep and stabilizing its timing by scheduling regular nightly periods of enforced bed rest and darkness to stabilize the timing and duration of sleep', *Biological Psychiatry* 43, 11 (1 June 1998), pp. 822–8; James Phelps <psycheducation.org/treatment/bipolar-disorder-light-and-darkness/dark therapy/> (Last accessed August 2017). Caramagno anticipates these findings in his assessment that Leonard's imposition of a rest regime may have been beneficial in alleviating or staving off illness (*The Flight of the Mind*, p. 19).

147. Phelps<psycheducation.org/treatment/bipolar-disorder-light-and-darkness/dark therapy/>

148. Wehr, 'Fostering sleep', p. 822.

149. Leonard Woolf, in Frederic Spotts (ed.), *Letters of Leonard Woolf* (New York: Harcourt Brace Jovanovich, 1950), p. 236.

150. Ibid. p. 236.

151. Whybrow, *A Mood Apart*, p. 152.

152. Whybrow, *A Mood Apart*, p. 153. See the chapter 'The Legacy of the Lizard' (pp. 127–55) for a review of this research into the effects of depression on the brain.

153. Dunn, *Antonia White*, pp. 75–86.

154. Ibid. p. 77.

155. Dunn observes that 'It was as if she was both in the belly of the beast and also detached, observing the processes of her madness and the treatment meted out to her from a distant perspective' (*Antonia White*, p. 80).

156. Whybrow, *A Mind Apart*, pp. 142–3.

157. See, for example, Barker, Campbell and Davidson (eds), *From the Ashes of Experience*; Chamberlin, *On Our Own*; Hornstein, *Agnes's Jacket*; and Read and Reynolds (eds), *Speaking Our Minds* for accounts of incarceration in locked wards and its long-lasting effects on inmates.

158. For an overview of this research, see Peter Stastny, 'Involuntary Psychiatric Interventions: A Breach of the Hippocratic Oath?', *Ethical Human Sciences and Services* 2, 1 (2000), pp. 21–41.

159. Goodwin and Jamison, *Manic-Depressive Illness*, p. 105.

160. Ibid. pp. 337–43.

161. Ibid. p. 43.

162. Woolf, in Anne Olivier Bell and Andrew McNeillie (eds), *The Diary of Virginia Woolf*, vol. 2 (New York: Harcourt Brace Jovanovich, 1978), p. 108.

163. Woolf, in Anne Olivier Bell and Andrew McNeillie (eds), *The Diary of Virginia Woolf*, vol. 5 (New York: Harcourt Brace Jovanovich, 1985), p. 64.

164. Unpublished diaries, 15 May 1937.

165. Unpublished diaries, 4 December 1937; 31 January 1938.

166. Qtd. in Dunn, *Antonia White*, p. 97. Victoria Walker traces White's attempts to engage Woolf and their single meeting in '"Exactly like a housemaid writing to Greta Garbo": Antonia White meets Virginia Woolf', in *Notes and Queries* 61, 1 (2014), p. 146.

167. Qtd. in Dunn, *Antonia White*, p. 129.

168. Jamison, pp. 106–7.

169. Qtd. in Jamison, p. 106.

170. Ibid. p. 106.

Chapter 2

1. Oliver Sacks, *The Man Who Mistook His Wife for a Hat: And Other Clinical Tales* (1985; New York: Touchstone, 1998), p. 121.

2. Jerome Bruner, 'The Remembered Self', in Ulric Neisser and Robyn Fivush (eds), *The Remembering Self: Construction and Accuracy in the Self-Narrative* (Cambridge: Cambridge University Press, 1994), p. 53.

3. Jerome Bruner, *Making Stories: Law, Literature, Life* (New York: Farrar, Straus and Giroux, 2002), p. 89.

4. Ibid. p. 85.

5. Valerie Raoul, Connie Canam, Angela Henderson and Carla Peterson (eds), *Unfitting Stories: Narrative Approaches to Disease, Disability and Trauma* (Waterloo: Wilfrid Laurier University Press, 2007), p. 112.

6. See Anne Hunsaker Hawkins, *Reconstructing Illness: Studies in Pathography*, 2nd edn (West Lafayette: Purdue University Press, 1999); and Arthur W. Frank, *The Wounded Storyteller*, 2nd edn (Chicago and London: The University of Chicago Press, 2013). Other discussions of illness, identity and narrative include Kathy Charmaz, *Good Days,*

Bad Days: The Self in Chronic Illness and Time (New Brunswick, NJ: Rutgers University Press, 1997); G. Thomas Couser, *Recovering Bodies: Illness, Disability, and Life-Writing* (Madison: University of Wisconsin Press, 1997); Ann Jurecic, *Illness as Narrative* (Pittsburgh: University of Pittsburgh Press, 2012); Arthur Kleinman, *The Illness Narratives: Suffering, Healing, and the Human Condition* (New York: Basic Books, 1988); and Shlomith Rimmon-Kenan, 'The Story of "I": Illness and Narrative Identity', *Narrative* 10, 1 (2002), pp. 9–27.

7. Both Hawkins and Kleinman discuss narrative models in the context of illness and identity. See also Hilary Clark (ed.), *Depression and Narrative: Telling the Dark* (Albany: State University of New York Press, 2008).

8. For discussions of the difficulties associated with shaping narratives of mental illness, see Ann Hudson Jones, 'Literature and Medicine: Narratives of Mental Illness', *Lancet* 350.974 (1997), pp. 359–61; Mary Elene Wood, *Life Writing and Schizophrenia: Encounters at the Edge of Meaning* (Amsterdam and New York: Rodopi, 2013), and the collections edited by Hilary Clark (*Depression and Narrative*), Dwight Fee (*Pathology and the Postmodern: Mental Illness as Discourse and Experience* [London: Sage, 2000]), and Valerie Raoul et. al. (*Unfitting Stories*). See also Caramagno's brilliant study of Virginia Woolf and manic depression, *The Flight of the Mind*.

9. Karp, *Speaking of Sadness*, p. 75.

10. Raoul, Canam, Henderson and Peterson, *Unfitting Stories*, p. 28.

11. Peter Brooks formulates this principle succinctly: 'mental health is a coherent life story, neurosis is faulty narrative' (*Psychoanalysis and Storytelling* [Oxford: Blackwell, 1994], p. 49).

12. Frank, *The Wounded Storyteller*, p. 97.

13. Ibid. p. 97.

14. Ibid. p. 105.

15. Frank, p. 114. He goes on to note that, for those with religious beliefs, 'the mystery of the chaos narrative is its opening to faith' (p. 114), as, indeed, was the case for White.

16. Matti Hyvärinen, Lars-Christer Hydén, Marjo Saarenheimo and Maria Tamboukou (eds), *Beyond Narrative Coherence* (Amsterdam and Philadelphia: John Benjamins Publishing Company, 2010), p. 7.

17. Charlotte Linde, *Life Stories: The Creation of Coherence* (New York and Oxford: Oxford University Press, 1993), p. 16.

18. Paul John Eakin, *The Ethics of Life-Writing* (Ithaca: Cornell University Press, 2004), p. 6.

19. Paul John Eakin, 'Breaking Rules: The Consequences of Self-Narration', *Biography* 24, 1 (winter 2001), p. 120.

20. Eakin also lists public condemnation and litigation as possible conse-
    quences. See 'Breaking Rules', p. 114.
21. Wood, *Life Writing and Schizophrenia*, p. 20.
22. Unpublished diaries, 24 August 1937.
23. Unpublished diaries, 22 February 1953; 20 April 1973.
24. Podnieks reads White's choice of names for herself – the first her mother's
    nickname for her, the surname her mother's maiden name – as a maternal
    identification that rejected her father (*Daily Modernism*, p. 218).
25. *Diary* 1, p. 19; unpublished diaries, 6 October 1935.
26. The unpublished diaries in particular develop this theme in reference to
    White's efforts to transform her chaotic twenties into fiction. See, for
    example, entries for 31 October 1965 and 21 November 1965.
27. Jamison, *An Unquiet Mind*, p. 68.
28. Whybrow, *A Mood Apart*, p. 19.
29. Caramagno, *The Flight of the Mind*, p. 72.
30. Goodwin and Jamison, *Manic-Depressive Illness*, p. 879.
31. Whybrow, *A Mood Apart*, p. 8.
32. Ibid. p. 54.
33. Ibid. p. 19.
34. Sheri L. Johnson and Randy Fingerhut, 'Life events as predictors of relapse,
    depression and mania in bipolar disorder', in Steven Jones and Richard
    Bentall (eds), *The Psychology of Bipolar Disorder: New Developments
    and Research Strategies* (Oxford: Oxford University Press, 2006), p. 51.
35. Whybrow, *A Mood Apart*, p. 13.
36. Tilman Habermas and Susan Bluck, 'Getting a Life: The Emergence
    of the Life Story in Adolescence', *Psychological Bulletin* 126, 5 (2000),
    p. 749.
37. Ibid. p. 749.
38. Dan P. McAdams, 'The Problem of Narrative Coherence', *Journal of
    Constructivist Psychology* 19, 2 (2006), p. 115.
39. Ibid. pp. 113–15; Habermas and Bluck, 'Getting a Life', pp. 750–1.
40. Habermas and Bluck, 'Getting a Life', p. 750.
41. McAdams, 'The Problem of Narrative Coherence', p. 113.
42. Habermas and Bluck, 'Getting a Life', p. 750.
43. Ibid. p. 750.
44. McAdams, 'The Problem of Narrative Coherence', p. 115.
45. Habermas and Bluck, 'Getting a Life', p. 751.
46. McAdams, 'The Problem of Narrative Coherence', p. 115.
47. Habermas and Bluck, 'Getting a Life', p. 751.
48. Ibid. pp. 751, 758.
49. Ibid. p. 762.
50. Ibid. p. 757.

51. McAdams, 'The Problem of Narrative Coherence', pp. 112, 111.

52. Unpublished diaries, 17 June 1953.

53. Unpublished diaries, 6 February 1956.

54. Unpublished diaries, 6 February 1956.

55. Unpublished diaries, 2 August 1955; *Diary* 1, p. 287; unpublished diaries, 26 September 1960.

56. Unpublished diaries, 2 August 1955.

57. Unpublished diaries, Good Friday 1962; 23 June 1963.

58. Charles Dickens, *David Copperfield* (Peterborough, ON: Broadview Press, 2001), p. 102.

59. The death of the little boy in *The Lost Traveller* encodes to some extent White's sense that she had 'killed my little boy' (unpublished dream diaries, 19 March 1949): not only is the boy named Charles in the novel, but Chitty reports that her mother came downstairs after writing the scene and announced 'I've just killed a little boy' (*Now to My Mother*, p. 158).

60. Unpublished diaries, 26 November 1952; 11 August 1962.

61. Unpublished diaries, 12 June 1955.

62. McAdams, 'The Problem of Narrative Coherence', p. 123.

63. Habermas and Bluck, p. 762.

64. Irene Patelis-Siotis, 'Cognitive-behavioral therapy: applications for the management of bipolar disorder', *Bipolar Disorder* 3 (2001), p. 105.

65. Ibid. p. 105.

66. Ibid. pp. 105–6.

67. Randy S. Milden, 'Affective Disorders and Narcissistic Vulnerability', *American Journal of Psychoanalysis* 44 (1984), p. 347.

68. Mark Freeman, 'Beyond Narrative: Dementia's Tragic Promise', in Lars-Christer Hydén and Jens Brockmeier (eds) *Health, Illness and Culture: Broken Narratives* (New York and London: Routledge), p. 171.

69. Mark Freeman, 'Afterword: "Even Amidst": Rethinking narrative coherence', in Hyvärinen, Hydén, Saarenheimo and Tambouko (eds), *Beyond Narrative Coherence*, p. 173.

70. Michael S. Gazzaniga, *The Mind's Past* (Berkeley: University of California Press, 1998), pp. 1–2.

71. Gazzaniga, 'The Storyteller in Your Head', *Discover* (spring 2012); *The Mind's Past*, pp. 1–2.

72. Ibid. p. 2.

73. Jonathan Gottschall, *The Storytelling Animal: How Stories Make Us Human* (Boston: Houghton Mifflin Harcourt, 2012), p. 99.

74. Galen Strawson attacks the 'narrativist orthodoxy' of scholarship on narrative identity, proclaiming himself an 'episodic' who lives in the here and now ('Against Narrativity', *Ratio* XVII [4 December 2004],

pp. 428–52). James Phelan concedes that he and many other scholars are guilty of 'narrative imperialism' and of making 'unsustainable extravagant claims' about the centrality of narrative in constructions of identity ('Who's Here? Thoughts on Narrative Identity and Narrative Imperialism', *Narrative* 13 [2005], pp. 205–10). In a spirited response, Paul John Eakin points out that such arguments conveniently ignore the real anguish of those who must live without a sense of continuous existence, such as Oliver Sacks' patient with Korsakov's syndrome, a man who literally must make himself up from moment to moment ('Narrative Identity and Narrative Imperialism: A Response to Galen Strawson and James Phelan', *Narrative* 14, 2 [May 2006], p. 185). Eakin stresses again the prescriptive and normative social pressure that underwrites the narrative construction of self: 'identity narratives, delivered piecemeal every day, function as the signature for others of the individual's possession of a normal identity [. . .] Failures of narrative competence, triggered by various forms of memory loss and dementia, may entail institutional confinement. When we prescribe what it takes to count as a person, and we certainly do so tacitly when we follow such behavioral norms, we enter dangerous territory' (p. 182). White's anguish over self-fragmentation, intensified by her use of her life as the scaffolding for her fiction, lends weight to Eakin's argument.

75. Phyllis Chesler's *Women and Madness* (Garden City, NY: Doubleday, 1972) and Showalter's *The Female Malady* initiated the study of how discourses of mental illness reproduce gender bias. See also Lisa Appignanesi, *Mad, Bad and Sad: A History of Women and the Mind Doctors, 1800 to the Present* (London: Virago, 2008) and Jane M. Ussher, *Women's Madness: Misogyny or Mental Illness?* (New York and London: Harvester Wheatsheaf, 1991).

76. Showalter, *The Female Malady*, p. 55. See also Valentine, *Psychoanalysis, Psychiatry and Modernist Literature* for an analysis of how modernist aesthetics took shape in the context of the emergence of psychoanalysis and psychiatry.

77. Cited in Showalter, *The Female Malady*, p. 125.

78. See in particular Showalter, *The Female Malady*, pp. 195–218, and Ussher, *Women's Madness*, pp. 97–209.

79. Showalter, *The Female Malady*, pp. 203, 204.

80. Ibid. p. 205.

81. Ibid. p. 204. Katherine Conley has disputed the notion that the iconic figure of the schizophrenic woman necessarily disempowered women artists in her study of women writers working within the context of surrealism, arguing that 'the positive qualities of this figure counterbalance the negative ones in a mix that, while ambiguous, can help explain part of the attraction of surrealism for women' (*Automatic Woman:*

The Representation of Woman in Surrealism [Lincoln and London: University of Nebraska Press, 1996], p. 3).

82. White notes her enjoyment of *Nadja* in her diary (*Diary* 1, p. 80). She had just met a group of younger poets, including David Gascoyne, who wrote the first English introduction to surrealism and may have discussed the novel with her.

83. The psychologist Gail A. Hornstein notes that contemporary psychiatrists view schizophrenia as an illness that 'scrambles transmissions between different parts of the brain': the schizophrenic's speech acts are thus viewed as 'a jumble of incoherent phrases produced by the random firing of faulty brain circuits'. To imagine that such phrases mean anything is 'like thinking you could decipher the static on a bad telephone line' (*Agnes's Jacket*, p. xiii). Wood similarly notes that 'In both popular and medical representations of schizophrenia, the words people diagnosed with schizophrenia speak or write are not heard as story but as jumbled, random linguistic units disconnected from meaning and from the kind of social interrelatedness that gives sense to story-telling' (*Life Writing and Schizophrenia*, p. 13). Marta Caminero-Santangelo has challenged the ubiquity of what she calls the 'subversive metaphor' of women's madness in feminist theory – that is, the idea that women's madness represents a liberating resistance and protest – by underscoring the fact that those diagnosed with mental illnesses are typically silenced: 'In order to use madness as a metaphor for the liberatory potentials of language, feminist critics must utterly unmoor it from its associations with mental illness as understood and constructed by discourses and practices both medical and popular' (*The Madwoman Can't Speak: Why Insanity Is Not Subversive* [Ithaca and London: Cornell University Press, 1998], p. 2).

84. Wood, *Life Writing and Schizophrenia*, p. 10.

85. Recently, scholars have shown that women did define themselves as active artists within the context of surrealism. Conley's *Automatic Woman* explores several women writers, including Leonora Carrington and Unica Zürn, contemporaries of White who wrote narratives of psychosis and incarceration. There is no evidence, however, that White knew these writers or their work. Jennifer Cizik Marshall explores Zürn's narratives in relation to her diagnosis of schizophrenia, which Marshall convincingly argues was, in fact, a misdiagnosis: Zürn, like White, suffered from manic depression. See 'The Semiotics of Schizophrenia: Unica Zürn's Artistry and Illness', *Modern Language Studies* 30, 2 (Autumn 2000), pp. 21–31. Other representative studies of women's role in surrealism include Whitney Chadwick, *Women Artists and the Surrealist Movement* (Boston: Little, Brown, 1985); and Susan Rubin Suleiman, *Subversive Intent: Gender, Politics, and the Avant-Garde* (Cambridge, MA: Harvard University Press, 1990).

86. Wood, *Life Writing and Schizophrenia*, p. 54.
87. Qtd. in Dunn, *Antonia White*, p. 201.
88. White's embrace of an illness identity follows the four stages Karp maps in his study of depression: 1) a period of 'inchoate feelings'; 2) an acknowledgement that 'something is really wrong with me'; 3) a 'crisis stage' that inaugurates medical intervention; 4) a stage of 'coming to grips with an illness identity' (Karp, *Speaking of Sadness*, p. 57).
89. Qtd. in Dunn, *Antonia White*, p. 202.
90. David Gascoyne, *Journal 1936–37* (London: Enitharmon Press, 1980)
91. Ibid.
92. Eugen Bleuler, *Dementia Praecox or The Group of Schizophrenias*, trans. Joseph Zinkin (New York: International Universities Press, 1950), p. 351.
93. I am much indebted here to Wood's succinct account of the diagnostic history of schizophrenia (*Life Writing and Schizophrenia*, pp. 8–10). Freud's doubt about the inaccessibility of schizophrenia to the 'talking cure' set the groundwork for the subsequent dismissal of the speech acts of those diagnosed with schizophrenia (p. 10). Given this history, it is surprising that White was taken on as an analysand in the 1930s, although Wood shows how American psychoanalysts such as Harry Stack Sullivan and Frieda Fromm-Reichmann developed innovative and often successful therapies with their supposedly inaccessible patients (pp. 10–11). In general, Wood remarks, American psychiatry remained open to psychoanalytic treatment with psychotic patients until the emergence of neurophysiological approaches in the later part of the twentieth century.
94. Wood, *Life Writing and Schizophrenia*, p. 9.
95. Ibid. p. 9.
96. Hopkinson, *Nothing to Forgive*, p. 14.
97. White references this second novel in her diary: 'I must not forget that my father was not at all unsympathetic about my 2nd book and I read it to him with no misgivings. But obviously he judged me by too high standards and felt that if I weren't George Meredith full grown . . . I was no good. He didn't really feel easy about anything I'd done until someone else had praised it' (*Diary* 1, p. 161). Chitty, however, suggests that White's sense of her father's judgement is inaccurate. She writes, 'It is not generally known that Antonia wrote a second novel at this time, apparently undismayed by the disastrous reception of the first [. . .] More remarkable still, her father liked it and said she might one day be a George Meredith. This was the highest praise he could

give' (*Now to My Mother*, p. 10). Chitty also expresses doubt about White's equation of her writer's block with her father's reaction to her first novel: 'There is just a possibility that my mother invented this pivotal episode in her life, or at least exaggerated it beyond recognition' (*Now to My Mother*, p. 7).

98. Podnieks points out that White frequently uses the word 'impotence' to record her difficulties with writing: it dominates her descriptions during and after her analysis in the 1930s, reflecting her connection of writing with the father's pen/penis (*Daily Modernism*, pp. 200–1).

99. Caramagno, *The Flight of the Mind*, p. 63.

100. Ibid. p. 63.

101. Podnieks has written extensively about the scope and importance of White's diaries, noting that they are on a scale with those of Virginia Woolf. See *Daily Modernism*, pp. 165–224.

102. White's description of the 'dullness' of daily life and her craving for 'violent shocks' recalls Woolf's similar description of 'shocks' that intrude on the 'cotton wool' of daily life in 'A Sketch of the Past' (p. 70).

103. Chitty describes the diaries and her editorial decisions in her introduction to the two volumes she edited for publication. She explains there her incorporation of these singular notebooks into the diary proper: 'none of these (with the exception of the first few pages of the Benedicta diary and the French passages of the Nicholson diary) differs greatly from the normal diaries, and they have been incorporated chronologically with the rest' (Introduction, pp. 3–4).

104. In *Daily Modernism*, Podnieks discusses White's method of keeping notebooks as 'a form of Freudian case study that documents herself and her life' and a means of 'investigating the different levels of her consciousness' (p. 166). Podnieks describes White as exploiting psychoanalysis 'as a modernist literary aesthetic' (p. 166). My focus here is on the ways in which psychoanalysis functioned as a master narrative.

105. Margaret Drabble, 'Review of *Antonia White Diaries, 1926–1957*', *Vogue* (British) (September 1991), pp. 102–3. Lessing may have known of White's unusual mode of using different notebooks to record different aspects of herself: White reviewed Lessing's first novel, *The Grass is Singing*, for *The New Statesman*; Chitty reports that White felt 'special enthusiasm' for it (*Now To My Mother*, p. 159). White and Lessing did become acquainted with each other, although the extent of that acquaintance is not documented by White, her daughters or Dunn.

106. Ibid. pp. 102–3.
107. Dunn, *Antonia White*, p. 327.
108. Ibid. p. 318.
109. A letter to Emily Coleman in 1939, as analysis was coming to an end, anticipates White's return to the Church as a way of repairing the fundamental broken springs of being: 'A true belief in God would be the strongest spring of action and happiness' (qtd. in Dunn, *Antonia White*, p. 243).
110. Charlotte Linde, *Life Stories: The Creation of Coherence* (New York and Oxford: Oxford University Press, 1993), p. 164.
111. Ibid. p. 189.
112. Ibid. p. 189.
113. Jerome Bruner, 'Life as Narrative', in *Social Research* 71, 3 (Fall 2004), p. 694.
114. Ibid. p. 694.
115. Ibid. pp. 694, 708.
116. Hilde Lindemann Nelson, *Damaged Identities, Narrative Repair* (Ithaca and London: Cornell University Press, 2001), pp. 158–60.
117. Ibid. p. 159.
118. Ibid. pp. 159–60.

Chapter 3

1. Podnieks, *Daily Modernism*, p. 89; Valentine, *Psychoanalysis, Psychiatry, and Modernist Literature*, p. 64.
2. Podnieks, *Daily Modernism*, pp. 89, 188. Podnieks explores the parallels between Freud's case history of Dora and White's diary at length (pp. 180–8).
3. For discussions of Catholicism in White's work, see Benson, '"Varieties of Disbelief"'; and O'Mara, 'Trust Amid Sore Affliction'. For discussions of spirituality more generally, see Chait, 'The Psychospiritual in the Literary Analysis of Modernist Texts' and 'Site also of Angst and Spiritual Search'. For discussions of White and Joyce, see Bowen, 'Introduction', p. vii; Podnieks, *Daily Modernism*, pp. 206–16; and Rose, 'Antonia White', pp. 239–40.
4. See Newton, 'Sexual Trauma, Psychosis and Betrayal'; and Wells, 'Strand by Strand'.
5. Wells notes that White was interested in 'reconciling the two discourses of psychoanalysis and religion in order to understand her own neurosis' but that once she reconverted to Catholicism she 'began to embrace the religious discourse with more passion' ('Strand by Strand', p. 50).

Podnieks, on the other hand, describes White's ongoing use of psycho-analysis as a strategy of self-analysis and as an aesthetic strategy (*Daily Modernism*, pp. 180–8).

6. Unpublished diaries, 1 December 1965.
7. Chitty, editorial note, *Diary* 1, p. 193.
8. Unpublished diaries, 9 December 1965.
9. Unpublished diaries, 8, 11 and 14 January 1966. White reports the title as 'A Psycho-analytical Approach to Aesthetics'.
10. See Philippe Ployé, 'Inpatient Psychotherapy and Prenatal Regression', *British Journal of Psychotherapy* 22, 4 (2006), pp. 483–95.
11. See Janet Sayer's account of how women analysts influenced and shaped psychoanalysis, particularly after Freud's death: *Mothers of Psychoanalysis: Helene Deutsch, Karen Horney, Anna Freud, Melanie Klein* (Harmondsworth: Penguin, 1992).
12. Unpublished diaries, 1 December 1965.
13. See Marvin Richard O'Connell, *Critics on Trial: An Introduction to the Catholic Modernist Crisis* (Catholic University Press, 1995).
14. See Dunn for a summary of these doubts (*Antonia White*, pp. 397–400).
15. Podnieks explores White's equation of the pen and the penis in *Daily Modernisms*, pp. 200–1. Chait explores the relationship between sexuality and spirituality in White's writing in 'The Psychospiritual in the Literary Analysis of Literary Texts' and 'Site also of Angst and Spiritual Search'.
16. White seems to have known little about psychoanalysis before entering treatment: in fact, she was hostile and resistant, writing in her diary that she had never known anyone it had helped. See, for example, *Diary* 1, p. 34.
17. Abraham's paper was delivered to the 1920 Sixth International Psycho-analytic Congress to great acclaim. James Glover, an important figure in British psychoanalytic circles, was in attendance and became 'a total convert': he and his brother Edward subsequently underwent analysis with Abraham and James returned to London to 'normalise' the Med-ico-Psychological Clinic by incorporating it into the British Psycho-Ana-lytical Society, founded in 1913 by Ernest Jones. See Showalter for a discussion of this process (*The Female Malady*, pp. 198–9). James died in his thirties in 1926 and his brother Edward took over many of his duties in the British Psycho-Analytical Society.
18. Karl Abraham, 'Manifestations of the Female Castration Complex', rpt. Jean Strouse (ed.), *Women and Analysis: Dialogues on Psycho-analytic Views of Femininity* (New York: Grossman Publishers, 1974), pp. 109–10.
19. Ibid. p. 110.

20. Ibid. p. 110.
21. Ibid. p. 111.
22. Ibid. p. 112.
23. Ibid. p. 113.
24. Ibid. p. 113.
25. Ibid. p. 113.
26. Ibid. p. 114.
27. Ibid. pp. 114–15.
28. Ibid. p. 117.
29. Ibid. p. 116.
30. Ibid. p. 116.
31. Ibid. p. 123.
32. 'The great enjoyment many women obtain from using a hose for watering the garden is characteristic, for here the unconscious experiences the ideal fulfilment of a childhood wish' ('Manifestations', p. 122).
33. Ibid. p. 122.
34. Ibid. p. 124.
35. Ibid. p. 125.
36. Ibid. p. 116.
37. Ibid. p. 125.
38. Although I have been unable to discover who Carroll's training analyst was, Carroll had close ties with Edward Glover, who had been drawn to psychoanalysis through his brother James and through Abraham's paper. Glover and Carroll worked together at the Institute for the Scientific Treatment of Delinquency, which Glover founded (as the Association for the Scientific Treatment of Criminals) in 1931; Carroll became an important force in this work, joining Glover there in spring 1933. (The name changed twice more, becoming the Institute for the Study and Treatment of Delinquency in 1951 and then the Centre for Crime and Justice Studies in 1999.) Carroll was elected an associate member of the British Psycho-Analytical Society in 1932 and became a full member in 1936: he was thus still under the supervision of a training analyst when White began treatment with him and Glover may have been his supervisor. Glover wrote Carroll's obituary (*International Journal of Psychoanalysis* 38 [1957], pp. 277–9) when Carroll died suddenly aged 56 in November 1956. My thanks to Joanne Halford, archivist of the Institute of Psychoanalysis, for providing information on Carroll (personal communication, 25 August 2015).
39. Dunn, *Antonia White*, p. 88. In fact, this man, Jim Dougal, had had polio.

40. Ibid. p. 129.

41. Ibid. pp. 109–10.

42. Sigmund Freud, 'Inhibitions, Symptoms and Anxiety', in James Strachey (ed. and trans.), *The Standard Edition of the Complete Psychological Works of Sigmund Freud* (vol. 20) (London: The Hogarth Press and the Institute of Psychoanalysis, 1959), p. 90. In 'Antonia White and the Subversion of Literary Impotence', Jeffery discusses this essay in relation to White's writer's block, arguing that the connection between writing and the sexual act 'explains the inhibition experienced by White when attempting to write creatively' after the repudiation of her adolescent novel (p. 75).

43. Ibid. p. 75.

44. Dunn, *Antonia White*, p. 177.

45. Podnieks has read these passages of the writing woman as abnormal, odd or monstrous as evidence of White's conflicts about combining femininity and artistry (*Daily Modernisms*, pp. 198–206). But it is significant that these passages proliferate during her analysis. While the break-up of her marriage may have also contributed to White's sense of failed femininity, this analysis – with its insistent linking of White's illness to her repressed rage about 'castration' – certainly intensified White's conflicts about artistry.

46. White typically uses the word 'odd' to mark sites of puzzlement, connections that she has not yet explained to her own satisfaction. The word may also carry the lingering meaning it did at the end of the nineteenth century in Britain, when there was concern about increasing numbers of 'surplus' or 'odd' women who could not fulfil their 'natural' roles. The end of the First World War reignited this hysteria, when the 1921 census revealed that there were 1.75 million more women than men as a result of the losses in the war. One headline proclaimed 'Problem of the Surplus Women – Two Million Who Can Never Become Wives'; polemicist Anthony M. Ludovici decried the 'surplus woman' as 'malign', 'deficient' and 'wretched'. See Virginia Nicholson, *Singled Out: How Two Million Women Survived without Men After the First World War* (New York: Viking, 2008), pp. 22–3, 58. For other discussions of the cultural bias against single women, see Sheila Jeffreys, *The Spinster and her Enemies: Feminism and Sexuality, 1880–1930* (Melbourne: Spinifex Press, 2003). This cultural equation of the single woman with abnormality is one that clearly affected White's sense of herself as humiliated and 'mutilated' by her third divorce.

47. Abraham, 'Manifestations', p. 125.

48. Ibid. p. 126.

49. Ibid. p. 126.

50. See in particular Broe, 'My Art Belongs to Daddy', pp. 41–86, esp. pp. 73–6; and Podnieks, *Daily Modernism*, pp. 165–224, esp. pp. 188–92. Dunn concludes that, 'although there is little reason to believe there was any kind of genital contact between them, there was an erotic element in his love and interest in her, combined with a heavy-handed expression of power invested with the weight of paternal disapproval and reinforced by the threat of supernatural retribution' (*Antonia White*, p. 219).

51. Dunn, *Antonia White*, pp. 215, 217.

52. Sigmund Freud, 'Femininity', in Strouse (ed.), *Women and Analysis*, p. 91.

53. See Podnieks, *Daily Modernisms*, pp. 200–1, for a discussion of White's obsession with pens.

54. Qtd. in Dunn, *Antonia White*, pp. 209–10.

55. In her last analytic treatment in the 1960s, White puzzles over the fact that 'Money has never come up in this analysis as it did all the time with Carroll' (*Diary* 2, p. 167), a sign that Freudian orthodoxy concerning money has weakened.

56. Hopkinson develops an unprofessional but accurate reading of her mother's weight fluctuations: 'Her tendency to swell up when her life was dull and without stimulation and to lose weight when happy or in love, had been a problem since her twenties'; Hopkinson notes that the weight gain White experienced at the end of analysis was the most extreme it had ever been (*Nothing to Forgive*, p. 184).

57. Qtd. in Hopkinson, *Nothing to Forgive*, p. 178.

58. The phrase 'unquiet mind' references Jamison's memoir of her illness, *An Unquiet Mind*.

59. Podnieks considers White's reconversion a response to exile, but she links it to a sense of homelessness and modernist exile, rather than as a response to experiencing an 'unquiet mind' (*Daily Modernisms*, p. 214).

60. Freud, *The Future of an Illusion*, in James Strachey (ed.), *The Standard Edition of the Complete Psychological Works of Sigmund Freud* XXI (London: Hogarth Press and The Institute of Psychoanalysis, 1961), p. 14.

61. Mark Edmundson, *The Death of Sigmund Freud: The Legacy of His Last Days* (London: Bloomsbury, 2007), p. 233.

62. Ibid. p. 233.

63. Podnieks notes this correspondence, although she does not read White's reconversion as a response to internal chaos but as a response to modernist exile (*Daily Modernisms*, pp. 212–14).

64. White tried to discuss her 'Garden of Eden' troubles with local priests on several occasions: they both identified her problems as emotional rather than intellectual (*Diary* 2, pp. 185, 201).

65. Podnieks writes that White here identifies with the 'original mother' and accepts responsibility for the Fall of Man (*Daily Modernisms*, p. 219). The passage also speaks to White's sense of internal corruption, which was intensified if not actually generated by her almost constant state of agitated depression or dysphoric mania.

66. Podnieks reads this passage as 'writing beyond the ending of perhaps the greatest patriarchal narrative in history, replacing it with a modernist ending in which women may empower themselves to "name and control"' (*Daily Modernisms*, p. 219). But White records this entry during the late 1940s, when she was highly unstable, as I show later in this chapter. It speaks to a manic inflation of her sense of her own depravity.

67. Chitty, *Now to My Mother*, p. 155. The entire dream in the unpublished dream diaries details the dreamer's uncertainty about whether the ravisher is the father or someone deputised by him because the father does not believe it is appropriate for him to carry out the act. The dreamer understands that she is never going to be able to know the actual ravisher. The dream also situates the ravishment inside the ark of the covenant, again underscoring White's literalising of religious narratives in her representations (unpublished dream diaries, 6 November 1947).

68. In one of her many retellings of her father's repudiation of her and her adolescent novel, White describes the lifelong barrier that resulted: 'To the end of his life he refused to discuss the matter or to let me state my side of the case. Thus for fifteen years there was a cloud between us which was never entirely dissolved' (*The Hound and the Falcon*, p. 155).

69. 'Sed Tantum Dic Verbo', in *Strangers*, p. 159. According to Hopkinson, White wrote the poem soon after starting her analysis with Kingsmill (*Nothing to Forgive*, p. 230); she recorded the Ritual Rape Dream on 6 November 1947 (unpublished dream diaries).

70. White cites this verse verbatim in *The Hound and the Falcon*, p. 93.

71. Jon Bloom, 'Desiring God', 16 December 2013 <www.desiringgod.org/articles/when-a-sword-pierces-your-soul> (last accessed August 2017).

72. Chait, 'The Psychospiritual in the Analysis of Modernist Texts', p. 65.

73. Unpublished diaries, 7 July 1949; 1 June 1949.

74. Hopkinson, *Nothing to Forgive*, p. 233.

75. Frieda Fordham, *An Introduction to Jung's Psychology* (1953; Harmondsworth: Penguin, 1986), p. 49.

76. Qtd. in Dunn, *Antonia White*, p. 293.
77. Hopkinson, *Nothing to Forgive*, p. 233.
78. Ibid. p. 233.
79. Chitty, *Now to My Mother*, p. 153.
80. Hopkinson, *Nothing to Forgive*, p. 233.
81. Ibid. p. 238.
82. Ibid. p. 240.
83. Jung, *Modern Man in Search of a Soul* (1933; London: Redwood Burn Limited, 1978), p. 20.
84. Ibid. p. 19.
85. Ibid. pp. 19–20.
86. Ibid. p. 25.
87. Ibid. pp. 25–6.
88. Ibid. p. 230.
89. Fordham, *An Introduction to Jung's Psychology*, p. 98.
90. Ibid. p. 107.
91. Ibid. p. 107.
92. Jung, *Modern Man in Search of a Soul*, pp. 80–1.
93. Ibid. p. 250.
94. Qtd. in Chitty, *Now to My Mother*, p. 152.
95. Fordham, *An Introduction to Jung's Psychology*, p. 55.
96. Ibid. p. 56.
97. Ibid. pp. 56–7.
98. Ibid. p. 58.
99. Ibid. p. 58.
100. Unpublished diaries, 5 March 1951.
101. Jung, *Modern Man in Search of a Soul*, p. 268.
102. Ibid. p. 269.
103. Ibid. p. 273.
104. Ibid. p. 279.
105. Ibid. p. 280.
106. Ibid. p. 273.
107. Ibid. p. 277.
108. Ibid. p. 277.
109. Jung notes, for example, that, of the hundreds of patients he had treated over the years, most were Protestant, whereas he treated 'not more than five or six believing Catholics' (*Modern Man in Search of a Soul*, p. 264). A questionnaire he sent out queried whether people in spiritual distress consulted a clergyman or a doctor: 57 per cent of Protestants opted for the doctor whereas only 25 per cent of Catholics did (p. 265). Jung ends this chapter by stating his firm conviction 'that

a vast number of people belong to the fold of the Catholic Church and nowhere else, because they are suitably housed there' (*Modern Man in Search of a Soul*, p. 282).

110. Chitty attests to the close friendship between White and Father Victor in *Now to My Mother*, pp. 144–64. In the interests of clarity, I will refer to Father White as Father Victor.

111. Ann C. Lammers, 'Jung and White and the God of terrible double aspect', *Journal of Analytical Psychology* 52, 3 (2007), pp. 255, 256. See also Clodagh Weldon, *Father Victor White, O.P.: The Story of Jung's White Raven* (Chicago: Chicago University Press, 2007).

112. Lammers, 'Jung and White', p. 257.

113. John P. Dourley, 'The Jung–White Dialogue and why it couldn't work and why it won't go away', *Journal of Analytical Psychology* 52, 3 (2007), p. 279.

114. Unpublished dream diaries, 3 April 1948.

115. Unpublished dream diaries, 7 July 1949.

116. Unpublished dream diaries, 5 June 1949; 7 July 1949.

117. Unpublished dream diaries, 5 June 1949.

118. Unpublished diaries, 24 September 1965.

119. Unpublished diaries, 9 December 1965. Both the published and unpublished diaries suggest Galway's careful monitoring for excitement during this period.

120. Unpublished diaries, 12 January 1966.

121. Hanna Segal, 'A Psychoanalytic Approach to Aesthetics', John Phillips and Lyndsey Stonebridge (eds), *Reading Melanie Klein* (London and New York: Routledge, 1998), p. 209.

122. Ibid. p. 209.

123. Stephen A. Mitchell, *Relational Concepts in Psychoanalysis: An Integration* (Cambridge, MA and London: Harvard University Press, 1988), p. 181.

124. Unpublished diaries, 12 January 1966.

125. Unpublished diaries, 23 November 1965.

126. Ibid. Klein wrote extensively on manic depression, in essence viewing mania as a defence against the psychic reality of depressive feelings. See 'A Contribution to the Psychogenesis of Manic-Depressive States' and 'Mourning and Its Relation to Manic-Depressive States' in Juliet Mitchell (ed.), *The Selected Melanie Klein* (New York: Macmillan, 1986), pp. 115–45 and pp. 146–74 respectively. See also Segal's discussion of Klein's conceptualisation of manic defences in *Introduction to the Work of Melanie Klein*, 2nd edn (New York: Basic Books, 1974), pp. 82–91.

127. Unpublished diaries, 8 January 1966.
128. Ibid.
129. Ibid.
130. Klein, 'Mourning', p. 172.
131. Ibid. p. 172.
132. Ibid. p. 173.
133. Unpublished diaries, 23 November 1965.
134. Unpublished diaries, 24 October 1966.
135. In addition to numerous entries in the published diaries (*Diary* 2, pp. 147, 161, 181, 185, 250), entries also appear in the unpublished diaries (18 November 1966; 26 July 1967; 11 November 1967; 19 May 1968; 27 May 1968; 17 November 1968; 4 October 1970).
136. White discusses this article in her unpublished diaries, 18 November 1966.

Chapter 4

1. Flood, 'Autobiographical Novels', p. 133.
2. Qtd. in Carmen Callil, 'Introduction', *Beyond the Glass* (New York: The Dial Press, 1979), np.
3. Ibid. np.
4. Two significant exceptions are Flood and O'Mara, who both identify ways in which the later novels expand on themes latent in *Frost in May*. See Flood, 'Autobiographical Novels', p. 133; and O'Mara, 'Trust Amid Sore Affliction', p. 38.
5. Qtd. in Callil, 'Introduction', np.
6. White complains about her inability to invent throughout her diary. She also longs for the 'real power' of invention, as in the following passage: 'My first two crude attempts [at novels] were really much more on the right lines because they were imaginative: the trouble was I knew nothing about anything' (*Diary* 1, p. 101).
7. Chitty, *Now to My Mother*, pp. 157–8.
8. Qtd. in Callil, 'Introduction', np.
9. Ibid. np.
10. Chitty, *Now to My Mother*, p. 157.
11. Callil, 'Introduction', np.
12. Discussions of the series and White's biography are often interwoven. See, for example, Penny Brown, *The Poison at the Source*, pp. 121–50; Flood, 'Autobiographical Novels', pp. 131–49; Sandra Jeffery, 'Antonia White and the Subversion of Literary Impotence', pp. 73–81; Podnieks, *Daily Modernism*, pp. 176–98; and Ellen Cronan Rose, 'Antonia White', pp. 239–48.

13. My discussion of the thematic continuity of the series is much indebted to a number of excellent interpretations, including Brown, *The Poison at the Source*, pp. 121–50; Flood, 'Autobiographical Novels', pp. 131–49; O'Mara, 'Trust Amid Sore Affliction', pp. 33–43; and Rose, 'Antonia White', pp. 239–48.

14. A number of scholars have noted White's equation of conversion with coercion as well as the sacrifice of the daughter's sexuality to the father. See in particular Flood, who explains that 'the theme of conversion is a complicated one in White's books, for beneath its religious meaning lies the more sinister one of changing the person into someone else, someone more acceptable to him who forces the change' ('Autobiographical Novels', p. 133). For discussions of the sacrifice of the daughter's sexuality, see, in addition to Flood, Brown, *The Poison at the Source*; Chait, 'Site'; and Rose, 'Antonia White'.

15. Lizzie Hutton has developed the theme of expulsion in the novels in detail, arguing that 'the sense of irrevocable expulsion – with its reverberating effects on the sense of self – is not merely a function of early childhood sensitivity, though perhaps it is most precisely captured and remembered there'. Instead, the series insists upon 'the disturbing fact of human isolation, which a fitful reality [. . .] can force upon any one of us at random. See 'The Example of Antonia White', *New England Review* 26, 1 (2005), p. 125.

16. Paulina Palmer explores in detail White's 'alternative female sexual economy' in *Frost in May*, focusing in particular on the complex homoerotic relationships between Nanda, her close friend Léonie and two older girls. See 'Antonia White's *Frost in May*: A Lesbian Feminist Reading', in Susan Sellers (ed.), *Feminist Criticism: Theory and Practice* (New York: Harvester Wheatsheaf, 1991), pp. 89–108. As Palmer notes, 'Instead of treating female erotic relations explicitly, White creates a metonymic discourse' in which 'the facts of sexual arousal and response are not represented directly by reference to intimate parts of the body' but indirectly by reference to less culturally loaded body parts and to nature (p. 103). Palmer discusses in detail the ways in which motifs of freedom and imprisonment are played out on the female body (p. 104).

17. See Flood, 'Autobiographical Novels', p. 133.

18. Brown, *The Poison at the Source*, p. 128.

19. Unpublished diaries, 1 June 1937.

20. A passage in *The Lost Traveller*, in which Claude begins to assault Clara's friend Patsy, has often been cited as evidence that White was an incest victim. See Broe, 'My Art Belongs to Daddy', p. 44; and Podnieks, *Daily Modernisms*, pp. 191–2. Marcia Anne Newton explores the theme of incest in the novels extensively in her unpublished dissertation, 'Sexual

Trauma, Psychosis, and Betrayal in Antonia White's Autobiographical Fiction' (University of Sheffield, 2014).

21. Brown identifies Claude's 'latent homosexual tendencies' and observes that they 'suggest a sexual ambivalence which in turn affects his views of Clara's relationships with men' (*The Poison at the Source*, p. 132). In 'Site', Chait explores the homoeroticism of Claude in the fourth novel and notes its initial mention in *The Lost Traveller* (p. 155). Isabel does not, however, seek out Callaghan because of Claude's interest, as Chait suggests: instead, Claude seeks out Callaghan only after Isabel has begun a flirtation with him in *The Lost Traveller*. Claude's attraction to other men is mediated through Isabel and Clara and is signalled by his likening those men (Callaghan, Archie) to the lost Larry.

22. See, for example, Sandra Chait, 'Psychospiritual', pp. 63–4; and Flood, 'Autobiographical Novels', p. 137.

23. Chait notes the 'obvious Freudian connotation of "tower"' ('Psychospiritual', p. 63). White may also be alluding to Yeats's 'A Prayer for my Daughter', which is set in a tower and which voices similarly controlling attitudes towards the daughter's sexuality.

24. Tim Ashley, 'Wagner's *Tannhäuser*', *The Guardian*, 11 December 2010.

25. Ibid.

26. Ibid.

27. Ibid.

28. Oscar Wilde, *The Picture of Dorian Gray* (Peterborough, ON: Broadview Press, 2005), p. 168.

29. Chait observes that Claude's reference to himself as having 'a touch of Dr Middleton . . . and, I fear, more than a touch of Sir Willoughby' situates Clara between the father and lover of Clara Middleton in Meredith's novel ('Site', p. 155). Chait further notes that the discussion of Claude's relationship to O'Sullivan in *Beyond the Glass* includes the information that 'Clara received her name at Larry's [O'Sullivan's] insistence and against Isabel's wish because of the mutual love Claude and Larry held for the heroine' of Meredith's novel ('Site', p. 155).

30. Ellis Hanson, *Decadence and Catholicism* (Cambridge, MA: Harvard University Press, 1998), p. 11. For other representative studies of Wilde and 'decadent Catholicism', see Martin Lockerd, '"A Satirist of Vice and Follies": Beardsley, Eliot, and Images of Decadent Catholicism', *Journal of Modern Literature* 37, 4 (2014), pp. 143–65; Shushma Malik, 'All Roads Lead to Rome? Decadence, Paganism, Catholicism and the Later Life of Oscar Wilde', *Cahiers victoriens et édouardiens* 80 (automne 2014): pp. 2–14 (online); and Ronald Schuchard, 'Wilde's Dark Angel

and the Spell of Decadent Catholicism', in Constantin-George Sandulescu (ed.), *Rediscovering Oscar Wilde* (Savage, MD: Barnes and Noble, 1994), pp. 371–96.

31. Hanson, *Decadence and Catholicism*, p. 18.
32. Ibid. pp. 23–4.
33. Ibid. p. 24.
34. See Malik, 'All Roads Lead to Rome?' for a description of Wilde's path to conversion.
35. White's familiarity with the classics may have informed her choice of the word 'fascinate' here, for the root of the word comes from Fascinum, an old Roman god of fertility. The *fascinus*, a winged phallic object often worn as a protective charm, was an emblem of 'fertility, abundance and orgiastic excess' as well as 'masculine generative power' more generally. See Gemma Angel's 'Fascinus and the Winged Phallus Tattoo' on the Researchers in Museums blog at University College, London <http//blogs.ucl.ac.uk/researchers-in-museums/2013/01/07/fascinus-the-winged-phallus-tattoo> (last accessed 12 January 2017).
36. In his case history of Dora, for example, Freud identifies picklocks and keys as phallic and rooms (or apartments) as standing for female genitals: 'The question whether a woman is "open" or "shut" can naturally not be a matter of indifference. It is well known, too, what sort of "key" effects the opening in such a case' ('Fragment of an Analysis of a Case of Hysteria', in James Strachey [ed.], *The Standard Edition of the Complete Psychological Works of Sigmund Freud* [vol. 7] [London: Hogarth Press and The Institute of Psychoanalysis, 1953], p. 67).
37. This suggestion that the loss of the father could induce psychological breakdown has, of course, biographical parallels, for White wrote the early chapters of the novel shortly after her father's death and at a time when she was beginning to deteriorate mentally.
38. Wilde, *Dorian Gray*, p. 59.
39. Wilde, *Dorian Gray*, pp. 75–6.
40. Adrienne Harris, '"Fathers" and "Daughters"', *Psychoanalytic Inquiry* 28 (2008), p. 41.
41. Ibid. p. 43. See also Haydée Faimberg, *The Telescoping of Generations: Listening to the Narcissistic Links between Generations* (London and New York: Routledge, 2005).
42. Sigmund Freud, '"Civilized" Sexual Morality and Modern Nervousness', in Philip Rieff (ed.), *Sexuality and the Psychology of Love* (New York: Collier Books, 1953), pp. 20–40.

43. See especially 'The Most Prevalent Form of Degradation in Erotic Life', in *Sexuality and the Psychology of Love*, pp. 58–63.

44. Christine C. Kieffer, 'Selfobjects, Oedipal Objects, and Mutual Recognition: A Self-Psychological Reappraisal of the Female "Oedipal Victor"', *The Annual of Psychoanalysis* 32 (2004), p. 72.

45. Kieffer, 'Selfobjects', p. 75. See also Judith Lewis Herman, with Lisa Hirschman, *Father–Daughter Incest* (Cambridge, MA: Harvard University Press, 1981), particularly the chapter on the seductive father (pp. 109–28).

46. Kieffer, 'Selfobjects', p. 75.

47. Ibid. p. 76.

48. Ibid. p. 77.

49. Ibid. p. 74.

50. Ibid. p. 74.

51. Ronald Britten, 'Forever Father's Daughter: The Athene-Antigone Complex', in Alice Etchegoyen and Judith Trowell (eds), *The Importance of Fathers: A Psychoanalytic Re-evaluation* (London and New York: Routledge, 2001), pp. 108, 197.

52. Ibid. pp. 109, 114.

53. The unhappy wife in Yeats's play mirrors Isabel: like Isabel, she prefers to read and dream rather than devote herself to domestic concerns, for which she receives harsh criticism from her mother-in-law. Claude's mother voices similar complaints about Isabel: '"I often wonder if your mother wouldn't be happier if she took some interest in household things. It doesn't seem natural, somehow, a woman spending so much time lying on a sofa and reading, the way she does"', she tells Clara (*The Lost Traveller*, p. 96).

54. See O'Mara, 'Trust Amid Sore Affliction' for a particularly insightful reading of the Catholic doctrine involved in Isabel's transformation, especially pp. 38–9.

55. Flood, 'Autobiographical Novels', p. 139.

56. Ibid. p. 139.

57. Ibid. p. 137.

58. Brown notes the significance of Isabel's intervention, although she views it as an alternative to Clara's prayers to the Virgin Mary instead of as a possible answer to them (*The Poison at the Source*, p. 136).

59. Chitty, *Now to My Mother*, pp. 157–8.

60. St Augustine, 'Exposition on Psalm LVI', *Expositions on the Psalms* (Christian Classics Ethereal Library <www.ccel.org/ccel/schaff/npnf108.ii.LVI.html>last accessed August 2017).

61. O'Mara, 'Trust Amid Sore Affliction', p. 38.

62. Ibid. p. 39.
63. Qtd. in Callil, 'Introduction', np.
64. Jamison, *Touched with Fire*, p. 126.
65. Karl Jaspers, *General Psychopathology*, 7th edn, trans. J. Hoenig and Marian W. Hamilton (Manchester: Manchester University Press, 1972), p. 447.
66. Ibid. p. 577.
67. See Vandivere, 'Framed Liminalities', for a particularly illuminating discussion of these passages ('Framed Liminalities', pp. 51–2).
68. 'Bipolar Disorder (*DSM IV-TR* 296.0-296.89) <https://www.brown.edu/Courses/BI_278/Other/Clerkship/. . ./Bipolar%20Disorder.pdf> p. 1 (last accessed August 2017).
69. 'Bipolar Disorder', p. 2.
70. Ibid. p. 2.
71. Ibid. p. 2.
72. Caramagno notes that mood swings are associated with fevers: 'In fact, the more severe the depression, the higher the temperature; moreover, in some patients, manic phases produced even higher oral temperatures than did depression' (*The Flight of the Mind*, p. 315 n.20).
73. Ibid.
74. See Hinshaw, *The Years of Silence are Past*, p. 83. Hinshaw observes that when his father began personalising the world in this manner he knew that his father had passed from the hypomanic to the acute stage of mania.
75. Qtd. in Goodwin and Jamison, *Manic-Depressive Illness*, p. 35.
76. 'Bipolar Disorder', p. 2.
77. Goodwin and Jamison, *Manic-Depressive Illness*, p. 36.
78. Statistics vary; the ones cited here are from Julie Nordgard, Sidse M. Arnfred, Peter Handest and Josef Parnas, 'The Diagnostic Status of First-Rank Symptoms', *Schizophrenia Bulletin* 34, 1 (January 2008), p. 138. This topic is controversial; for a review of the issues involved, see Goodwin and Jamison, *Manic-Depressive Illness*, pp. 99–104.
79. Evelyne Keitel, *Reading Psychosis: Readers, Texts and Psychoanalysis*, trans. Anthea Bell (Oxford: Basil Blackwell, 1989), p. 5.
80. 'Bipolar Disorder', p. 3.
81. Numerous scholars have noted the connection between Clara's return to the other side of Looking-Glass World through reading and writing. See, for example, Brown, *The Poison at the Source*, p. 148; and Flood, 'Autobiographical Novels', pp. 147–8.
82. Valentine, 'Mad and Modern', p. 132.
83. Ibid. p. 134.

84. Flood, 'Autobiographical Novels', p. 141.
85. Archie's uncharacteristically angry reaction suggests that he grasps Clara's implication of (symbolic) castration: 'Instead of kissing her as he usually did whenever he left the house, he went out abruptly, slamming the kitchen door' (*The Sugar House*, p. 188).
86. Abraham, 'Manifestations of the Female Castration Complex', p. 124.
87. Flood, 'Autobiographical Novels', pp. 143–4.
88. Wolfgang Schivelbusch, *The Railway Journey: The Industrialization of Time and Space in the 19th Century* (Berkeley and Los Angeles: University of California Press, 1986), p. 114.
89. Freud, 'Three Essays on Sexuality', pp. 201–2.
90. Marylaura Papalas, 'Speed and Convulsive Beauty: Trains and the Historic Avant-garde', *Studies in 20th and 21st Century Literature* 39, 1, Article 2. http://dx.doi.org/10.4148/2334-4415.1818 (last accessed August 2017).
91. Ibid.
92. Flood compares the irrevocable changes associated with this shock to the shock of the father's repudiation of Nanda in *Frost in May*: 'This striking repetition of Nanda's sense of catastrophic change in herself as the result of her father's rejection suggests the connection in White's mind of the heroine as writer and as boy killer' ('Autobiographical Novels', p. 142). It also suggests the loss of 'masculine' agency, both in sexuality and artistry. Flood's article appeared before the publication of White's diaries, but her insight is corroborated by a passage in White's diary after the publication of *The Sugar House*: 'How appalled my father would be if he knew the results of that fifteenth birthday. Yet I often feel as if I had never been a "whole" person since that day' (*Diary* 1, p. 263).
93. Blake's epigram appears with the title 'Abstinence' in *The Complete Poetry and Prose of William Blake*, ed. David V. Erdman (New York: Doubleday, 1988), p. 474.
94. Jung, 'On the Psychogenesis of Schizophrenia', in Herbert Read, Michael Fordham and Gerhard Adler (eds) and R. F. C. Hull (trans.), *C. G. Jung: The Collected Works*, vol. 3, *The Psychogenesis of Mental Disease* (London: Routledge and Kegan Paul, 1960), p. 235.
95. See Vandivere, 'Framed Liminalities', pp. 46–69.
96. Robert Louis Stevenson, *The Strange Case of Dr Jekyll and Mr Hyde*, in Stephen Greenblatt et al. (eds), *The Norton Anthology of English Literature* vol. E: *The Victorian Age*, 8th edn (New York and London: Norton, 2006), pp. 1645–85.
97. Showalter, *The Female Malady*, p. 211. Vandivere has discussed the link between Carroll and White extensively in 'Framed Liminalities' (pp. 54–6).

98. William Empson, *Some Versions of Pastoral* (Harmondsworth: Penguin, 1995), p. 277.

99. David Gascoyne, *A Short Survey of Surrealism* (1935; London: Enitharmon Press, 2000), p. 94. The association of British surrealism with Alice in Wonderland is reflected in Salvador Dali's stunning illustrations for a 1969 edition of *Alice in Wonderland*, reprinted by Princeton University Press in 2015; and by a 1982 exhibition in Paris at the Galerie 1900–2000, 'Les enfants d'Alice: peinture surréaliste en Angleterre, 1930–1960'. The exhibition and the exhibition catalogue of the same title, edited by Michel Rémy, renewed interest in British surrealism.

100. Catriona McAra, 'Surrealism's Curiosity: Lewis Carroll and the *Femme-Enfant*', *Papers of Surrealism* 9 (summer 2011): pp. 1, 5, 7 (online).

101. Ibid. p. 9.

102. Whitney Chadwick, 'An Infinite Play of Mirrors: Women, Surrealism, and Self-Representation', in Whitney Chadwick (ed.), *Mirror Images: Women, Surrealism, and Self-Representation* (Cambridge, MA and London: The MIT Press, 1998), p. 10.

103. Dore Bowen, 'Exquisite Correspondence: A Dialogue with Whitney Chadwick', *Afterimage* 26, 6 (May/June 1999), p. 8.

104. Louis A. Sass discusses the schizophrenic 'truth-taking stare' that signals schizophrenia: the world may seem 'horrifying in some insidious but ineffable way', and the stricken individual may 'stare at himself in a glass, as if transfixed by the strangeness of his own reflections – the so-called *signe du miroir*' (*Madness and Modernism: Insanity in the Light of Modern Art, Literature, and Thought* [Cambridge, MA and London: Harvard University Press, 1992]), p. 44.

105. Whitney Chadwick, 'Leonora Carrington: Evolution of a Feminist Consciousness', *Woman's Art Journal* 7, 1 (spring–summer 1986), p. 38.

106. Vandivere, 'Framed Liminalities', p. 51.

107. For a comparative selection of commentaries on this passage, see Bible Hub <biblehub.com/commentaries/1_corinthians/13-12.htm> (last accessed August 2017).

108. In an essay published in 1954, while *Beyond the Glass* was in press, White discusses the limitation of human vision within a Catholic context: 'The great paradoxes, the great mysteries remained, but faith, though it could not resolve or penetrate them, could accept them and even rejoice in them since in eternity God would give us vision. Meanwhile, even on earth, He occasionally gives us glimpses of insight into them, if only to reveal the depth upon depth still hidden' ('Antonia White', in F. J. Sheed (ed.), *Born Catholics*, [London: The Catholic

Book Club, 1954], p. 46). See also her explicit reference to this Biblical passage in *The Hound and the Falcon* (pp. 163–4). This reference, which White claims to quote as she wrote it down at the time, is an excellent example of how much White revised diary passages for publication, for it is an extensively reworked version of an entry of 18 August 1941 (*Diary* 1, p. 177).

109. Bible Hub <biblehub.com/commentaries/1_corinthians/13-12.htm> (last accessed August 2017).

110. *DSM-5*, p. 303.

111. Ibid. pp. 302–3.

112. Ibid. pp. 302–3.

113. Janet Frame, *Janet Frame: An Autobiography* (*To the Is-Land* [1982]; *An Angel at My Table* [1984]; *The Envoy from Mirror City* [1985]) (Auckland: Vintage, 1989), p. 241.

114. Jung, 'On the Psychogenesis of Schizophrenia', p. 234.

115. Juan Terblanche, 'Between Two Shattered Mirrors: A Jungian Exploration of Anthony Mannix's Artworks', in Patrick Ebewo, Ingrid Stevens and Mzo Sirayi (eds), *Africa and Beyond: Arts and Sustainable Development* (Cambridge Scholars Press, 2014), p. 230.

116. White explicitly connects Richard Crayshaw to Clara's psychic conflicts through allusions to Jungian psychology. Before she meets him, her friend Clive shows her his photograph. When Clara says she feels she has seen Crayshaw before, Clive responds, '"In your dreams, probably. He's obviously an Archetype"' (*Beyond the Glass*, p. 107). Richard thus embodies the collective unconscious aspects of Clara's personal unconscious conflicts.

117. Brown, *The Poison at the Source*, p. 145.

118. Freud, 'The Dissection of the Psychical Personality', in James Strachey (ed.), *The Standard Edition of the Complete Psychological Works of Sigmund Freud* (vol. 22) (London: Hogarth Press and the Institute of Psychoanalysis, 1964), p. 59.

119. Valentine, 'Mad and Modern', p. 128.

120. Ibid. p. 126.

121. Ibid. p. 128.

122. Ibid. p. 126.

123. Hal Foster, *Compulsive Beauty* (Cambridge, MA: The MIT Press, 1993), p. 81.

124. See, for example, Flood, 'Autobiographical Novels', p. 148; Valentine, 'Mad and Modern', pp. 33–4.

125. Other commentators who have explored the parallels between the convent and the asylum include Brown, *The Poison at the Source*, p. 147; and Flood, 'Autobiographical Novels', p. 149 n.15.

126. Vandivere discusses the looking glass, mirror writing and allusions to Carroll extensively in 'Framed Liminalities' (pp. 54–7). Valentine reads the mirror and writing through a Lacanian lens in 'Mad and Modern' (pp. 132–4).
127. Flood, 'Autobiographical Novels', p. 148.
128. O'Mara, 'Trust Amid Sore Affliction', p. 39.
129. Ibid. p. 35.
130. Ibid. p. 40.
131. Ibid. p. 41.

Epilogue

1. Dunn, *Antonia White*, p. 217.
2. White's difficulties were increased by the fact that she had 'invented' the little boy's death at the end of *The Lost Traveller*, a death she connected with her abortion (*Diary* 1, p. 225).

Bibliography

Abraham, Karl (1927), 'Notes on Manic-Depressive Insanity', in Ernest Jones (ed.), Douglas Bryan and Alix Strachey (trans.), *Selected Papers of Karl Abraham*, London: Hogarth Press, pp. 137–56.

Abraham, Karl (1974), 'Manifestations of the Female Castration Complex', in Jean Strouse (ed.), *Women and Analysis: Dialogues on Psychoanalytic Views of Femininity*, New York: Grossman Publishers, pp. 109–35.

Allitt, Patrick (1997), *Catholic Converts: British and American Intellectuals' Turn to Rome*, Ithaca: Cornell University Press.

American Psychiatric Association (2013), *Diagnostic and Statistical Manual of Mental Disorders*, 5th edn, Washington, DC and London: American Psychiatric Publishing.

Angel, Gemma, 'Fascinus and the Winged Phallus Tattoo', University College, London, <http://blogs.ucl.ac.uk/researchers-in-museums/2013/01/07/fascinus-the-winged-phallus-tattoo> (last accessed January 2017).

Appignanesi, Lisa (2008), *Mad, Bad and Sad: A History of Women and the Mind Doctors, 1800 to the Present*, London: Virago.

Ariza, M. Alvarez, R. Mateos Alvarez and G. E. Berrios (2009), 'A review of the natural course of bipolar disorders (manic-depressive psychosis) in the pre-drug era: Review of studies prior to 1950', *Journal of Affective Disorders*, 115: pp. 293–301.

Armstrong, Tim (2000), 'Two Types of Shock in Modernity', *Critical Quarterly* 42, 1: pp. 61–73.

Ashley, Susan A. (2003), 'Railway Brain: The Body's Revenge against Progress', *Proceedings of the Western Society for French History* 31: pp. 177–96.

Ashley, Tim (2010), 'Wagner's *Tannhäuser*', *The Guardian*, <http://www.theguardian.com/music/2010/dec/11/richard-wagner-tannhauser-opera> (last accessed January 2017).

Saint Augustine, 'Exposition on Psalm LVI', *Expositions on the Psalms*, Christian Classics Ethereal Library www.ccel.org/ccel/schaff/npnf108.ii.LVI.html (last accessed March 2017).

Barker, Phil, Peter Campbell and Ben Davidson (eds) (1999), *From the Ashes of Experience: Reflections on Madness, Survival and Growth*, London: Wiley-Blackwell.

Bauer, Mark S. (2002), 'Psychosocial Interventions for Bipolar Disorder: A Review', in Mario Maj, Hagop S. Akiskal, Juan José Lopez-Ibor and Norman Sartorius (eds), *Bipolar Disorder*, John Wiley and Sons, pp. 281–357.

Benjamin, Jessica (1991), 'Father and daughter: Identification with difference – a contribution to gender heterodoxy', *Psychoanalytic Dialogues* 1, 3: pp. 277–99.

Benson, Julietta (1993), '"Varieties of Disbelief": Antonia White and the Discourses of Faith and Scepticism', *Literature and Theology: An Inter-disciplinary Journal of Theory and Criticism* 7, 3: pp. 284–301.

Blake, William (1988), in David V. Erdman (ed.), *The Complete Poetry and Prose of William Blake*, New York: Doubleday.

Bleuler, Eugen, (1950), *Dementia Praecox or The Group of Schizophrenias*, Joseph Zinkin (trans.), New York: International Universities Press.

Bloom, Jon (2013), 'Desiring God' <www.desiringgod.org/articles/when-a-sword-pierces-your-soul> (last accessed 17 April 2017).

Boose, Lynda E. and Betty S. Flowers (eds) (1989), *Daughters and Fathers*, Baltimore and London: The Johns Hopkins University Press.

Bowen, Dore (1999), 'Exquisite Correspondence: A Dialogue with Whitney Chadwick', *Afterimage* 26, 6: pp. 8–9. Online.

Bowen, Elizabeth (1978), 'Introduction', Antonia White, *Frost in May*, London: Virago, pp. v–x.

Britten, Ronald (2001), 'Forever Father's Daughter: The Athene-Antigone Complex', in Alice Etchegoyen and Judith Trowell (eds), *The Importance of Fathers: A Psychoanalytic Re-evaluation*, London and New York: Routledge, pp. 107–18.

Broe, Mary Lynn (1989), 'My Art Belongs to Daddy: Incest as Exile, The Textual Economics of Hayford Hall', in Mary Lynn Broe and Angela Ingram (eds), *Women's Writing in Exile*, Chapel Hill and London: University of North Carolina Press, pp. 41–86.

Brooks, Peter (1994), *Psychoanalysis and Storytelling*, Oxford: Blackwell.

Brown, Penny (1992), *The Poison at the Source: The Female Novel of Self-Development in the Early Twentieth Century*, London: Macmillan.

Bruner, Jerome (1994), 'The Remembered Self', in Ulric Neisser and Robyn Fivush (eds), *The Remembering Self: Construction and Accuracy in the Self-Narrative*, Cambridge: Cambridge University Press, pp. 41–54.

Bruner, Jerome (2002), *Making Stories: Law, Literature, Life*, New York: Farrar, Straus, Giroux.

Bruner, Jerome (2004), 'Life as Narrative', *Social Research* 71, 3: pp. 691–710.

Callil, Carmen (1979), 'Introduction', Antonia White, *Beyond the Glass*, London: Virago, np.

Caminero-Santangelo, Marta (1998), *The Madwoman Can't Speak: Why Insanity Is Not Subversive*, Ithaca and London: Cornell University Press.

Caplan, Eric Michael (1995), 'Trains, Brains, and Sprains: Railway Spine and the Origin of Psychoneuroses', *Bulletin of the History of Medicine* 69, 3: pp. 387–419.

Caramagno, Thomas C. (1992), *The Flight of the Mind: Virginia Woolf's Art and Manic-Depressive Illness*, Berkeley, Los Angeles and London: University of California Press.

Carroll, Lewis (2015), *Alice in Wonderland*, Princeton: Princeton University Press.

Chadwick, Whitney (1985), *Women Artists and the Surrealist Movement*, Boston: Little Brown.

Chadwick, Whitney (1986), 'Leonora Carrington: Evolution of a Feminist Consciousness', *Woman's Art Journal* 7, 1: pp. 37–42.

Chadwick, Whitney (1998), 'An Infinite Play of Empty Mirrors: Women, Surrealism, and Self-Representation', in Whitney Chadwick (ed.), *Mirror Images: Women, Surrealism, and Self-Representation*, Cambridge, MA and London: The MIT Press, pp. 2–35.

Chait, Sandra (2000), 'The Psychospiritual in the Literary Analysis of Modernist Texts', in Heather Walton and Andrew W. Hass (eds), *Self/Same/Other: Revisioning the Subject in Literature and Theology*, Sheffield, England: Sheffield Academic Press, pp. 54–69.

Chait, Sandra (2005), 'Site also of Angst and Spiritual Search', in Elizabeth Podnieks and Sandra Chait (eds), *Hayford Hall: Hangovers, Erotics, and Modernist Aesthetics*, Carbondale: Southern Illinois University Press: pp. 150–69.

Chamberlin, Judi (1978), *On Our Own: Patient-Controlled Alternatives to the Mental Health System*, New York: McGraw-Hill.

Charmaz, Kathy (1997), *Good Days, Bad Days: The Self in Chronic Illness and Time*, New Brunswick, NJ: Rutgers University Press.

Chesler, Phyllis (1972), *Women and Madness*, Garden City, NY: Doubleday.

Chitty, Susan (1985), *Now to My Mother: A Very Personal Memoir of Antonia White*. London: Weidenfeld and Nicolson.

Clark, Hilary (2008), 'Introduction', in Hilary Clark (ed.), *Depression and Narrative: Telling the Dark*, Albany, NY: State University of New York Press.

Cohen, Margaret (2008), 'Review Essay: *The Prenatal Theme in Psychotherapy* by Philippe Ployé', *British Journal of Psychotherapy* 24, 2: pp. 221–8.

Conway, Martin A. (ed.) (1997), *Recovered Memories and False Memories*, Oxford, New York and Tokyo: Oxford University Press.

Conley, Katharine (1996), *Automatic Woman: The Representation of Woman in Surrealism*, Lincoln: University of Nebraska.

Cooper, Arnold M. (1989), 'Will Neurobiology Influence Psychoanalysis?', in Arnold M. Cooper, Otto E. Kernberg and Ethel Spector Person (eds), *Psychoanalysis: Towards the Second Century*, New Haven: Yale University Press, pp. 202–18.

Couser, G. Thomas (1997), *Recovering Bodies: Illness, Disability, and Life-Writing*, Madison: University of Wisconsin Press.

Della Salla, Sergio, Clara Calia, Maria Fara De Caro and Robert D. McIntosh (2014), 'Transient involuntary mirror writing triggered by anxiety', *Neurocase: The Neural Basis of Cognition* <http//dx.doi.org/10.1080/13554794.2014.969278> (last accessed 17 October 2014).

Derby, Irving (1933), 'Manic-Depression "Exhaustion" Deaths', *Psychiatric Quarterly* 7: pp. 436–9.

Dima, Danai and Gerome Breen (2015), 'Polygenic risk scores in imaging genetics: Usefulness and applications', *Journal of Psychopharmacology*, DOI: 10.1177/0269881115584470.

Dourley, John P. (2007), 'The Jung-White Dialogue and why it couldn't work and won't go away', *Journal of Analytical Psychology* 52, 3: pp. 275–95.

Drabble, Margaret (1991), 'Review of *Antonia White Diaries, 1926–1957*', *Vogue* (British): pp. 102–3.

Dunn, Jane (1998), *Antonia White: A Life*, London: Jonathan Cape.

Eakin, Paul John (1999), *How Our Lives Become Stories: Making Selves*, Ithaca and London: Cornell University Press.

Eakin, Paul John (2001), 'Breaking Rules: The Consequences of Self-Narration', *Biography* 24, 1: pp. 113–27.

Eakin, Paul John (ed.) (2004), *The Ethics of Life-Writing*, Ithaca: Cornell University Press.

Eakin, Paul John (2006), 'Narrative Identity and Narrative Imperialism: A Response to Galen Strawson and James Phelan', *Narrative* 14, 2: pp. 180–7.

Edmundson, Mark (2007), *The Death of Sigmund Freud: The Legacy of His Last Days*, London: Bloomsbury.

Edwards, Lee R. (1989), 'Schizophrenic Narrative', *Journal of Narrative Technique* 19: pp. 25–30.

Empson, William (1995), *Some Versions of Pastoral*, Harmondsworth: Penguin.

Faimberg, Haydée (2005), *The Telescoping of Generations*, London and New York: Routledge.

Farnham, Frank R. and Henry G. Kennedy (1997), 'Acute excited states and sudden death', *British Medical Journal* v. 315 n. 7116.

Fee, Dwight (ed.) (2000), *Pathology and the Postmodern: Mental Illness as Discourse and Experience*, London: Sage.

Fieve, Ronald R. (1975), *Moodswing*, New York: Bantam.

Flood, Jeanne A. (1983), 'The Autobiographical Novels of Antonia White', *Critique*: pp. 131–49.

Fordham, Frieda (1986), *An Introduction to Jung's Psychology*, Harmondsworth: Penguin.

Foster, Hal (1993), *Compulsive Beauty*, Cambridge, MA: The MIT Press.

Foucault, Michel (1973), *Madness and Civilization: A History of Insanity in the Age of Reason*, Richard Howard (trans.), New York: Vintage.

Fowke, Alex, Susan Ross and Katie Ashcroft (2012), 'Childhood Maltreatment and Internalized Shame in Adults with a Diagnosis of Bipolar Disorder', *Clinical Psychology and Psychotherapy* 19: pp. 450–7.

Frame, Janet (1989), *Janet Frame: An Autobiography*, Auckland: Vintage.

Frank, Arthur W. (1995), *The Wounded Storyteller: Body, Illness, and Ethics* 2nd edn, Chicago and London: University of Chicago Press.

Frank, Ellen (2005), *Treating Bipolar Disorder: A Clinician's Guide to Interpersonal and Social Therapy*, New York and London: Guilford Press.

Freeman, Mark (2008), 'Beyond Narrative: Dementia's Tragic Promise', in Lars-Christer Hydén and Jens Brockmeier (eds), *Health, Illness and Culture: Broken Narratives*, New York and London: Routledge, pp. 169–84.

Freeman, Mark (2010), '"Even Amidst": Rethinking Narrative Coherence' in Matti Hyvärinen, Lars-Christer Hydén, Marja Saarenheimo and Maria Tamboukou (eds), *Beyond Narrative Coherence*, Amsterdam and Philadelphia: John Benjamins, pp. 167–86.

Freud, Sigmund (1953a), '"Civilized" Sexual Morality and Modern Nervousness', in Philip Rieff (ed.), *Sexuality and the Psychology of Love*, New York: Collier Books, pp. 20–40.

Freud, Sigmund (1953b), 'Fragment of an analysis of a case of hysteria', in James Strachey (ed.), *The Standard Edition of the Complete Psychological Works of Sigmund Freud* (vol. 7), London: Hogarth Press and the Institute of Psychoanalysis, pp. 7–122.

Freud, Sigmund (1957), 'Two Instances of Pathogenic Phantasies Revealed by the Patients Themselves', in James Strachey (ed.), *The Standard Edition of the Complete Psychological Works of Sigmund Freud* (vol. 11), London: Hogarth Press and the Institute of Psychoanalysis, pp. 236–7.

Freud, Sigmund (1959), 'Inhibitions, Symptoms and Anxiety', in James Strachey (ed.), *The Standard Edition of the Complete Psychological Works of Sigmund Freud* (vol. 20), London: Hogarth Press and the Institute of Psychoanalysis, pp. 87–174.

Freud, Sigmund (1961), *The Future of an Illusion*, in James Strachey (ed.), *The Standard Edition of the Complete Psychological Works of Sigmund Freud* (vol. 21), London: Hogarth Press and the Institute of Psychoanalysis, pp. 3–56.

Freud, Sigmund (1963), 'The Most Prevalent Form of Degradation in Erotic Life', in Philip Rieff (ed.), *Sexuality and the Psychology of Love*, New York: Collier Books, pp. 58–63.

Freud, Sigmund (1964a), 'The Dissection of the Psychical Personality', in James Strachey (ed.), *The Standard Edition of the Complete Psychological Works of Sigmund Freud* (vol. 22), London: Hogarth Press and the Institute of Psychoanalysis, pp. 57–80.

Freud, Sigmund (1964b), in James Strachey (ed.), *Moses and Monotheism. The Standard Edition of the Complete Psychological Works of Sigmund Freud* (vol. 23), London: Hogarth Press and the Institute of Psychoanalysis, pp. 3–137.

Freud, Sigmund (1974), 'Femininity', in Jean Strouse (ed.), *Women and Analysis: Dialogues on Psychoanalytic Views of Femininity*, New York: Grossman Publishers, pp. 73–94.

Gascoyne, David (1980), *Journal 1936–37*, London: Enitharmon Press.

Gascoyne, David (2000), *A Short Survey of Surrealism*, London: Enitharmon Press.

Gazzaniga, Michael S. (1998), *The Mind's Past*, Berkeley: University of California Press.

Gazzaniga, Michael S. (2012), 'The Storyteller in Your Head', *Discover*.

Glover, Edward (1957), 'Obituary for Dennis Carroll', *International Journal of Psychoanalysis* 38: pp. 277–9.

Goffman, Erving (1961), *Asylums: Essays on the Social Situation of Asylum Patients and Other Inmates*, New York: Doubleday.

Goodwin, Frederick K. and Kay Redfield Jamison (2007), *Manic-Depressive Illness: Bipolar Disorders and Recurrent Depression* 2nd edn, Oxford and New York: Oxford University Press.

Gottschall, Jonathan (2012), *The Storytelling Animal: How Stories Make Us Human*, New York: Houghton Mifflin Harcourt.

Haaken, Janice (1998), *Pillar of Salt: Gender, Memory and the Perils of Looking Back*, New Brunswick, NJ and London: Rutgers University Press.

Habermas, Tilmann and Susan Bluck (2000), 'Getting a Life: The Emergence of the Life Story in Adolescence', *Psychological Bulletin* 126, 5: pp. 748–69.

Hacking, Ian (1995), *Rewriting the Soul: Multiple Personality Disorder and the Sciences of Memory*, Princeton: Princeton University Press.

Hanson, Ellis (1998), *Decadence and Catholicism*, Cambridge, MA: Harvard University Press.

Harris, Adrienne (2008), '"Fathers" and "Daughters"', *Psychoanalytic Inquiry* 28, 1: pp. 39–59.

Hawkins, Anne Hunsaker (1999), *Reconstructing Illness: Studies in Pathography* 2nd edn, West Lafayette: Purdue University Press.

Henke, Suzette (2000), *Shattered Subjects: Trauma and Testimony in Women's Life Writing*, New York: St Martin's Press.

Herman, Judith Lewis, with Lisa Hirschman (1981), *Father-Daughter Incest*, Cambridge, MA: Harvard University Press.

Hinshaw, Stephen P. (2002a), 'Growing Up in a Family with Bipolar Disorder: Personal Experience, Developmental Lessons, and Overcoming Stigma', in Mario Maj, Hagop S. Akiskal, Juan José López-Ibor and Norman Sartorius (eds), *Bipolar Disorder*, Sussex: John Wiley and Sons, pp. 525–56.

Hinshaw, Stephen P. (2002b), *The Years of Silence are Past: My Father's Life with Bipolar Disorder*, Cambridge: Cambridge University Press.

Hopkinson, Lyndall (1988), *Nothing to Forgive: A Daughter's Life of Antonia White*, London: Chatto and Windus.

Hornstein, Gail A. (2012), *Agnes's Jacket: A Psychologist's Search for the Meaning of Madness*, Ross-on-Wye: PCCS Books.

Hubert, Renée Riese (1994), *Magnifying Mirrors: Women, Surrealism, and Partnership*, Lincoln: University of Nebraska Press.

Hutton, Lizzie (2005), 'The Example of Antonia White', *New England Review* 26, 1: pp. 121–9.

Hyvärinen, Matti, Lars-Christer Hydén, Marja Saarenheimo and Maria Tamboukou (eds) (2010), *Beyond Narrative Coherence*, Amsterdam and Philadelphia: John Benjamins.

Jamison, Kay Redfield (1993), *Touched with Fire: Manic-Depressive Illness and the Artistic Temperament*, New York: Free Press.

Jamison, Kay Redfield (1999), *Night Falls Fast: Understanding Suicide*, New York: Knopf.

Jamison, Kay Redfield (2011), *An Unquiet Mind: A Memoir of Moods and Madness*, London: Picador.

Jaspers, Karl (1972), J. Hoenig (ed.) and Marian W. Hamilton (trans.), *General Psychopathology* 7th edn, Manchester: Manchester University Press.

Jeffery, Sandra (2005), 'Antonia White and the Subversion of Literary Impotence at Hayford Hall', in Elizabeth Podnieks and Sandra Chait (eds), *Hayford Hall: Hangovers, Erotics, and Modernist Aesthetics*, Carbondale: Southern Illinois University Press, pp. 70–88.

Jeffreys, Sheila (2003), *The Spinster and her Enemies: Feminism and Sexuality, 1880–1930*, Melbourne: Spinifex Press.

Johnson, Sheri L. and Randy Fingerhut (2006), 'Life Events as predictors of relapse, depression and mania in bipolar disorder', in Steven Jones and Richard Bentall (eds), *The Psychology of Bipolar Disorder: New Developments and Research Strategies*, Oxford: Oxford University Press, pp. 47–72.

Jones, Ann Hudson (1997), 'Literature and Medicine: Narratives of Mental Illness', *The Lancet* 350.974, pp. 359–61.

Jung, Carl G. (1933), *Modern Man in Search of a Soul*, London and Henley: Routledge.

Jung, Carl G. (1960), 'On the Psychogenesis of Schizophrenia', in Herbert Read, Michael Fordham and Gerhard Adler (eds) and R. F. C. Hull (trans.), *C. G. Jung: The Collected Works* (vol. 3), London: Routledge and Kegan Paul.

Jurecic, Ann (2003), *Illness as Narrative*, Pittsburgh: University of Pittsburgh Press.

Kapfhammer, Hans-Peter (2006), 'Somatic symptoms in depression', *Dialogues in Clinical Neuroscience* 8, 2: pp. 229–30.

Karp, David A. (1996), *Speaking of Sadness: Depression, Disconnection, and the Meanings of Illness*, New York and Oxford: Oxford University Press.

Keitel, Evelyne (1989), *Reading Psychosis: Readers, Texts and Psychoanalysis*, Oxford: Blackwell.

Kieffer, Christine C. (2004), 'Selfobjects, Oedipal Objects, and Mutual Recognition: A Self-Psychological Reappraisal of the Female "Oedipal Victor"', *The Annual of Psychoanalysis*, 32: pp. 69–80.

Klein, Melanie (1986a), 'A Contribution to the Psychogenesis of Manic-Depressive States', in Juliet Mitchell (ed.), *The Selected Melanie Klein*, New York: Macmillan, pp. 115–45.

Klein, Melanie (1986b), 'Mourning and its Relation to Manic-Depressive States', in Juliet Mitchell (ed.), *The Selected Melanie Klein*, New York: Macmillan, pp. 146–74.

Kleinman, Arthur (1988), *The Illness Narratives: Suffering, Healing, and the Human Condition*, New York: Basic Books.

Laing, R. D. (1967), *The Politics of Experience*, New York: Pantheon.

Laing, R. D. (1972), *The Politics of the Family and Other Essays*, New York: Vintage Books.

Laing, R. D. (1976), *The Divided Self*, Harmondsworth: Penguin Books.

Lammers, Ann C. (2007), 'Jung and White and the God of terrible double aspect', *Journal of Analytic Psychology* 52, 3: pp. 253–74.

Lee, Hermione (1980), 'Introduction', in Antonia White, *Strangers*, New York: Dial Press, pp. i–vii.

Linde, Charlotte (1993), *Life Stories: The Creation of Coherence*, New York and Oxford: Oxford University Press.

Liu, Richard T. (2010), 'Early life stressors and genetic influences on the development of bipolar disorder: The roles of childhood abuse and brain-derived neurotrophic factors', *Child Abuse and Neglect* 34, 7: pp. 516–22.

Lockerd, Martin (2014), '"A Satirist of Vices and Follies": Beardsley, Eliot, and Images of Decadent Catholicism', *Journal of Modern Literature* 37, 4: pp. 143–96.

Malik, Shushma (2014), 'All Roads Lead to Rome? Decadence, Paganism, Catholicism and the Later Life of Oscar Wilde', *Cahiers victoriens et édouardiens* 80: pp. 2–14.

Mann, Stephen C., Stanley N. Caroff and Henry R. Bleier (1986), 'Lethal Catatonia', *American Journal of Psychiatry* 143: pp. 1374–81.

Mansell, Warren and Rebecca Pedley (2004), 'The ascent into mania: A review of psychological processes associated with the development of manic symptoms', *Clinical Psychology Review* 28: p. 496.

Marneros, Andreas (2001), 'Origin and development of concepts of bipolar mixed states', *Journal of Affective Disorders* 67: pp. 229–40.

Marneros, Andreas and Frederick K. Goodwin (2016), 'Bipolar disorders beyond major depression and euphoric mania', in Andreas Marneros and Frederick K. Goodwin (eds), *Bipolar Disorder: Mixed States, Rapid Cycling and Atypical Forms*, Cambridge: Cambridge University Press, pp. 1–44

Marshall, Jennifer Cizik (2000), 'The Semiotics of Schizophrenia: Unica Zürn's Artistry and Illness', *Modern Language Studies* 30, 2: pp. 21–31.

Masurel-Marray, Claire (2012), 'Conversions to Catholicism among Fin de Siècle Writers: A Spiritual and Literary Genealogy', *Cahiers victoriens et édouardiens* 76: pp. 105–25.

Matus, Jill L. (2001), 'Trauma, Memory, and Railway Disaster: The Dickensian Connection', *Victorian Studies* 43, 3: pp. 413–36.

McAdams, Dan P. (2006), 'The Problem of Narrative Coherence', *Journal of Constructivist Psychology* 19, 2: 109–25.

McAra, Catriona (2011), 'Surrealism's Curiosity: Lewis Carroll and the *Femme-Enfant*', *Papers of Surrealism* 9: pp. 1–25. Online.

McNally, Kieran (2009), 'Eugene Bleuler's Four As', *History of Psychiatry* 12, 2: pp. 43–59.

McNally, Kieran (2013), 'Dementia praecox revisited', *History of Psychiatry* 24, 4: pp. 507–9.

Meissner, William (1984), *Psychoanalysis and Religious Experience*, New Haven: Yale University Press.

Miklowitz, David J. (2008), *Bipolar Disorder: A Family-Focused Treatment Approach* 2nd edn, New York and London: Guilford Press.

Milden, Randy S. (1984), 'Affective Disorders and Narcissistic Vulnerability', *American Journal of Psychoanalysis* 44: pp. 345–53.

Mitchell, Juliet (ed.) (1986), *The Selected Melanie Klein*, New York: Macmillan.

Mitchell, Stephen A. (1988), *Relational Concepts in Psychoanalysis: An Integration*, Cambridge, MA and London: Harvard University Press.

Murray, Alex (2013), 'Recusant Poetics: Rereading Catholicism at the *Fin de Siècle*', *English Literature in Transition, 1880–1920* 56, 3: pp. 355–73.

Nelson, Hilde Lindemann (2001), *Damaged Identities, Narrative Repair*, Ithaca: Cornell University Press.

Newton, Marcia Anne (2014), 'Sexual Trauma, Psychosis, and Betrayal in Antonia White's Autobiographical Fiction: A Critical Examination of the Freudian Perspective', Diss. University of Sheffield.

Nicholson, Virginia (2008), *Singled Out: How Two Million Survived without Men After the First World War*, New York: Viking.

Nordgaard, Julie, Sidse M. Arnfred, Peter Handest and Josef Parnas (2008), 'The Diagnostic Status of First-Rank Symptoms', *Schizophrenia Bulletin* 34, 1: pp. 137–54.

O'Connell, Marvin R. (1995), *Critics on Trial: An Introduction to the Catholic Modernist Crisis*, Washington, DC: Catholic University of America Press.

O'Mara, Philip F. (1988), 'Trust Amid Sore Affliction: Antonia White's Novels', *Cithara: Essays in the Judaeo-Christian Tradition* 28, 1: pp. 33–43.

Palmer, Paulina (1991), 'Antonia White's *Frost in May*: A Lesbian Feminist Reading', in Susan Sellers (ed.), *Feminist Criticism: Theory and Practice*, New York: Harvester Wheatsheaf, pp. 89–108.

Papalas, Marylaura, 'Speed and Convulsive Beauty: Trains and the Historic Avant-garde', *Studies in 20th- and 21st-Century Literature* 39, 1 (Article 2) <http://dx.doi.org/10.4148/2334-4415.1818> (last accessed 15 January 2017).

Patelis-Siotis, Irene (2001), 'Cognitive-behavioral therapy: applications for the management of bipolar disorder', *Bipolar Disorder* 3: pp. 1–10.

Perring, Christian (2006), 'Telling the Truth about Mental Illness: The Role of Narrative', in Nancy Nyquist Potter (ed.), *Trauma, Truth and Reconciliation: Healing Damaged Relationships*, Oxford: Oxford University Press, pp. 257–76.

Phelan, James (2005), 'Who's Here? Thoughts on Narrative Identity and Narrative Imperialism', *Narrative* 13: pp. 205–10.

Ployé, Philippe (2006a), 'Inpatient Psychotherapy and Prenatal Regression', *British Journal of Psychotherapy* 22, 4: pp. 483–95.

Ployé, Philippe (2006b), *The Prenatal Theme in Psychotherapy*, London: Karnac Books.

Podnieks, Elizabeth (2000), *Daily Modernism: The Literary Diaries of Virginia Woolf, Antonia White, Elizabeth Smart, and Anaïs Nin*, Montreal: McGill-Queen's University Press.

Podnieks, Elizabeth, and Sandra Chait (eds) (2005), *Hayford Hall: Hangovers, Erotics, and Modernist Aesthetics*, Carbondale: Southern Illinois University Press.

Porter, Roy (1987), *A Social History of Madness: The World Through the Eyes of the Insane*, New York: Weidenfeld and Nicolson.

Post, Robert M. et al. (2014), 'Verbal abuse, like physical and sexual abuse, in childhood is associated with an earlier onset and more difficult course of bipolar disorder', *Bipolar Disorders* 17, 3: pp. 323–30.

Raoul, Valerie, Connie Canam, Angela D. Henderson and Carla Peterson (eds) (2007), *Unfitting Stories: Narrative Approaches to Disease, Disability, and Trauma*, Waterloo: Wilfrid Laurier University Press.

Read, Jim, and Jill Reynolds (eds) (1996), *Speaking Our Minds: An Anthology*, New York: Palgrave Macmillan.

Rimmon-Kenan, Shlomith (2002), 'The Story of "I": Illness and Narrative Identity', *Narrative* 10.1: pp. 9–27.

Rose, Ellen Cronan (1991), 'Antonia White: Portrait of the Artist as a Dutiful Daughter', *Literature, Interpretation, Theory* 2, 3: pp. 239–48.

Sacks, Oliver (1998), *The Man Who Mistook His Wife for a Hat: And Other Clinical Tales*, New York: Touchstone.

Sass, Louis A. (1987), 'Introspection, Schizophrenia, and the Fragmentation of the Self', *Representations* 19: pp. 1–34.

Sass, Louis A. (1992), *Madness and Modernism: Insanity in the Light of Modern Art, Literature, and Thought*, Cambridge, MA and London: Harvard University Press.

Sass, Louis A. (2000/2001), 'Schizophrenia, Modernism, and the "Creative Imagination": On Creativity and Psychopathology', *Creativity Research Journal* 13, 1: pp. 55–74.

Sayers, Janet (1991), *Mothering Psychoanalysis: Helene Deutsch, Karen Horney, Anna Freud and Melanie Klein*, London and New York: Penguin.

Schacter, Daniel L. (1996), *Searching for Memory: The Brain, the Mind, and the Past*, New York: Basic Books.

Scheff, Thomas (1966), *Being Mentally Ill*, Chicago: Aldine.

Scheff, Thomas (1975), *Labeling Madness*, Englewood, NJ: Prentice-Hall.

Schivelbusch, Wolfgang (1986), *The Railway Journey: The Industrialization of Time and Space in the 19th Century*, Berkeley and Los Angeles: University of California Press.

Schott, G. D. (2007), 'Mirror writing: neurological reflections on an unusual phenomenon', *Journal of Neurology, Neurosurgery and Psychiatry* 78, 1: pp. 5–13.

Schuchard, Ronald (1994), 'Wilde's Dark Angel and the Spell of Decadent Catholicism', in Constantin-George Sandulescu (ed.), *Rediscovering Oscar Wilde*, Savage, MA: Barnes and Noble, pp. 371–96.

Segal, Hanna (1974), *An Introduction to the Work of Melanie Klein* 2nd edn, New York: Basic Books.

Segal, Hanna (1998), 'A Psychoanalytic Approach to Aesthetics', in John Phillips and Lyndsey Stonebridge (eds), *Reading Melanie Klein*, London and New York: Routledge, pp. 203–22.

Shorter, Edward (1997), *A History of Psychiatry: From the Era of the Asylum to the Age of Prozac*, New York, Chichester, Brisbane, Toronto, Singapore and Weinheim: John Wiley and Sons.

Shorter, Edward (2009), 'The History of Lithium Therapy', *Bipolar Disorder* 11, 2: pp. 4–9.

Showalter, Elaine (1985), *The Female Malady: Women, Madness, and English Culture, 1830–1980*, New York: Pantheon.

Solomon, Andrew (2002), *The Noonday Demon: An Anatomy of Depression*, New York and London: Vintage.

Sontag, Susan (2001), *Against Interpretation and Other Essays*, New York: Macmillan.

Stastny, Peter (2000), 'Involuntary Psychiatric Interventions: A Breach of the Hippocratic Oath?', *Ethical Human Sciences and Services* 2, 1: pp. 21–41.

Stastny, Peter, and Peter Lehmann (eds) (2007), *Alternatives Beyond Psychiatry*, Berlin: Peter Lehmann.

Stevenson, Robert Louis (2006), in Stephen Greenblatt et al. (eds), *The Strange Case of Dr Jekyll and Mr Hyde*, *The Norton Anthology of English Literature* 8th edn, Volume E: *The Victorian Age*, New York and London: Norton.

Strauss-Noll, Mary Therese (2000), 'A Passionate and Troubled History: Antonia White and Her Father', *Pennsylvania English*, 22, 1–2: pp. 129–42.

Strawson, Galen (2004), 'Against Narrativity', *Ratio* 17: pp. 428–52.

Styron, William (2001), *Darkness Visible: A Memoir of Madness*, London: Vintage.

Suleiman, Susan Rubin (1988), 'A Double Margin: Reflections on Women Writers and the Avant-Garde in France', *Yale French Studies* 75: pp. 148–72.

Suleiman, Susan Rubin (1990), *Subversive Intent: Gender, Politics, and the Avant-Garde*, Cambridge, MA: Harvard University Press.

Szasz, Thomas (1970), *Ideology and Insanity*, Garden City, NY: Anchor Books.

Terblanche, Juan (2014), 'Between Two Shattered Mirrors: A Jungian Exploration of Anthony Mannix's Artworks', in Patrick Ebewo, Ingrid Stevens and Mzo Sirayi (eds), *Africa and Beyond: Arts and Sustainable Development*, Cambridge: Cambridge Scholars Press, pp. 230–47.

Ussher, Jane M. (1991), *Women's Madness: Misogyny or Mental Illness?*, New York and London: Harvester Wheatsheaf.

Valentine, Kylie (2003a), 'Mad and Modern: A Reading of Emily Holmes Coleman and Antonia White', *Tulsa Studies in Women's Literature* 22, 1: pp. 121–47.

Valentine, Kylie (2003b), *Psychoanalysis, Psychiatry and Modernist Literature*, Basingstoke and New York: Palgrave Macmillan.

Van Schoonhetan, Anna Bentinck (2015), *Karl Abraham: Life and Work, A Biography*, London: Karnac Books.

Vandivere, Julie (2005), 'Framed Liminalities: Antonia White's *Beyond the Glass* and Emily Coleman's *The Shutter of Snow*', in Elizabeth Podnieks and Sandra Chait (eds), *Hayford Hall: Hangovers, Erotics, and Modernist Aesthetics*, Carbondale: Southern Illinois University Press, pp. 46–69.

Walker, Victoria (2014), '"Exactly like a housemaid writing to Greta Garbo": Antonia White Meets Virginia Woolf', *Notes and Queries* 61, 1: p. 146.

Watson, Stuart, et al. (2014), 'Childhood Trauma in Bipolar Disorder', *Australian and New Zealand Journal of Psychiatry* 48, 6: pp. 564–70.

Wehr, Thomas A. (1987), 'Sleep Production as a Final Common Pathway in the Genesis of Mania', *American Journal of Psychiatry* 144, 2: pp. 201–4.

Wehr, Thomas A., et al. (1998), 'Fostering Sleep and stabilizing its timing by scheduling regular nightly periods of bed rest and darkness to stabilize the timing and duration of sleep', *Biological Psychiatry* 43, 11: pp. 822–8.

Weldon, Clodagh (2007), *Father Victor White, O.P.: The Story of Jung's White Raven*, Chicago: University of Chicago Press.

Wells, Sherah (2009), 'Strand by Strand: Untying the Knots of Mental and Physical Illness in the Correspondence and Diaries of Antonia White and Emily Holmes Coleman', in Vera Kalitzkus and Peter L. Twohig (eds), *The Tapestry of Health, Illness and Disease*, Amsterdam and New York: Rodopi, pp. 43–55.

White, Antonia (1954), 'Antonia White', in F. J. Sheed (ed.), *Born Catholics*. London: The Catholic Book Club, 1954. 34–49.

White, Antonia (1978), *Frost in May*, London: Virago.

White, Antonia (1979a), *The Lost Traveller*, London: Virago.

White, Antonia (1979b), *The Sugar House*, London: Virago.

White, Antonia (1979c), *Beyond the Glass*, London: Virago.

White, Antonia (1980), *The Hound and the Falcon: The Story of a Reconversion to the Catholic Faith*, London: Virago.

White, Antonia (1981), *Strangers*, New York: Dial.

White, Antonia (1983), *As Once in May*, ed. Susan Chitty, London: Virago.

White, Antonia (1991), *Diaries 1926–1957*, ed. Susan Chitty, London: Constable.

White, Antonia (1992), *Diaries 1958–1979*, ed. Susan Chitty, London: Constable.

White, Victor (1960), *Soul and Psyche: An Enquiry into the Relationship of Psychotherapy and Religion*, New York and London: Harper and Brothers.

Whybrow, Peter (2015), *A Mood Apart: Depression, Mania and Other Afflictions of the Self*, New York: Basic Books.

Wilde, Oscar (2005), *The Portrait of Dorian Gray*, Peterborough, ON: Broadview Press.

Wiley, Harold (1970), 'Breton, Schizophrenia and Nadja', *The French Review* 43, 1: pp. 100–6.

Wood, Mary Elene (2013), *Life Writing and Schizophrenia: Encounters at the Edge of Meaning*, Amsterdam and New York: Rodopi.

Woolf, Leonard (1950), *Letters of Leonard Woolf*, ed. Frederic Spotts, New York: Harcourt Brace Jovanovich.

Woolf, Leonard (1964), *Beginning Again: An Autobiography of the Years 1911 to 1918*, New York: Harcourt Brace Jovanovich.

Woolf, Leonard (1967), *Downhill All the Way: An Autobiography of the Years 1919 to 1939*, New York: Harcourt Brace Jovanovich.

Woolf, Virginia (1985), *Moments of Being* 2nd edn, ed. Jeanne Schulkind, San Diego, New York and London: Harcourt Brace Jovanovich.

Woolf, Virginia (1978–85), *The Diary of Virginia Woolf*, ed. Anne Olivier Bell and Andrew McNeillie, 5 vols, New York: Harcourt Brace Jovanovich.

Index